A HISTORY OF THE
SHELTON FAMILY
OF
ENGLAND AND AMERICA

Including all spellings of the name Sheldon, Shenton, Skelton,
Skilton, Schylton, Shilston, Felton, Melton, Chilton, Chelton,
Chilston, Carlton, Carleton, Charlton, etc.

by

MILDRED CAMPBELL WHITAKER
(Mrs. Alexander Edward Whitaker)

of

St. Louis, Missouri

Mildred Campbell Whitaker

To

the Memory of My Mother

GENEVIEVE SHELTON CAMPBELL

"None knew her but to love her,

None named her but to praise;"

and

to Her Father

JOHN GILMORE SHELTON

Worthy scion of a noble race

still described by all who knew him

as a "magnificent Virginia Gentleman".

No higher tribute could be paid him.

FOREWORD

*T*HIS History has been twenty years "aborning", and has meant a great outlay of money, a tremendous amount of work and an inexhaustible supply of patience. The information on various family lines, contained in my "Genealogy" published in 1927, were given me by descendants of these lines and presumed to be accurate; but the early records prove many errors were made.

I have made personal research for data of all lines contained in this book and have had access, not only to county records, land grants, etc., but to family bibles, executor's papers, old personal letters, wills, deeds, etc., never published and in possession of members of the Shelton family, which has enabled me to straighten out this much, at least, of the tangled and much involved family history. There is too much "I" but as the work was all personal this could not be avoided; the constant repetition of "the author" seemed too stilted.

Such quantities of data have been acquired that it has been a difficult task to select just what to use, that would prove most helpful in enabling the various branches of the family in the clearing up of their own lines. I trust the selection will prove to have been a wise one.   M. C. W.

CONTENTS

LIST OF ILLUSTRATIONS

THE
SHELTONS
OF
ENGLAND
AND
AMERICA

THE SHELTONS
of
ENGLAND AND AMERICA

HERE is no family among all of those represented by the early colonists which has a background to surpass the *Shelton* family; and no history has been so neglected and dreadfully mixed up, largely due to the various spellings used in the records. These various spellings occur in the English and Irish records as well as those in America. In England, in the earlier centuries, the history was too well known to cause confusion and the spellings were used interchangeably: four spellings — Chilton, Skelton, Shelton and Sheldon — were used in the same notice of a birth, marriage or death. I have several hundred notes from "The Gentleman's Magazine" and other early English records, which show this to be a fact. However, although carelessness in the spelling in those days is proverbial, a new explanation has been recently given me. It seems that one of the evidences of culture in early days was the number of ways a man could spell his *name*. Whatever the reason, it has, unfortunately, caused errors to be made in the histories of Americans of such prominence as *Thomas Jefferson* and *Patrick Henry,* both of whom married members of the Shelton family, and for twenty years I have attempted to ascertain the *facts,* as it is too late to correct the *records.*

My grandfather, John Gilmour Shelton, was born in Lancaster County, Virginia, March 1, 1802. He lived in

Virginia until he was past thirty years of age; he was
twenty-four when Thomas Jefferson died. Grandfather
knew Jefferson well, since both he and Patrick Henry had
married Sheltons of my *grandfather's family;* he knew all
of the Shelton traditions and history and we, his descendants, were brought up on the knowledge of the family
connections.

The errors in all of the published lives and histories of
Jefferson and *Henry,* determined me to work until I could
establish the *facts.*

In 1927, I published a book* containing my *own* Shelton
line from the year 792 to the present and as many col-
lateral lines as I could feel reasonably sure of at that time;
it being impossible to get a correct history from the
existing data without help from family records.

No sooner had the book been published, than letters from
descendants of the Sheltons from all over the country
poured in. Some of these spelled their name *Chilton,*
some *Chelton,* some *Sheldon,* some *Skelton, Carleton* and
Charlton, but all, with *one* exception, claimed to be *Sheltons,*
and I have proven them to be right.

The exception occurs in the Jones-Gilliam line, which
has its descent from the marriage of Sally (Sarah) Shelton
(daughter of James Shelton and Jane Meriwether) to
Colonel Thomas Jones, and the marriage of her sister,
Lucy, to Robert Gilliam.

To each one of the records quoted to me by Judge Lewis
Jones of Kentucky and Mr. R. D. Gilliam of Petersburg,
Virginia, to prove that their descent is from a separate

* "Genealogy of the Campbell, Noble, Gorton, Shelton, Byrd, Gilmore and
Allied Families", The Mound City Press Company, St. Louis, Missouri.

BOOK PLATE OF MERIWETHER AND REUBEN SHELTON,
FROM THEIR BIBLE, IN POSSESSION OF THE JONES
FAMILY OF KENTUCKY

From a tracing made by Catesby Jones

family in Virginia, in which the spelling occurs *Skelton*, at least half a dozen records exist to prove that *all* descended from these Virginia families are *Sheltons*. The confusion arose from the fact that *Reuben, James* and *Meriwether Shelton* of Hanover, Goochland and Essex Counties, Virginia, used the old English "H" in their signatures. This was written with a hook that made it look like the present "K". The name, however, was pronounced "Shelton". A tracing of the arms of Meriwether Shelton, with his own signature, is given here.[1]

These arms are the same carried by Sir Ralph Shelton[2] in 1334 at the Dunstable Tournament. My tracing was copied from an old Shelton bible in the possession of the Jones family of Kentucky. The "H's" in the first and last names are *identical*, and the arms are the same as those

---

(1) The Arms of Meriwether and Reuben Shelton, as emblazoned on this bookplate, are: "Azure, on a fesse between three fleur de lis, or." with the crest, "a cornish chough's head erased sa. in beak an acorn or. stalked and leaved, vert." which is the arms of Skelton (Armathwait Castle, co. Cumberland, temp. Edward I) except that in the latter the crest is, A peahen's head erased, sa, in the beak an acorn, or. stalked and leaved, vert." In the Shelton bible the bird's head may be a peahen, I am not sure. I have every coat of arms of both the Skelton and the Shelton families in England. There are forty-seven Shelton arms, and that of Thomas Shelton, Esq. (temp. Edward III; his dau. and heir, Elizabeth, mar. John Belgrave, of Belgrave, Co. Leicester,) (Visitation of Leicester, 1619) is "Sa. three escallops, ar." That of Shelton, Co. Stafford, the same. These are the only arms of Shelton which have the "escallops" and none of the others have the same "tinctures".

(2) I can not find when the arms used by this Ralph, and later by Sir John Shelton and his wife, Anne Boleyn (and later still by the Hanover County, Virginia, Sheltons) were granted. In "Norfolk Families", Rye states: "Ralph de Chelton, at the Dunstable Tournament in *1334*, bore arms: "Arg, on a bend Az; 3 fleur de lys of the field."

I have made several attempts to get a record from the College of Arms, but they act as though they had never heard of a Shelton family. Burke gives these same arms, with a different crest, but he also gives it for *Skelton*, without any explanation that the families are one and the same.

used by my own grandfather. These arms are given as "Shelton" in Burke's Encyclopedia of Heraldry but, according to the record in the College of Arms, Burke has given the wrong crest. The same arms were used by the Cumberland *Skeltons*, a branch of the "House of Shelton" of Norfolk, England; the *Sheldons* of Derbyshire, Warwickshire and Worcestershire, are all descended from the Norfolk house.

There was a "Shelton" in Bedfordshire in 792. Either the villages took their names from the family, or the family took its name from the villages; in Norfolk, it is written in Domesday Book as "Seltun" but seems to have always been *called "Shelton"*. Blomefield, in his history of the family, states: "So numerous were the branches and so nobly connected its principal line that few private families, even in feudal times, could surpass the *Sheltons* in opulence and alliance." An old manuscript in the British Museum contains the Shelton arms with forty-seven impalements all beautifully emblazed.

I have *proven* the Sheltons, Shentons, Shiltons, Sheldons, Feltons, Carltons, Carletons, Charltons, Chiltons, Skeltons, Skiltons, Shilstons and Schyltons in Bedfordshire, Berkshire, Cumberland, Derbyshire, Northampton, Nottinghamshire, Hampshire, Lincolnshire, Cambridgeshire, Oxfordshire, Shropshire, Wiltshire, Devonshire, Staffordshire, Leicestershire, Yorkshire, Sussex, Kent, Essex, Surry, Worcestershire and Warwickshire, England, (and the Irish families of the same names) to be descendants of the *Norfolk* and *Suffolk Sheltons*. There probably are *many in other counties* descendants of the same family, as they had huge grants of land from the Crown in all parts of England.

SIR DUDLEY CARLETON, VISCOUNT DORCHESTER—FROM
A PORTRAIT IN THE NATIONAL PORTRAIT GALLERY IN
LONDON, ENGLAND

Sir Richard Shelton,[1] Solicitor General and later King's Counsel, and Sir Guy Carleton,[2] who succeeded Clinton in command of the English forces in the American Revolution, were descendants of the Norfolk *Sheltons,* as were *Viscount Dorchester (Sir Dudley Charlton,* or *Carleton,* Ambassador to Venice, to the States General and to France,

(1) Sir Richard Shelton, K. C., d. in 1647; his wife was Lettice Fisher and their eldest son and heir was John Shelton, who married Elizabeth Salvin of "Croxdale", Durham Co. They had Thomas, called Chilton in the records, of Newbottle, Durham, who married Grace Punshon and had Thomas Chilton, Jr., (Shelton), who married Isabel (called Sibell), dau. of Thomas Byrtfield; Sir Richard Shelton and Lettice Fisher also had a son, Richard, who was living in 1650 (some records state he succeeded his father as King's Councillor), and a son Robert, called "Robert of Bermingham", Warwickshire, who married Mary Temple in 1642.

(2) From Dublin Records, Vol. 13. "Sir Guy Carleton descended from the English family of "Shelton" in Cumberland, from whence they came to Ireland. He was the third son of Christopher Shelton, Esq. of "Newry", Co. Down, who died in Ireland in 1738, leaving a widow who became the third wife of the Rev. Thos. Skelton (Shelton) and died in 1757. Three brothers of this illustrious family lost their lives at "Marston Moor" in the 17th century, having espoused the loyal cause. Sir Guy was born at Strabane, Co. Tyrone, on September 3, 1724; he was with Gen. Wolfe at the siege of Quebec; in February, 1762, he was promoted to Colonel and embarked with the Earl of Albemarle for the siege of Havana, where he distinguished himself for bravery; he was severely wounded at Moro Castle and was appointed Lieutenant-General and later Governor of Quebec. In April, 1772, he was promoted to Major-General, and appointed Colonel of the 47th Regiment of Foot. This same year, he married Lady Mary Howard, sister of the Earl of Effingham. He was Commander-General at Crown Point and was created Knight of the Bath in July, 1776; in August, 1777, he was made Lieutenant-General. In 1781, he was appointed Commander in Chief in America, to succeed Clinton, and remained to the end of the war. He evacuated New York and returned to England. In April, 1786, he was appointed Governor of Quebec, Nova Scotia and New Brunswick, and as a reward for his long services, was raised to the Peerage as "Lord Dorchester of Dorchester, in Oxford; he returned to Kempshot near Basingstoke, in Hampshire, and later to his seat near Maidenhead, where he died November 10, 1808, aged 84; at this time, he was Colonel of the 4th Regiment of Dragoons, and a General in the army. He left numerous issue, and was succeeded by his grandson, Arthur Henry Carleton, who was a minor in 1808."

member of the Privy Council, Secretary of State, 1629, and
Vice Chamberlain of the Household), buried in Westminster
Abbey; *Sir Walter Charlton* F. R. S., physician to Charles
II; *Sir Job Charlton* of "The Park" parish of Whittington,
Shropshire, eminent lawyer, Chief Justice of Chester, 1662
—King's Sergeant 1668— Speaker of the House of Com-
mons, etc.; *Gilbert Sheldon,* Archbishop of Canterbury; *Sir
Joseph Sheldon,* Lord Mayor of London, *Sir Ralph Sheldon,*
the antiquarian, called "The Great Sheldon", who pre-
sented the exquisitely illumined "Windsor Visitations" to
the College of Arms; three Lord Mayors of Ireland, and
dozens of others distinguished in Church and State.

Sheltons have been in every great battle in England and
America, and have always served with distinction. In England, they are found in the personal retinue of their kings
and princes. They served through the entire French and
Norman campaigns, were in Spain with John of Gaunt, at
Crecy and Poitiers with Edward the III, at Monmouth with
Richard Coeur de Lion, with Henry IV and with Henry V
at Agincourt. The sword carried by *Sir Richard* at Agincourt is preserved with great pride and is said to rival that
of King Edward the III in Westminster Abbey.

This Sir Richard *"Skelton"* was High Sheriff of Cumberland and a Knight of the Bath. He was a brother of
Sir *Ralph Shelton* of Norfolk, and Sir *John Shelton,* whose
wife was Margaret Brus (Bruce). Through *this* marriage,
the Castle in Yorkshire, now called "Skelton", came into
this branch of the Shelton family of Suffolk and Norfolk.
It was a stronghold of the ancient Norman family of Brus.
Robert de Brus had Robert, Lord of Annandale, from
whom descended the Royal line of Scotland. Through the

TOMB OF SIR ROBERT HOUGHTON AND HIS WIFE LUCY SHELTON,
IN ST. MARY'S CHURCH, SHELTON, NORFOLK, ENGLAND

marriage with the Norman house of Brus, a *Shelton* laid claim to the Scottish throne.

In 1422 Sir Richard Shelton, called Skelton in the records, married the heiress to the Branthwaite Estates in Cumberland. Nicholas and Peter de Shelton (some records spell this *de Shelldonne*) were among the rebelling barons against King John and forfeited their great estates to the crown. These were restored by Henry III. One of the Sheltons founded and endowed an abbey in Northamptonshire; it was later suppressed and taken by Henry VIII. Henry de Shelldonne turned over his "Barony of Mortmain" to Edward I.

The Shelton name is spelled in such a variety of ways that, as one recent writer states, "the historians seem to be making sport of us", but the English history is consecutive and dates from "more than two hundred years before the Conquest"; and the *official records* prove *all* of these families of various spelling to be descended from the Suffolk and Norfolk *Sheltons*.

One of the early Sir Ralph Sheltons of Norfolk was "The Crusader". The Crusader's cross is used in the armorial glass and on the tombs at the old St. Mary's Church at *Shelton,* Norfolk, England, and old Carrow Abbey, Norfolk. The Sir Robert Houghton buried at St. Mary's, Shelton, Norfolk, married Lucy Shelton; both, with their children, are buried there and a large tomb bears their names and effigies. See plate on opposite page.

When King James escaped to France, Lieutenant John Shelton was one of the three men in his entourage. Frances Shelton was Maid of Honor to Queen Catherine. Many of the Sheltons were staunch supporters of the Stuart cause, and had to leave England to save their heads. Some found refuge in France, some in Spain, and some joined Charles II in Scotland.

John Skelton (Shelton) was "Page of Honor to Charles II". He was knighted and appointed Governor of Plymouth Citadel in 1666 and Deputy Lieutenant of the county. He married Bridget, daughter of Sir Peter Prideaux, and quartered his arms with those of the Earl of Bath. There is a memorial tablet to Sir John and his wife in St. Andrew's Church, Plymouth, England.

THE SHELTONS IN ENGLAND

MONG the early Sheltons on record in England, were Robert de Sheldonne and his brother, Guy, who fought with William the Conqueror; Baldwin de Shelton, who held land in Cumberland in 1066; a Shelton who held land in Bedfordshire in 792; and the Sheltons who were "in Suffolk and Norfolk more than two hundred years before the Conquest"; according to the history in the British Museum.

Thomas de Shelton was with Sir John Fitz Walter through the entire French campaign, 1347-56, and he and his brother William, and William's son, Robert, were in the personal retinue of the Prince of Wales. Thomas was given large grants in Essex, Cambridge and Norfolk, in the "Queen's Remembrance" list.

The first official records in Suffolk and Norfolk Counties are:

(1) John de Shelton, tied his Manor of Stradbrooke (there was an ancient Free Chapel founded at "Shelton Manor" in Stradbrooke, endowed with many lands), Suffolk, to the "Priory of Butley" in Norfolk. This was confirmed by his son:

(2) John de Shelton of "Stradbrooke", Suffolk and "Shelton", Norfolk.

(3) Nicholas de Shelton, "Lord of Stradbrooke Manor", son of John (2), married in 1215 and bought the estate

of "Weybridge Manor", Surry. He, with his brother Peter, were among the rebelling barons against King John and forfeited their great estates. His son, Nicholas, died in the service of the king. The second son of John (2), Ralph, succeeded as the estates were entailed according to the old English law.

(4) Ralph de Shelton (d. 1245) married in 1228, Katherine, daughter of Henry de Elleigh (also spelled Illeye in records) of Suffolk. Their sons were Ralph, Henry, Robert, (from whom descended the Lords of Powys—see page 11) John, Thomas and William who had a large grant in *Kent,* in 1296. I do not have the order of their births; the eldest son must have been Ralph (6).

(5) Nicholas, son of John (2) must have had his interest in his estates restored to him as he is on record as "Lord of Shelton" in 1257. His successor was

(6) Ralph, son of Ralph (4), who had sons Ralph, John, Henry and Robert (probably others); his successor to the estates in Norfolk and Suffolk was

(7) Henry, the second son of Sir Ralph (4) and brother of Sir Robert (8), who held Shelton "by the fee of Arundel" in 1270. In October, 1276, "Sir Henry de Shelton, Kt." is on record as "Overlord in Warwickshire and Leicestershire". His son, Sir Nicholas de Sheldon, was Knighted with Edward, Prince of Wales, May 22, 1306. In 1316, this Sir Nicholas held the fee of "Sheldon Hall", Warwickshire. Henry (7) also held "Brent Elleigh", and Barningham, Suffolk. He died in 1286, and his brother Robert succeeded him. This brother,

(8) Sir Robert Shelton, with his wife, in 1302 held "Shelton", "Barningham", Mundhaven", "Scole", and

"Brent Elleigh". Robert died August 25, 1306. He had sons: Alan, Ralph, Richard, John, Nicholas, Thomas, Hugh and Robert, among other children; his son

(9) Sir John Shelton, b. — 1280, succeeded to the Norfolk and Suffolk estates as Sir John de Shelton of "Stradbrooke"; he married 1st. Maud by whom he had sons John and Robert. His 2nd. wife was Hawys, dau. of the Prince of Powys of Wales. In 1316, he is on record as "Overlord of Weybridge, Surry, and Stradbrooke, Suffolk, Lord of Illeys, Cumberland, Suffolk and Silthorpe (?) in Nottinghamshire"

(10) Sir John Shelton, Kt, (son of Sir John (9) and his 1st wife Maud) and his wife, Agatha, daughter of Sir John Geddney of Lincolnshire, had the Norfolk and Suffolk estates settled on them by Sir John Shelton (9) on his marriage to Hawys, dau. of the Prince of Powys. This John (10) died very soon after his father's 2nd. marriage; he left a son Robert according to the record.

Owen AP. Griffith was created "First Prince of Powys" by Henry I—of England.

Sir Robert de Shelton, b-1244-5, d. Aug. 25, 1306, married Isabella (no surname given); in Cumberland, a record in 1268 reads, "Sir Robert de Carleton". They held "Brent Elleigh" Suffolk—tho 33rd of Edw. I. Vol. I, P. 297—Coppinger 15 "Suff. Man"

The eldest son and heir of Robert and Isabella, was Sir Alan (called) in records de Cherltone) of "Apley Castle". In 1327, he was granted the right to "embattle his Manor in Shropshire". His wife was Margery Fitz Aer—dau—of "Hugh of Apley Castle" and Whittingford. In the 9th of Richard II (1387) "Thomas Shelton of Apley Castle had license to go into Spain, with John of Gaunt".

Sir John *Shelton* 9th *recorded* "Lord of Shelton, Norfolk" is given in the Suffolk records of Coppinger in 1301 as "John de Skelton, son of Robert de *Schelton* and his wife Isabella". This Sir John had the "Lordship of Powys" conferred on him by Royal Charter in 1313 or 1314, this was either at the time of his marriage to Hawys, heiress of the Prince of Powys, or soon after. He was summoned to the Parliament of May 9-1324, as "John de Cherltone, Lord of Powys;" he was M. P. from 1313 until 1353, page to Edward I, Chamberlain of Edward II, Gentleman of the Bed-Chamber of Edward III, Chief Governor of Ireland and Justicicar 1337-38; he died in 1353 and he and his wife are buried in the Grey Friars in Shrewsbury. He was succeeded by his son, John, 7th. Lord of Powys, who married Maud, daughter of Roger de Mortimer, 1st Earl of March, by Joan, daughter of Piers de Joinville. This John Shelton was His Majesty's Chamberlain of Household, and died in 1360. His son, 8th. Lord Powys, was born in 1334 and died July 13, 1374; he married Joan daughter of Ralph, Earl of Stafford, by Margaret, daughter and heir of Hugh D'Audley, Earl of Gloucester. John was succeeded by his son, John, 9th Lord Powys, b. 4-25-1362 who d. s. p. Oct. 19, 1401 (will dated 1395); he was Justice of North Wales and married Alice, daughter of Richard FitzAllen, Earl of Arundel, by his first wife, Elizabeth, daughter of William de Bohun, Earl of Northampton. John died without issue at his castle of Pool in Wales.

He was succeeded by Edward, 10th Lord of Powys (who was a grandson of Sir Alan Shelton, son of Alan's son, John, who married Mary daughter of William Knightley "of Fawsley an ancient house of Northampton"). Edward was born in 1371 and married June 1, 1399, Eleanor, widow of Roger de Mortimer, Earl of March, and daughter of Thomas de Holland, Earl of Kent, by Alice, daughter of the Earl of Arundel.

Edward, 10th Lord Powys, K. G. died 10-23-1405; his daughter, Joyce, married, first Sir John Tibetot, Earl of Worcester; and second, Sir William Stanley, see pages 13 and 14.

From Thomas *Shelton* brother of Edward, 10th Lord of Powys descends the "Walton on Thames" family called *Charlton*. Although the descendants of this family are now called *Charlton* in the records, many of the Shropshire family were called, *Shelton*. I found a notice of the death of a "Sir John *Shelton*," at his home, "Apley Castle, Shropshire," in the obituaries of the late 1700's in England.

In 1566, Thomas Shelton was granted a 21-year lease on the Church and rectory of "St. Mary of the Abbey" in Chertsey, Surry.

The palace of the Archbishop of Canterbury is at Croyden, 10 miles south of London, on the London-Brighton Road; in 1573, Queen Elizabeth came here with her entire retinue, and stayed a week.

The Archbishop Gilbert Sheldon is buried in the church of "John the Baptist", Croyden; this was done at his own request.

In 1713, Edward called Carleton owned "Carshallton Manor" in Surry; and "Dorking" and "Milton Court" were owned by John Charleton, spelled here, Carlton, and his wife, Joyce, of "Walton-on-Thames"; they also owned the Manor of Pyford" in Godley Surry; the grant of 1548 acres included the "Park of Pyford".

D. Parkes del. 1794

G. Hollis sculp

GREY FRIERS, SHREWSBURY.

Where John de Cherltone, Lord of Powys, and his wife Hawys, daughter of the Prince of Powys, are buried

TOMB OF QUEEN ELEANOR, OF CASTILE, WIFE OF EDWARD I OF ENGLAND, IN THE LINCOLN CATHEDRAL IN ENGLAND
(See Magna Carta Chart for descent)

Charles I, in 1630, granted "Sandon Manor" to Dudley Carleton, Viscount Dorchester, who died in 1632; his heir was his nephew and namesake.

Dudley's elder brother, Sir John Carleton, conveyed the Manor later to William and Gerard Gore; John of "Walton-on-Thames", after the "Dissolution", received a grant from the King of the "Priory of Stoke D'Aberton" Surry. "Walton-on-Thames" had belonged to Gilbert de Clare and was known as "Walton Leigh". In 1540, Henry VIII bought the Manor from Sir John Shelton and in 1542 he gave John and his wife, Joyce, the Avowdson of the church of "St. Mary" Walton-on-Thames for 41 years.

In 1595, Edward Charleton owned the Manors of "Berewell" in Kingston, and "Chessington" and "Sayes" in Chertsey; there is a monument to his memory in the Church of St. Peter, in Chertsey.

—Victorian Histories of England.

Joyce Cherlton was an ancestor of *George Washington.* Her mother, Eleanor Holand, by her first marriage to Roger Mortimer, was ancestor of all monarchs of England from *Edward IV* to the present King, *George VI.* See chart pedigree below:

Edward I, King of England

:	:
Edmund of Woodstock	EDWARD II
:	:
Joan of Kent	EDWARD III
:	:
Thomas de Holand, Earl of Kent	Lionel of Clarence
who = Alice—dau—of the Earl of Arundel and had	:
:	Phillippa
	:
Edward Cherlton, K.G. — Eleanor Holand —	Roger de
10th Lord Powys, b. 1371,	Mortimer,
mar. 6/1/1399, d. 10/23/1405	Earl of March
:	:
Joyce Cherlton = (1) Sir John Tibetot	Anne Mortimer
•	:
(2) Sir William Stanley	Richard of York
	:
•	EDWARD IV
Joyce Tibetot = Sir Edmund Sutton	:
: • alias Dudley—son of	:
• John, Lord Dudley	

Margaret Sutton = John Butler	ELIZABETH
:	:
William Butler = Margaret,	MARGARET
:	:
Margaret Butler = Lawrence Washington	MARY, Queen of Scots
:	:
Lawrence Washington = Amphillis Twigdon	JAMES I
:	:
John Washington of Virginia = Ann Pope	Elizabeth
:	:
Lawrence Washington = Mildred Warner	Sophia
:	:
Augustine Washington = Mary Ball	GEORGE I
:	:
GEORGE WASHINGTON, Pres. of the United States	GEORGE II
	:
	Frederick
	:
The figure of Joyce Cherlton is 4½ feet long, and the	GEORGE III
entire picture 8 feet long, 42 inches wide.	:
	Edward, Duke of Kent
The Lady Joyce (Jocosa) is shown wearing the Robes	:
of the Garter, emblazoned with the Royal Arms of	VICTORIA
England and of Wales, by right of her father, Sir	:
Edward Cherlton, (Shelton) K.G., representative of	EDWARD VII
the royal line of Wales.	GEORGE V
	GEORGE VI

It is easy to understand how the descendants of Sir John *Shelton*, 6th Lord of Powys, became "Charltons". Sir John was summoned to Parliament as "Sir John de Cherltone, Lord of Powys". His son and successor is also on record as "de Cherltone"; the 3rd and 4th Sir John's, Lords of Powys, are called "Cherltone"; the 5th, Edward, grandson of Sir Allan, is recorded as "Charlton"; many of this line appear in the county records, as well as in the records of Oxford and Cambridge as *"Carleton"*.

In Cumberland, some records are "Schelton", which accounts for the "Skelton" which has been so hard to understand. Robert, ancestor of these Lords of Powys, is called "Carlton" in Cumberland records.

(11) Sir Ralph, second son of Sir Robert (8), came into possession of the Norfolk Estates in 1315. In 1310, Ralph's brother, John , and John's son, Robert, sold their "Manor of Haverland" to John's brother Nicholas and his wife, Alice, and *their* son, *Thomas* Shelton. From this

BRUSH FROM THE TOMB OF LADY JOYCE
CHERLTON (SHELTON)

Thomas, descend the "Sandyacres" Sheltons of Derby-shire. The John Shelton whose wife was Margaret Brus (Bruce) held "Brent Elleigh". After John's death, his widow relinquished her dowry in the Suffolk Estates and all of these estates reverted to Sir Ralph, Sr., of "Shelton". He and his wife, Joan, still held the Norfolk and Suffolk Estates at Ralph's death. They had three daughters: Joan, twelve; Margaret, five; and Isabel, six months old, when the father died; no sons. Sir Ralph was succeeded by his brother,

(12) Sir Richard, who, in turn, was succeeded by

(13) Sir John[1] of Skelton Castle, Cumberland, who was succeeded by his son Ralph. This

(14) Sir Ralph Shelton, b. in 1315, at his mother's death in 1334, was "Lord of the Manor". He was eighteen years of age then. In 1346, King Edward III granted him his Letters Patent, showing that he had been in the "King's own Company at Crecy". He was one of the Gentlemen sent to rescue the Black Prince when he was surrounded, and was knighted for his part in saving the life of the Black Prince. He was also in great favor with the King

(1) John de Schelton, son of Ralph Shelton (6) was Knight of the Shire of Cumberland in 1318.

His son, Adam de Skelton, held the same office in 1330, and he had Adam de Skelton, Proctor of Cambridge, who died in 1406. He had Anslem de Sheldon of "Sheldon Hall" Warwickshire, whose son and heir was Henry de Sheldon (1422). Henry had Sir Nicholas de Sheldon, who succeeded his father in 1442; he married Joane and had an only child, Henry de Shelton, born 1443, who married Beatrice de Peito, daughter of Sir John de Peito and his wife, Beatrice Shelton, daughter of Sir John Shelton of "Stradbrooke" and "Norfolk".

Sir John de Peito was a son of Sir John de Peito and his wife, Alinore of "Weston", Warwickshire. Henry Shelton died without issue and left his estates to "Sir John Shelton of Stradbrooke" and "Norfolk". After the

at Poitiers and was in personal attendance on Edward III in this battle.[2]

This Sir Ralph used the same arms as those afterwards used by the Hanover County, Virginia, Sheltons. He married, first Anne, daughter of Sir Ralph Burgulion of Great Snoring, Suffolk, his cousin. Through this marriage, he became heir to the great estates of Sir Ralph Burgulion. In 1346, he married Joan, daughter of Sir John de Plais of "Wetyng". She died in 1405. In the Battle of Poitiers, Ralph took prisoner John Rocourt and, later in 1356, obtained for him a safe conduct from the King. Sir Ralph built the *old* "Shelton Hall", a fortified castle, and the Church of St. Mary's at Shelton, Norfolk. (See photos and descriptions in my "Genealogy"). He died November 17, 1378 and he and his wife were buried in St. Mary's Church at Shelton, Norfolk, with life-size effigies in bronze on their tombs—these have been stolen or destroyed long since. Sir Ralph's son and heir, by his first wife, was

(15) Sir Ralph Shelton, Knt., who married Alice, daughter of Sir Thomas Uvedale, Knt., of "Tacolneston". In 1385, he attended John of Gaunt, Duke of Lancaster, on his great expedition into Spain, and was at the famous battle of Nazarett. In 1398, John, Ralph's son, released the Manor of "Gedney" in Lincolnshire to the Abbot of Ramsey. Ralph's (15) brothers were, besides John, William who

destruction, by fire, of "Shelton Hall", Norfolk, Warwickshire became the seat of the head of the Shelton "clan", now known as *Sheldon* in England.

(2) There is a magnificent painting, by our American artist Julian Story, in the Telfair Gallery at Savannah, Georgia, of this "Battle of Crecy". The author got a great thrill when she realized that in the group of gentlemen surrounding the "Black Prince" was her own ancestor, Ralph Shelton. See photo on opposite page.

THE BLACK PRINCE AT CRECY.—From the painting by Julian Story in the Telfair Gallery, Savannah, Georgia. One of the gentlemen in the group is Sir Ralph Shelton, who was knighted for saving the life of the Black Prince in this battle. The dead King of Bohemia is seen in the foreground.

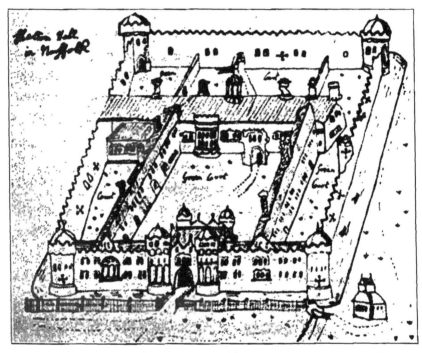

SHELTON HALL, SHELTON, NORFOLK, ENGLAND, DESTROYED
BY FIRE BEFORE 1600

married Catherine, daughter of Simon Baret of "Hardwick", and Robert. There may have been other sons but these are the only ones given in Suffolk Pedigrees. Sir Ralph was succeeded by his son,

(16) Sir Ralph Shelton, Knt. He was about 58 years old when Joan, widow of his grandfather, died in 1405. This Sir Ralph was on the "Voyage of St. Maloes de L'ifle", and on that into Scotland with Richard II, and that into Spain where Sir Hugh Hastings died. Ralph died April 25, 1424, and is buried in Great Snoring Church, Suffolk. His son, or brother Robert, who died in 1423, is buried in St. Mary's Church, Great Snoring. Ralph's (16) son

(17) Sir John Shelton, who had possession of the Norfolk and Suffolk estates in 1427 and died in 1431, also had possession of Skelton Castle, Yorkshire, and of Armathwaite Castle, Cumberland. His brother was Sir Richard (called Skelton) K.B., who married the heiress to the Branthwaite estates in 1422; he was with Henry V at Agincourt; it is *his* sword, at Armathwaite Castle, Cumberland, that is said to rival that of King Edward III at Westminster. Sir John Shelton's widow married Robert Allington. She died in 1479.[1]

(18) William Shelton, uncle of the Sir Ralph (16), was executor of Ralph's estate and his heir after Sir John (17). William, 18th Lord of the Manor, married Catherine, daughter of Simon Baret of "Hardwick". William died

(1) Robert Shelton was High Sheriff of Shropshire in 1471—his eldest son was William of "Apley Castle".

Sir John Shelton was High Sheriff of Gloucester in 1429 and of Hertfordshire in 1445.

In requisitions in Northampton in 1451 he is given as Sir Johannes Shelton.

in 1440; his wife, in 1456; both are buried in St. Mary's
Church, Shelton, Norfolk.

After the death of Sir John (17) William held "Shel-
ton", Norfolk, "Hardwick", "Nether-hall", "Over-hall",
"Great Snoring", "Thursford", and "Burgulion" in
Kerdeston, and "Brent Elleigh" and "Stradbrooke", Suf-
folk—all of these he left to Ralph, son and heir of Sir John
Shelton (17), whose widow had married Robert Allington.

(19) Sir Ralph Shelton, who was 49 years of age when
his mother died in 1479, had a grant from Henry VII of
"the Custody and Marriage of the Body and Lands of
Ralph, Brother and Heir of Robert Berney, Esq., of
Gunton". Sir Ralph was knighted in 1485 and created
Knight of the Garter in 1488. He was High Sheriff of
Norfolk. He married, first, Joan; there were no sons by
this marriage. His second wife was Margaret, daughter
of Robert Clere of Ormesby and his wife, Elizabeth,
daughter of Sir Thomas Uvedale; she died 1/16/1499 and
is buried at Bury Abbey, Suffolk. By Margaret Clere, Sir
Ralph had his son and heir

(20) Sir John Shelton, and Ralph, Richard,[1] Elizabeth
and Alice. Alice married Sir John Heveningham. This

(1) Richard was living in 1539 but I have no record of his wife or descendants. Elizabeth married Sir Richard Fitz Lewis of Dagenham. Ralph
married Mary, daughter and co-heiress of Robert Brome, of Norfolk, and widow
of John Jenny Esq. of Hardwick; she died in 1542—her husband Ralph was
living in 1539. Their eldest son and heir was Ralph Shelton Esq. of Brome
who died in 1592 and is buried at Brome; his wife was Prudence dau. and
co-heir of Edward Calthorpe Esq. of Kirkley Cone. Ralph had a sister Dorothy
Shelton of whom I have no further record. His son and heir Ralph Shelton
Esq. of Brome, was married twice; I have no record of the first wife, but his
second wife was Cecily—dau. Augustine Steward of Norwich; she died in
1612. Ralph's death is given as the same year in which his father died, 1592;
his will is dated 31. Oct-34 Eliz.

MOAT AROUND OLD SHELTON HALL, SHELTON, NORFOLK, ENGLAND

SHELTON TOMBS IN ST. MARY'S CHURCH, NORFOLK, ENGLAND THE TABLET IS A
MEMORIAL TO SIR RALPH SHELTON AND HIS WIFE, MARY WODEHOUSE.

ST MARY'S CHURCH, SHELTON, NORFOLK, ENGLAND

Sir John Shelton (20) was living in 1492, but was dead by 1500, the date of the death of his wife Margaret. His son and heir,

(21) Sir John Shelton, was High Sheriff of Norfolk in 1504. He was knighted in 1509, and was present as a Knight of the Bath at the Coronation of Henry VIII. He was "Governor of the Household" of the King. His wife, Lady Shelton, was "Governess to Princess (later Queen) Mary". Lady Shelton was Anne Boleyn, daughter of Sir William Boleyn of "Blicking", Wiltshire, and his wife, Margaret, daughter of Thomas Boteler (Butler), Duke of Ormond, and was an aunt of Queen Anne Boleyn. When Elizabeth was so persecuted during her sister's (Queen Mary's) reign, she fled to Sir John and Lady Shelton for protection. A pew in St. Mary's Church at "Shelton", Norfolk, is still called "Elizabeth's Pew". Later, when Elizabeth was crowned, she summoned her Aunt's family to London. They shared with her the Palace, and their descendants lived at the Court for Elizabeth's entire reign. Margaret, a daughter of Sir John Shelton and Anne Boleyn, was the "Cousin Madge", an attendant at the Court of the Queen, Anne Boleyn, who was commanded by her to distract the attentions of Henry when he was making love to Jane Seymour.

By his first wife Ralph had John Shelton, Gent. of Horning (who died in 1588, aged 33, and is buried in St. Martins of the Palace) and Edward Shelton, Gent. of Brome who married Anna. Both sons died before their father; Edward in 1589. By Cecily Steward, Ralph had 4 daughters, Thomasine, who married Thos. Uvedale, Gent., Grace who married John Thurlton of Brome, Mary who married Wm. Cook, Gent. of Linstead Suffolk and Frances, of whom I have no data. The estates of this Ralph Shelton of Brome including "Hardwick" reverted to the Norfolk and Suffolk Sheltons.

Madge married Sir Thomas Wodehouse of "Kimberley", Norfolk.

Sir John, Sr., (21) died December 21, 1539. *He* is the Sir John Shelton who had the grant of Carrow Abbey in 1538. It is now nearly 800 years since Carrow Abbey was founded, King Stephen having granted a piece of land by charter to two Nuns in 1146 on which this Benedictine Nunnery was built.

The Church, the oldest part of which dates from the 12th Century, with its adjoining conventual buildings must have been a striking landmark from its commanding position on rising ground overlooking the river Wensum. Some authorities think that the name Carrow is derived from the words "Car", a marshy spot, and "How", a hill. The carved stones, many of which are now placed in a Penthouse in the Cloister Garth, and the dimensions of the Church show that it must have been a beautiful and stately building.

The Nunnery clearly occupied an important position in medieval times. The right of levying toll upon all who entered the City on certain days was granted by King John. Two Bishops of Norwich, one of whom was Walter de Suffield, were consecrated in the Church. The Nunnery carried on its work for nearly 400 years until about 1539, when with the Dissolution of the Monasteries by Henry VIII the Church and most of the conventual buildings shared the fate of many another noble edifice.

The Prioress' House (now the northern wing of Carrow Abbey) fortunately escaped destruction, having been given by Henry VIII to Sir John Shelton, an uncle by marriage of Anne Boleyn. It had been built by the last (or the last but one) of the Lady Prioresses, Isabell Wygun, earlier in

CARROW ABBEY, NORFOLK, ENGLAND, GRANTED TO SIR JOHN SHELTON (21) BY HENRY VIII OF ENGLAND IN 1538

<u>Copied from</u>

"CARROW ABBEY", otherwise CARROW PRIORY, near NORWICH in the COUNTY NORFOLK.　　by WALTER RYE.

A description of the Hall and Parlour, and the stained glass in them. as they appeared to Anthony Norris about the year 17‥, is given by him in his collection.

1	<u>Shelton</u>.	Azure, a cross or.	
2	„	impaling <u>Harling</u>.	
3	„	„	<u>Ille</u> or <u>Illegh</u>, Ermine, two chevrons sable.
4	„	„	<u>Mellers</u>, Azure, in a bordure per pale wavy gules and argent; on a fess of the second, between three crowns or, three mascle conjoined(?) of the field.
5	„	„	<u>St Philibert</u>, Argent. three bendlets azure.
6	„	„	<u>Vaux</u>, Checky argent and gules.
7	„	„	<u>Burys</u>, Ermine, on a chief indented sable two lions rampant or.
8	„	„	<u>Gedding</u>. Argent three mullets sable.
9	„	„	<u>Uvedale</u> or <u>Qwdale</u>, Azure, a cross moline gules.
10	„	„	<u>Lowdham</u>, Argent. three inescutcheons, two and one. sable.
11	„	„	<u>Cockfield</u>, Azure, a cross checky argent and gules.
12	„	„	<u>Stapleton</u>, [blank shield, wrongly lettered <u>Stabylam</u>]
13	„	„	<u>Baret</u>, Argent, a fess between three mullets sable.
14	„	„	<u>Ufford</u>. Sable, a cross engrailed or.
15	„	„	<u>Brewse</u> [blank shield]
16	„	„	<u>Clere</u>.
17	„	„	<u>Marke</u>, Per pale ermine and azure, a lion rampant counter-changed within a bordure sable bezantée
18	„	„	<u>Boleyn</u>
19			[A blank shield, lettered <u>Shelton</u>, impaling <u>Woodhouse</u>, quartering <u>Barowe</u>
20	„	„	<u>Morley</u>.
21 22	} „	„	two blank shields.

The arms on the woman's side of the 12th and 15th shields are broken and destroyed, as was also the whole 19th shield; but the names which were painted on the glass under the arms, are still remaining. The two last were originally blank impalements.

Henry's reign, presumably on the site of an older house. She put her rebus, a "Y" and a "gun", on the spandrels of two of the outer doors and on those of the fire-place in the Parlour, a room panelled throughout in oak. The Guest Room is a finely proportioned one, of which the oak ceiling with its carved spandrels is one of the features.

Carrow Abbey passed into the hands of the Martineaus—members of a family which, like many others, traced descent from a Huguenot refugee, who found a haven in Norwich from religious persecution abroad. But in 1871, after the death of Miss Fanny Martineau, it was bought by the firm of J. & J. Colman. Soon afterwards excavating work was begun by Jeremiah James Colman (the father of the present occupiers, Ethel M. Colman and Helen C. Colman) and the foundation walls of the Church and adjoining portions of the Nunnery, which in course of time had become for the most part covered up, were unearthed. The Guest Room of the Prioress' house which had been divided up by another floor was also restored to its original proportions.

The modern southern wing, erected by James and Laura Stuart (the eldest daughter of Jeremiah James Colman), dates from 1899. The grant of the Abbey to Sir John Shelton (21) reads as follows:

"Grant in fee to Sir John Shelton of all messuages, etc., in and belonging to the late Priory of Carrowe"—1538— S. P. No. 967 (28) Vol. 5, p. 212, Coppinger's "Suffolk Manuscripts."

There was a very fine collection of Shelton Armorial Glass in the Abbey: part of which is shown on opposite page. The cross of the Crusades is used on all of these for

Shelton. In the British Museum are 47 coats of arms for "Shelton" all beautifully emblazoned.

In the will of Lady Anne Boleyn Shelton, proved January 8, 1556, there are legacies to "Sir John Shelton, son and heir", and to *"Sir Ralph, second son, and his wife Amy Wodehouse, daughter of Sir Roger Wodehouse, Knt. of "Kimberley", Norfolk."* From this marriage descends Gilbert *Sheldon*, Archbishop of Canterbury. Amy Wode-house *was a sister to the Thomas Wodehouse, who married* "Madge", or Margaret, Ralph Shelton's sister. Further legacies were left to Mary, daughter of Lady Shelton (who married, first, Sir Anthony Heveningham, Knt., and second, Philip Appleyard, Esq.) ; to Thomas, the third son, "Gentleman Porter of Her Majesty's Tower", (who married a Miss Appleyard) and to her daughters, Gabriella, Emma and Elizabeth, all three of whom d. s. p.[1] This *Thomas* Shelton's son, John, was Lord Mayor of Dublin in 1537; Thomas's descendants settled 'in Staffordshire and Cumberland, and from him descend a distinguished line of Sheltons in Ireland.

(22) Sir John Shelton, Knt., son of Sir John (21) and Anne Boleyn, was called "Sir John the Younger". He was High Sheriff of Norfolk from 1522 to 1525, inclusive. He held the Manors of "Shelton", "Stradbrooke", (some records say "Stratton"), "Sois", "Reeham", "Scole",

---

(1) I found no mention in the will of Lady Anne Boleyn Shelton of a daughter Anne, who is given in the H. S. Pedigrees. This Anne Shelton married 1st Sir Edmond Knevett Knt—and 2nd. Christopher Coote Esq. of BloNorton, son and heir of Richard Coote and Margaret Calthorpe. Their son Richard Coote married Elizabeth, daughter of Thomas Shelton of Norfolk.

The "Madge" who married Sir Thomas Wodehouse, also is not mentioned in the will of her mother. It is probable that settlements were made on them at the time of their marriages.

QUEEN ANNE BOLEYN, NIECE OF LADY ANNE BOLEYN SHELTON, WIFE OF
SIR JOHN SHELTON (21)—From a portrait by Johannes Corvus

MEMORIAL WINDOW IN ST. MARY'S CHURCH, NORFOLK,
ENGLAND, TO SIR JOHN SHELTON AND HIS WIFE, LADY
ANNE BOLEYN SHELTON

"Burgulion", "Barningham" (some records say "Birmingham"), "Great Snoring", "Carrow", "Brent Elleigh", and "Meldyng" (?) (spellings used in wills; probably "Wetyng"). He married Margaret, daughter of Sir Henry Parker, Jr., Knt., son of Henry[1], Lord Morley and his wife, Alice, daughter of Sir John St. John, Knt. of "Bletsoe".

Sir John Shelton (22) died November, 1558. This Sir John Shelton was one of the gentlemen who joined Queen Mary at Kenninghall in order to advance her to the throne. His daughter, Mary, was "Maid of Honor" and later, "Mistress of the Robes" to Queen Elizabeth. She married Sir James Scudamore of Hertfordshire,[2] and remained with the Queen until her death. Some of John's other children were his heir, Sir Ralph, and Anne who married Wm.—2nd son of Sir John Godslue, and Alice, who married Sir Thos. Josseline, of "Hide Hall" Herts.

(23) Sir Ralph Shelton[3] was High Sheriff of Norfolk in 1571. He was knighted by Queen Elizabeth in 1578. He

(1) Sir Henry Parker, Lord Morley, married Alice St. John, daughter of Sir John St. John of "Bletsoe", (and granddaughter of Sir Oliver St. John) whose wife was Margaret, daughter and heiress of Sir John Beauchamp of "Bletsoe". After the death of Sir Oliver, Lady Margaret married Sir John Beaufort, Duke of Somerset, and had an only daughter who became the mother of Henry VII. Margaret, daughter of Sir Henry Parker, Jr., married Sir John Shelton, Jr. and her sister, Jane, married George, Lord Rochford—brother of Queen Anne Boleyn. Lord Morley died 1556 or 1558 and his wife in 1552, aged 66. Both are buried at "Hallingbury".

(2) At her marriage, she gave *Canterbury* as her residence.

(3) H. S. Vol. 8, pg. 300 gives this Sir Ralph (23) as living in Warwickshire in the late 1500's—he died Oct. 3, 1580. I have only found three male heirs, but his will states that he left four sons. At the time of his death, he owned: "Shelton Overhall" in "Shelton", and "Shelton Netherhall" and diverse lands in Norfolk; Barrett, in Hardwicke, Snoring 2, Magna and Parva, Thursford 2 Magna and Parva and Barret's held by the Earl of Arundel; he names "son, Thomas, Porter of the Tower of London, heir."

married, first Mary, daughter of Sir William Wodehouse;
she died in 1568. In 1570, he married Anne, daughter of
Sir Thomas Barrow of "Barningham" Suffolk. Sir Ralph
died in 1580, and his widow married Sir Charles Cornwallis.
By Mary Wodehouse, his first wife, Sir Ralph had Edward,
who died in infancy, John, Ralph, Margaret,[1] Audrey and
Alice.

(24) Thomas, his heir, who was born in 1558, was another
"Gentleman Porter of Her Majesty's Tower". He died in
1595; no children are mentioned in his will. He is buried in
St. Peter's Church in the Tower of London; his first wife
was Elizabeth Flowerdew, dau. of Sir Edward Flowerdew;
no other marriage has been found. After death of Thos. in
1595 his widow is recorded as having married Sir Henry
Clere and died in 1608.

Thomas was succeeded by his brother

(25) Sir John Shelton who was born in 1559 and died
before 1606, when his brother, Ralph, owned the Norfolk
and Suffolk estates. This Sir John (25) was at the sacking
of Cadiz in Queen Elizabeth's reign. His first wife was

Sir Ralph (26), third son of the above Ralph (23), when he sold the
Norfolk estates in 1606, had all of the above manors and rent of ten others;
"Mooring Thorpe, Stratton, St. Mary, and Stratton St. Michael, Pulliam, St.
Mary's and Pulliam Market, Fritton, Hemphall, Denton, Alborough, Starston,
Barney, Tynetteshall, Eastbarsham, Westbarsham, Walsingham, Magna and
Parva, Hundringham and Kettleston". These are the spellings used in the
Court records; I have not attempted to locate these lands.

(1) Margaret born Dec. 24-1556 married Anthony Southwell, Esq. of St.
Faith's, Norfolk, who went with his brother Sir Thomas Southwell to Ireland
and died there in 1623 aged 46.

Audrey Shelton—b-June 10, 1568 married Sir Thomas Walsingham of
"Scadbury" Kent. Alice Shelton married three times, her first husband was
Thomas Waller, Esq. the second was William Wrool, and the third was
Tobias Wilkinson.

THEOBALD'S, THE FAVORITE RESIDENCE OF JAMES I, WHERE RALPH
SHELTON, FATHER OF THE FIRST JAMES SHELTON IN VIRGINIA,
WAS KNIGHTED IN 1607. HIS FIRST WIFE WAS JANE WEST,
DAUGHTER OF THE FIRST LORD de la WARR.

Joane Maleverer,[1] by whom he had Alice and Robert[2] and Richard of "Rowley Regis" Staffordshire, who had a son John Shelton of "Rowley Regis" and "Abberton Manor" Worcestershire, whose — dau — Clare married Cornelius Worley.

Sir John (25) married in 1597, his 2nd wife Elizabeth, dau. of Edward, Lord Cromwell. John was succeeded by (26) Sir Ralph Shelton, the third son of Sir Ralph Shelton and Mary Wodehouse, who was born in 1560. He married first, Jane West, daughter of the first Lord Delaware; second, in 1606, Dorothy Jermy(n), a daughter of sir Robert Jermy(n). Ralph was knighted at Theobald's in 1607. He was killed at the Isle of Rhe in 1627/8. According to records in the British Museum, he was "Minister to

(1) Joane (or Jane, records differ) was a daughter of Sir John Maleverer of "Allerton", Yorkshire, and his wife, Isabel Markenfeld.

(2) Robert, son of this Sir John Shelton, was called in records, Robert of "Birmingham" Warwickshire; he married Mary Temple, daughter of Edmund Temple of "Temple Hall" Leicestershire. Robert died in 1642; his brother, Sir Richard, was Solicitor General later K. C. to Charles I. Richard died in 1647 and it is his daughter, Lucy, who with her husband, Sir Robert Houghton and their two children, are buried in St. Mary's Church Shelton, Norfolk, and have a large memorial tomb there. (See cut, opposite page 7.)

Sir Richard Shelton K. C. matriculated as "son of John Shelton of Birmingham Warwickshire."

The Staffords Vist. give the Sir John Shelton of "West Bromwich" Staffordshire who married, first, Mary Knightley of "Fawsley" Northampton as son of the above Robert. He was a son of Sir John Shelton father of Edward Lord of Powys and was a brother of Edward. There was no issue to this marriage, according to the Visitations. Sir John's second wife was Elizabeth Holland, daughter of Cornelius Holland of "Windsor" Berkshire. Sir John died in 1663, at the age of 47; he is buried in Westminster Abbey. His wife, who later married Dr. Walter Needham, M. D., was buried beside him, on 2/13/1679. Sir John, by his second wife, had five daughters; Mary, Phoebe, Anne, Katherine and Barbara, and one son, John Shelton, born 1658, Fellow at Queen's College 1674. He married Mary Prickman of All Hallows in the Wall, London, on March 21, 1675.

Spain'', ''Secretary to the Prince of Wales'', and ''was one of the entourage of the Earl of Carlisle on the trip to France in 1612 to arrange for the marriage of Charles I with the sister of the French King''. From this, Sir Ralph, the American line descends.

Sir John Shelton, Mayor of Dublin in 1604, and Sir Richard Shelton of Staffordshire, Solicitor General to Charles I, later King's Counsel, Sir Charles ''Skelton'' who went down with his ship ''The Coronation'' in 1691, his brother Henry ''Skelton'', ''Major General of His Majesties' Forces'', who followed James II to Paris and died there, were all descendants of Sir John Shelton and his wife, Anne Boleyn. Sir Charles *supposedly* died without issue. He and Sir Henry are registered at Cambridge as ''Sons of Maurice *Shelton* of Shelton Hall, Norfolk''. Maurice was a son of Sir Ralph Shelton by his second wife, Anne Barrows. I have found no record of Henry's descendants, if he left any.

Sarah, daughter of above Maurice Shelton, married Robert Suckling and became the great-grandmother of Horatio, Lord Nelson. *Thomas Shelton,* son of Sir Ralph (26), invented the first process of shorthand in 1630. This was used by Samuel Pepys in his ''Diary''. This Thomas was the author of the best translation of ''Don Quixote''. It was translated in 1612, in forty days, for a friend who could not read Spanish. In 1620, his revised edition was published. It was *Sampson Shelton who built the clock* at Greenwich that sets the time for the world. The ''Poet Laureate'', John *''Skelton'',* who is buried in Westminster Abbey—(it was he who wrote ''Who Killed Cock Robin?'')—was John *Shelton,* son of Margaret and William *Shelton*

HENRY STUART, PRINCE OF WALES, K. G ACCORD-
ING TO RECORDS IN THE BRITISH MUSEUM, SIR
RALPH SHELTON WAS SECRETARY TO THIS PRINCE.

WHITEHALL IN THE REIGN OF JAMES I

of Dis, Norfolk. Their son, the poet, was born at Dis in 1460. He received the degree of "Laureate" at both Oxford and Cambridge. Erasmus styles him "The one light and ornament of British Letters". He was tutor to Prince Henry (later, Henry VIII) in 1490. The odium connected with his name is unjust, as it has been proven that the scurrilous book, "Merrie Tales", attributed to him on account of his gift of satire, was not written by him.[1]

Dozens of Sheltons have been on the student rolls of Oxford, Cambridge and Dublin Universities ever since the founding of these institutions. Neither the English genealogists nor I have ever been able to find all of the data about the descendants of Sir Ralph Shelton, killed at the "Isle of Rhe". He held the Norfolk and Suffolk estates in 1606 when he sold the *land* (Shelton Hall had burned down in the late 1500's) to Sir Robert Gardner, Knt.

I have never found his will. Blomefield erroneously states he died s. p., and gives his wife as Dorothy Jermyn. He did not marry her until 1606, and may not have had issue by her. His first wife was Jane West, daughter of the first Lord Delaware, and it was a son of this wife that founded the American line.

Jane was Ralph's first wife, but he was her *fourth* husband, although there was very little difference in their ages. He was born in 1560 and she, I think, in 1558. The H. S. Visitations in an account of this marriage, give him as Ralph Sheldon Esq. of "Beoley" Worcestershire. Ralph

---

(1) Another John; The Reverend John Shelton, who died at his home in Queen's square 1/31/1828, aged 56, was canon of Westminster Abbey and is buried in the "Dark Cloister". He was a son of John Shelton, Gentleman, B. A. Oxford 1795 of St. Helen's, Worcestershire, who was a Proctor of St. Helen's where he and his wife, Mary, are buried.

Shelton son of Sir John Shelton and Anne Boleyn, in 1539, was "granted all land and appurtenances of John Amerye and of the Monastery of Bordsley in Worcestershire". Ralph and his uncle William Shelton, receiver for the King, had large grants in Worcestershire and Warwickshire 1539 to 1547.

I had never been able to believe that a family of such prominence in England as the Shelton family could have died out with the founding of the American line. My grandfather had always said that one of the Sheltons was an Archbishop of Canterbury. I could find no *Shelton,* but did find Gilbert *Sheldon.* In tracing him back, I found him to be "our *Shelton* Archbishop".

Ralph *Shelton,* son of Sir John of Norfolk, and his wife, Anne Boleyn, married Amy Wodehouse, daughter of Sir Roger Wodehouse. They had a son, Roger, of Staunton, Staffordshire. Roger had three sons: Gilbert, the Archbishop of Canterbury, Ralph *Shelton,* who married Mary Perks of Devonshire; and Roger, who d. s. p. Roger's arms are given on the Cambridge records as the same as those used by the Sheltons in Virginia.

Ralph's daughter, Catherine, niece of the Archbishop of Canterbury, married John Dolben, Archbishop of York. Her brothers were John, Joseph and Daniel. Joseph was Lord Mayor of London and one of the heirs of the Archbishop, who died in 1681 and was buried at Croyden. Joseph's brother, Daniel, inherited the estates of his uncle whose will is in the English College at Rome, filed as "Gilbertius Sheldonius".

The South-east-Prospect of WESTON in Warwickshire, The Seat of Edward Viscount Weston.

Many of the records of the early days are in Latin so the retention of the "D" for the "T" is very easy to understand.

At the Coronation of Charles I, Gilbert Sheldon (*Shelton*) was Bishop of London, but he officiated for Archbishop Juxon who was old and infirm, at the Coronation of Charles.

Gilbert was made Archbishop of Canterbury on the death of Juxon and, in 1662, he is spoken of as "one of the most powerful men in England".[1]

After finding the Archbishop had come down in history as a *Sheldon,* I started to search for data on *that* name and found the missing *Shelton* families in the *Sheldons* of "Beoley", "Spechley", "Broadway", "Birmingham", and "Abberton" Manors, etc., in Worcestershire; "Sheldon Hall," "Skilts Studley" and "Weston" Manors, etc. in Warwickshire; "Apley Castle", Shropshire, "West Bromwich" and "Wolverhampton", Staffordshire; "Rowley Regis", and dozens of others.

The main line of the Norfolk family had been living in

(1) Gilbert Sheldon (Shelton) was elected Archbishop of Canterbury, August 11, 1663; he was a native of the parish of Staunton, Staffordshire, (The noted English novelist, Arnold Bennett was born at "Shelton" Staffordshire, May 27, 1867 and died there March 27, 1931) and is on record as "the youngest son of Roger *Shelton* of Staffordshire; he was born July 19, 1598 and died Nov. 9, 1677. At his own request, he was buried in the Church at Croyden (near the tomb of Archbishop Whitgrift) instead of in Westminister Abbey. He was a B. A. of Cambridge, 1619, and was Chancellor 1667-1669; he built the Sheldonian Theatre opened there in 1669.

"John Shelton of Croyden, married Lady Katherine Phipps, d. l. of Sir Constantine Phipps and daughter of the Duchess of Buckingham by her first husband the Earl of Anglesea. "The Rt. Hon. Lady Catherine Sheldon wife of John Sheldon Esq. of Croyden died January 22, 1736" Gent. Mag. Vol. 6, page 56.

Warwickshire, after old "Shelton Hall", Norfolk, burned down.[1]

(1) "Charlton House" (an entire room of which is in the St. Louis Art Museum in Forest Park), "Chilton House", "Rye House" and "Boxley" in Kent were homes of Shelton descendants.

William de Sheltone (spelled de Sheldonne in some records) had a large grant in Kent in 1296, including all the monastery lands. The "Leonard *Chilton* of Cadiz, Spain", who had a grant of arms in 1576 as "son and heir of John *Chilton* of Rye, Kent", had quartering of *Shelton* and *Barrowe* on his arms, so he was evidently descended from Sir Ralph (23) *Shelton* and his second wife, Anne Barrowe. John of Rye appears on records as *Shelton, Charleton* and *Chilton*. He may have been a descendant of Henry, son of Maurice Shelton of Shelton Hall, Norfolk, whose line I have not attempted to trace. I have found several Shelton-Leonard marriages. "Charlton House", Kent, was granted to the See of Canterbury by Henry VIII.

The sons of Edward Sheldon (Shelton) of "Weston" and "Beoley" gained distinction in their generation, in the royal service. Lionel was chaplain to Anne, Duchess of York; he died in 1673.

Dominick was Colonel of Horse in the army of James II in Ireland and Ralph was an equery to James II; Ralph died in 1723, aged 90.

Another Ralph Shelton was killed in an Indian campaign at Calcutta, April 26, 1709. He was only 37 years old, having been born in 1672. In the English records in the Gentleman's Magazine, I found a "Mr. Shelton of Shelton Hall, Warwickshire" in the 1600's besides the "Mr. Shelton of Shelton Hall, Warwickshire" in the obituaries in 1780; so, some of the family must have been known by their correct name.

The Manor of "West Bromwich", Staffordshire, was sold by Sir Edward Stanley to Richard Shelton, Solicitor, later K. C. to Charles I; in 1660, Sir Richard's son held the same office. Richard, Sr., died in 1647; his wife was Lettice Fisher. Their son and heir, John Shelton, Queen's College 1642, married Elizabeth Salvin of Croxdale, Durham County. Their son, Thomas ('called Chilton in the records) of "Newbottle, Durham", married Grace Punshon and had Thomas Chilton, Jr., who married Isabel (called Sibell), daughter of Thomas Byrtfield.

"Wendelbury" and "Wolverhampton" were also Shelton homes. The ancestor of the "Rowley Regis" Sheltons in Richard II's time, had lands in Birmingham. Richard of "Rowley Regis" had three sons: Richard, John and Maurice. John was living in the reign of Edward IV; he married Mary and had Clare, who married Cornelius Wirley of Handsworth, Staffordshire. From Maurice, second son of Richard (2) descend the Sheltons of "Beoley".—Ped. in Vaile's History, given by the Somerset Herald, John Charles Brookes.

The "Visitations" and the "Victorian Histories" are very contradictory about the owners of these estates. The former gives the Sir Ralph Sheldon (Shelton) whose first wife was Jane West, as the owner of "Beoley" in the late 1500's. I do not think this is correct, as Ralph Shelton, ancestor of the American family of Sheltons, bought the "Manor of Breforton" from Ambrose Dudley, Earl of Warwick, in 1589. The record states, "In Hilary term of 1589, the estate left me by my brother, the Earl of Leicester". In 1573, the "Manor of Costen Hackett" was conveyed to this same Ralph Shelton by *Jane Parker*. He owned the "Manor of Upton Wolde" in 1608, and the "Manor of Redditch"; in 1577 he sold the "Manor of Bentley" to Henry Field. The Victorian Histories state that "John Nevill, Lord Latimer, sold "Beoley Manor" to William Shelton in 1549; William had acquired other land in Beoley in 1544. This William married Mary Willington, eldest daughter and co-heir of William Willington of "Barcheson" Warwickshire. Their son, Ralph, married Anne, daughter of Sir Robert Throckmorton; William settled "Beoley" on this son, Ralph, who died in 1613. I think this is correct as the other Ralph was killed at the Isle de Rhe July 22nd, 1628. The estate may have reverted to this brother Ralph at William's death, and the statement that William settled it on his son Ralph, be another error.

In one record, the William (3) who bought "Beoley" in 1549 is given as a "son of Ralph Shelton"; in another he is given as a brother of Ralph Shelton, which seems to be correct.

William of "Beoley" appears to have been the son of John Shelton of "Rowley Regis", Staffordshire. William fought with Richard III on Bosworth Field, and for his adherence to Richard's cause, his lands were confiscated but were restored before his death in 1517, when he died "seized as Chief Manor of Balsford Hall", which he bequeathed to his brother, Ralph.

Extract from "BURKE'S ARMORY".

Sheldon. (formerly of Rowley Regis Co. Stafford: Warwickshire and Beoly co. Worcester and now of Brailes House, co. Warwick).

A very ancient and eminent family represented by Henry James Sheldon of Brailes House, Esq., son and heir of the late Edward Ralph Charles Sheldon of Brailes, Esq., M. P., by Marcella his wife, only daughter of and heiress of Thomas Meredith Winstanley of Lissen Hall, co. Dublin, Esq., grandson of Ralph Sheldon of Weston House, co. Warwick Esq., and Jane his wife, daughter of Admiral Francis Holburne of Menstrie: and great-grandson of William Sheldon, Esq., who was son of Edward Sheldon, Esq., by Elizabeth his wife, daughter of Sir John Shelley, of Mitchell Grove, co. Sussex, bart.

Arms.—Sa a fesse ar. betw. three sheldrakes ppr.

Crest.—A sheldrake ppr.

Motto.—Optimum pati.

In Genl. Bulwer's pedigree of the Sheltons of Norfolk and Suffolk, Sir

Richard Shelton, K. C. is given as the son of Henry, son of the first Thomas Shelton to be "Gentleman Porter of Her Majesty's Tower" (The third son of Lady Anne Bolyn and Sir John Shelton (21); this Thomas is given as founder of the Staffordshire and Rowley Regis Sheltons.

William Shelton, temp. of Henry VIII, introduced tapestry weaving into England. At "Weston", one of the Shelton Estates, three large tapestries lined the walls; these were purchased in 1814 by the Earl of Oxford, after the death, in 1812, of the wife of "Ralph Shelton of Weston", M. P. for Wilton. Baldwin Shelton of "Broadway" was brother of William of "Weston" Warwickshire.

"In 1595, Ralph Shelton conveyed "Breforton Manor" to John Watson and his wife, Anne; this was the year Ralph's brother, Thomas, died. Sir John Shelton of Norfolk and Suffolk was the John Shelton of "Abberton Manor", Worcestershire, and of "Rowley Regis", Staffordshire. John gave "Abberton" to his son, William, who d.s.p. in 1517 and left it to his brother, Ralph Shelton, whose sons William and Francis owned it in 1544. The Sir John Shelton of "West Bromwich" is buried in Westminster Abbey; his widow married Dr. Needham and is buried beside him.

"On February 13, 1679, Mrs. Elizabeth Needham, formerly wife of Sir John Shelton of West Bromwich, Staffs., buried in Westminster Abbey beside her first husband." "At All Hallows in the Wall, London, Mch 21, 1675, John Shelton, aged 17, of West Bromwich Staffs. to Miss Mary Prickman; consent of mother, Mrs. Elizabeth Needham". "At West Bromwich Manor, aged 102, Mr. John Shelton, Feb. 26, 1802, leaving nine children, 51 grandchildren, 95 great-grandchildren and 5 of the fourth generation".—These notes from H. S. Pub. and "Gentleman's Magazine".

"The 'Carltons' of Apley Castle, Shropshire, are evidently from the 'Lord of Powys' Sheltons, called 'Charlton'; in 1587, 'Francis of Apley Castle' was married to Elizabeth, daughter of the Earl of Rutland; and Anne, daughter of William Carlton of 'Apley', was married in 1501 to Randolph Grosvenor, grandson of Sir Thomas Grosvenor; Francis Carlton of Apley married Dorothy, fourth daughter of Oliver Lord St. John who died October 23, 1642. Richard, grandson of Anne (daughter of William of Apley) and Randolph Grosvenor of Belliport, was married to Ursula, daughter of Francis Carlton of Apley. Elizabeth, another daughter of Francis Carlton (Shelton) of Apley, was married to John Manners, 4th Earl of Rutland, who died Feb. 24, 1588; their first son died young, the other sons: Roger, Francis, Sir George and Sir Oliver, were, successively, Earls of Rutland.

In "British Family Names" by Barber, is the following record:
  "Skelton, a local name in Cumberland and Yorkshire; also *Shelton* from Shelton in Norfolk and Skelton in Yorkshire.
  In 'Domesday Book', it is Seltun."
In "Camden's Brittania" is this:
  "Skelton, seat of the ancient family of Brus (Bruce) of

ARMS OF THE SHELTONS CALLED SKELTONS,
OF ARMATHWAITE CASTLE, CUMBERLAND

I found a very good record of this family in the "Victorian Histories of England" in the third and fourth volumes, on Worcestershire. The volumes three and four on Warwickshire have not as yet been published. No explanation, however, is vouchsafed by the compiler about the confusion caused by the two spellings. The reading matter will be about the *Sheldons,* and in the footnotes, which refer to the court records, these people will all be called *Shelton.* It is most amazing. In the obituaries, published in London in 1780, there is a *John Shelton of Shelton Hall,* Warwickshire.

William Shelton, brother of the Sir John who married Anne Boleyn, was "Receiver for the King" for the Monastery Lands". He was an uncle of the Thomas Shelton (who married 1st a Miss. Appleyard), whose son was the Sir John Shelton, Lord Mayor of Dublin in 1537. This Sir John had a son, Henry Shelton, who had a son, Launcelot, registered at Cambridge as of "Armathwaite Castle", Cumberland. From him descends the family called *Skelton.*

Launcelot Shelton's son and heir was "John Shelton" of "Birmingham" and "Salford Manors". He matriculated at Cambridge (Queen's College) in 1594.

Henry Shelton's son, Peter, brother of Launcelot, married three times. From Peter and his second wife, Mary Leigh, descend the *Skeltons* of Yorkshire, two of whom were Lord Mayors of Leeds. Peter also used the arms used in Virginia by the Hanover County *Sheltons.*

In 1690, some of the Yorkshire *Sheltons* used a coat of

Yorkshire. Village of Skelton a few miles N. W. of York; below Skengrave, is "Kilton Castle" and contiguous to this is "Skelton Castle" of the ancient family of the Barons Brus, descended from Robert Brus, a Norman Knight, from whom the royal family of Scotland derived."

arms with the Crusader's Cross, blue, on a field of gold; the quartering and crest are both a red lion rampant. I have not been able to find out *when* or *to whom* these arms were issued.

John, son of Launcelot Shelton, married, first Julia Musgrave, and second Barbara Fletcher. By Julia, he had two sons. By his second wife, he had John, buried at Cambridge in 1639 as "Jonah Skilton", and Marmaduke (called Skelton), later of Yorkshire. Large grants of the Monastery Lands were made by Henry VIII to the *Sheltons* in many counties in England.

When Thomas Shelton, eldest son and heir of Sir Ralph and Mary Wodehouse and the second Thomas Shelton to be "Gentleman Porter of Her Majesty's Tower", died in 1595, his brother, Sir John of Rowley Regis, Staffordshire, succeeded to his estates in Norfolk and Suffolk. This was the John whose first wife was Jane (or Joane) Maleverer by whom he had Alice and a son, Robert Shelton. His second wife was Elizabeth, daughter of Sir Edward Cromwell. The record reads as follows: "The Right Worshipful Sir John *Shelton* Knight, and the Ryght Worshipful Elizabeth Crumwell, eldest daughter of the Ryght Hon'rable Edward Ld. Crumwell, were maryed this day." (Dec. 31, 1597).

I have not been able to find a record of the death of this Sir John, but his brother, Ralph, was in possession of the Norfolk Estates *before* 1606, when he sold them. I also found Carltons, Charltons, Charletons, etc. of England and Ireland to be descendants of the Suffolk and Norfolk Sheltons, as well as the Chiltons, Heltons, Cheltons, de Cherletons, Shiltons, Skiltons, Sheldons, Feltons, Skeltons,

D Parkes del.1810.

Shelton Oak, near Shrewsbury.

etc. The English records are worse than our early American ones, and it is simply maddening to try to unravel this mix-up. One has to have all of the data to do so. A few records cause more confusion than ever. Most of the records of the Shrewsbury family, Shropshire, are spelled Charlton, many Carleton and yet the old oak there is called the "Shelton Oak".[1] See photo on opposite page.

A man as prominent as the Chanter, later Assistant Dean

(1) "About a mile and a half from Shrewsbury, where the Pool road diverges from that which leads to Oswestry, there stands an ancient decayed Oak. There is a tradition that Owen Glendwr ascended this tree to reconnoitre; and finding that the King was in great force, and that the Earl of Northumberland had not joined his son Hotspur, he fell back to Oswestry, and, immediately after the battle of Shrewsbury, retreated precipitately to Wales."

This tree is now in a complete state of decay, and hollow, even the larger ramifications. It is visited by many people, from the above tradition. A gentleman whom I accompanied was so charmed with the old tree, that he gave it the name of *Owen Glendwr's Observatory*, and wrote the annexed inscription for a brass plate to be fixed to the tree:

"On July xxii,

A. D. mcccciii.

OWEN GLYNDWR.

ascended this Tree to reconnoitre,

on his march to Shrewsbury,

to join the daring Hotspur

against King Henry IV.;

but, finding his friends were defeated,

returned from this spot

into Wales."

The following are the dimensions of the Shelton Oak:

	Ft.	in.
Girt at bottom, close to the ground	44	3
Ditto, 5 feet from the ground	25	1
Ditto, 8 feet ditto	27	4
The height of the tree to A.	41	6

Within the hollow of the tree, at the bottom, there is sufficient room for at least half a dozen to take a snug dinner; and he, whose signature follows, would have no objection to make one of the party, and drink to the memory of Owen Glyndwr.

Yours, &c.   D. PARKES.

of Westminster Abbey, has come down to posterity as
George *Carleton*. He was a grandson of Dr. Henry *Shelton*
of "Hastings", Sussex, and a brother of Theophilus Shelton
(Clare 1707) of St. Paul's, Shadwell, who married Elizabeth Dryden, December 31, 1704; they were sons of Theophilus, Sr. of "Wakefield", Yorkshire. The children of this
George "Carleton" are buried in Westminster Abbey, as
are many others of the Shelton family. Several of this
family are buried in St. Margaret's, and Thomas Shelton,
who died in 1595, is buried in St. Peter's Church, in the
Tower of London.

A recent writer, previously referred to, says that "in the
Cathedrals the Shelton monuments jostle those of their
Kings".

"*Samuel Skelton*, born in England in 1584, pastor of the
Church in Salem, Massachusetts, U. S. A. in 1629, was
Samuel *Shelton*.[1] I have his matriculation and record at

(1) William Skelton, St. John's College, Cambridge, 1563, B. A. and M. A.,
died 1602. He was Rector of Coningsby, Lincolnshire. The Cambridge Roster
reads: "also *Shelton*, son of John and Joyce *Carleton* of Walton-on-Thames".
George, son of the above William, was born in 1578 at E. Barwick and died
in 1636. He succeeded his father as "Rector of Coningsby". His brother,
Samuel's, record at Cambridge is filed "Skelton (also Shelton)". Samuel's
son, Benjamin, is on the Cambridge roster as *Skelton* and *Charlton*. He is
given as of "Fobbing", Essex County, England. He had a son, Nathaniel,
registered at Oxford, 1637, and Queen's College, Cambridge, 1644. He also
had a brother by the name of Nathaniel. Benjamin had a son, John, born
in England, but baptized by his father, Samuel, in Salem, Massachusetts,
in 1639; *this John* is registered at Cambridge as *Charlton* (Queen's College,
1653). He was Chaplain to the Bishop of Lincoln and Canon of Lincoln
Cathedral. Benjamin's son, Nathaniel, later Bishop of Somerset, had a
son, John, born in Salem, Massachusetts, and baptized by Samuel Skelton
in 1648. I think it was the Nathaniel *Shelton* born in England in 1615
who is called *Felton* in the New England records, who married Mary
Skelton in Salem in 1633. He was a Lieutenant and died 7/30/1705, aged 90.
His wife died in May 8, 1701, aged 75. Their children were: John, *Nathaniel*,

College as Shelton. A daughter of this Dr. Shelton, Susannah (b. 1613/14) married in 1635/36, the first John Marsh in America, from whose brother, George, descended the Colonel Jonathan Marsh of the American Revolution. This Samuel "Skelton" was a brother of George "Shelton" (Clare 1602) and was "Chaplain to the Earl of Lincoln" in 1622; I have not been able to find a record of his first marriage. He married his second wife, Susannah Travis, April 27, 1619, at Sempringham, England, and sailed for New England May 4, 1629. He died in Salem, Massachusetts, August 2, 1634. He had two sons (left in England) by a former marriage: Benjamin and Nathaniel *Shelton*. One of these had a son, John, baptized in Salem, Massachusetts, U. S. A., in 1639. Dr. *Skelton's* son, Samuel, went back to England in 1649 and died there as *Shelton*. His sister, Elizabeth (b. 1618) married Robert Sanford of Boston, Massachusetts. Her sister, Mary (b. 1616), married Nathaniel *"Felton"*. There is no doubt in my mind that this Nathaniel was *Shelton*, a cousin of Mary's, although I have not tried to trace it back.

Edward *Chilton*, Attorney General of Virginia and Car-

Ruth, Hannah, and a daughter, Elizabeth, widow of Thomas Watkins. Nathaniel was the son of Nathaniel (called Skelton, a brother of Samuel) and his wife, Eleanor. Nathaniel, Sr., died in England, and his widow came to Salem and joined the Church there about 1637. Their children were Benjamin, Nathaniel, Judith and Margaret. Judith married John Ingersoll, who was born in England in 1625, and died in Salem, Massachusetts, in 1683. Margaret married, first Christopher Waller. She was married to her second husband, Robert Fuller, before 1687. Both were living in 1697. The John *Felton* who killed the Duke of Buckingham was a Lieut. John *Shelton* of Norfolk. The John called *Felton*, who, with his wife and children and servants came from Barbados in 1680 to visit his cousins in Salem, Massachusetts, was John *Shelton*, a grandson of the "James Shelton, Gentleman", founder of the American line, who moved from Virginia to Bermuda and died in Barbados in 1668.

olina, 1692-1698 and, later, in 1699, Attorney General of
Bermuda, was Edward *Shelton*. I have his entry at the law
courts in England, and his first marriage in England under
his right name. His second wife was Hannah Hill, daughter
of Sir Edward Hill of "Shirley", Virginia. There is no
known American issue, and this record has also come down
wrong to posterity. This Edward was a son of James and
Eleanor *Shelton* and a grandson of our first James in
America. (Will filed in London, June 1674, of St. Leonard's
Shoreditch P. P. C. Wills and Administrations, 1668-1678).
This James and Eleanor, and son, Edward, went to Bermuda in 1674 to take possession of the estate of James
Shelton, the founder of the Virginia line of Sheltons, who
died in Barbados, May 28, 1668. James' father, Sir Ralph
Shelton, was a member of the Parliament of 1611, and
signed the petition circulated by the "London Company
for Virginia" in 1610 and was a member of the second and
third Virginia Companies in 1609 and 1611. On April 16,
1620, "Sir Ralph Shelton, Kt." was a witness to the will of
Thos. Benet, Citizen and Alderman of London, of Castle
Wycrofte, Devonshire. (No. 435, pg. 148—Soam's Reg.
1620, abs. of wills—Pro. Court of Canterbury).

CHANCERY RECORDS AND ENGLISH WILLS

HANCERY Inquisition post mortem (Ser. 2) Vol. 119 No. 127. Norf.

Writ 12 Feb. 1 Eliz. [1559] of diem clausit extremum, on *Sir John Shelton, Knt.*

Inq. at Guildhall, Norwich, 4 March 1 Eliz. [1559]

John Shelton, Knt., was seised of the priory and manor of Carrowe and on 21 Aug. 5 Edw. VI [1551] enfeoffed Henry Parker, John Clare, Thomas Woodhouse, Edmund Wyndham, Knights, Thomas Woodhouse, Esq., and others (named) thereof to the use of (1) Dame Anne Shelton, widow mother of the said John for life (2) the said John for life (3) Ralph Shelton, Esq., son and heir apparent of the said John, and the heirs male of the said Ralph (4) the heirs male of the said John (5) the heirs of the body of the said Ralph (6) the right heirs of John.

John died 15 Nov. last [i. e. 1558].

The said Ralph S., Esq., is his son and heir, aged 22 at the time of his father's death.

Chancery Inquisition post mortem (Ser. 2) 196 No. 32.

Inquisition at the Guildhall, Norwich, 25 Ap. 24 Eliz. [1582] Norfolk

on *Ralph Shelton, Knt.*

He was seised of the site of the priory of Carrowe, and

of the manor of Carrowe. About 11 years since he agreed with Thomas Barrowe, Esq., that, in consideration of a marriage to be solemnized between Anne Barrowe, daughter of the said Thomas, and the aforementioned Ralph, the said Ralph should convey the said priory and manor to William Butts and Nicholas Bacon, Knts., to the said Thomas Barrowe and William Barrowe gents in fee simple to the use of (1) the said Ralph and Anne for their lives in survivorship (2) the heirs male of Ralph on the body of the said Anne (3) the right heirs of Ralph. The priory and manor are held in chief.

Ralph afterwards married Anne and conveyed the premises to Butts and the rest by fine levied Easter in 15 days, 13 Eliz. [i. e. 1571]. Afterwards Ralph and Anne had issue William Shelton. Ralph died 3 Oct. 22 Eliz. [i. e. 1580]. Anne survives. William, the son and heir, was aged 5½ at his father's death.

The said Ralph, under the style of Ralph Shelton of Shelton, Esq., by deed 20 Feb. 10 Eliz. [i. e. 1568] granted to Richard Davy of Lincoln's Inn gent. an annuity of 26s. 8d. out of Carrowe manor for life.

Ralph held no other manors or lands in Norfolk at his death.

––––

Chancery Inquisition post mortem (Ser. 2) Vol. 204 No. 154. Writ for inquiry as to lands of *Sir Ralph Shelton*, Knt.,
    deceased 11 Feb. 26 Eliz. [1584]. He died Oct. 3, 1580.
Inquisition in 'Le Sherehowse', Norwich, 28 Ap. 26 Eliz.
    [   ].
The said Sir Ralph Shelton died seised of the manors of

Shelton Overhall[1] and Shelton Netherhall[1] in Shelton and diverse lands there, the manor of Barrettes[1] in Hardwicke, the manors of Snoringe[2], Snoringes[2] and Thursford[2] in Snoring Magna and Parva and Thursford.[2]

He died seised of them in demesne as of fee 3 Oct. 22 Eliz. at Snoringe [i. e. 1580].

Thomas Shelton, Esq., son and heir of the said Ralph has received the profits since then.

Thomas Shelton, elder son (filius senior) of the said Sir Ralph is his next heir and was 22 when his father died.

———

Chan. Inq. p. m. (Ser. 2) 205 No. 170.

Writ 10 Feb. 26 Eliz. [1584] of diem clausit extremum on
   William Shelton, son of Ralph Shelton, deceased, Knt.,
   a minor in the Queen's custody.

Inquisition at the Guildhall, Norwich, 27 Ap. 26 Eliz. [1584].

The jurors say that the father, Sir Ralph S., was seised of Carrowe Priory and manor and made settlement of it (as in Inq. 196/32), that Ralph died 3 Oct. 22 Eliz. and that Anne still survives.

No other lands or hereditaments came to the Queen's hands by reason of the minority of Henry Shelton, brother and heir of the said William Shelton.

William died 12 Dec. 26 Eliz. [1583].

Henry Shelton is his brother and next heir, viz., 2nd son of the said Ralph on the body of Anne [Barrow]. He was aged seven when his brother William died.

(1) Held of the Earl of Arundel as of Formset Manor.
(2) Held of Sir Thomas Gawdyne, Knt of Cantley Manor.

P. C. C. 61 Drake

Thomas Shelton 'gentleman Porter of her majesties Tower
  of London'

To Thomas Catcher, woollen draper of Cannon streete,
London, in consideration of debt I owe him, and other
causes, all my goods, debts and bonds, on condition he pay
Mr. Albeny draper £6, Symonde my man £4, and on condition he see me conveniently buried without pomp.

Dated:—25 May 1594.

Witn.:—'John Catcher Alder, Thomas Catcher yonger'.
2 Aug. 1596 Administration (with will) to Thomas Catcher
  one of the creditors of Thomas Shelton deceased.

———

Manchester Papers (P.R.O.) 241 [Probably 1608].
      "Adventurers to Virginia"
        (showing their Shares).
Sr. Ralph Shelton.   £12. 10s.
        [No other Shelton].

———

Exchequer K. R. Special Commission Norf. 1628.

Commission, 18 May 43 Eliz. [1601] to Thomas Talbott
and others to the effect that Ralph Shelton late of Shelton
Co. Norf. Esq. by a bond of 29 July 11 Eliz. [i.e. 1569] was
bound to the Queen, together with William Mynne of Wy-
genhall Esq. in £200 payable on a certain day now past,
and has not paid.

The Commissioners are to inquire as to what lands the
said Ralph had and as to their value.

Inquisition taken at Wymondham 12 Aug. 43 Eliz. [1601].

The said Ralph was seised on 29 July 11 Eliz. and afterwards of the manors of Shelton Upperhall, Netherhall and Barwicks (sic) of the clear yearly value of £60; of divers lands in Shelton in tenure of Jn. Stannowe, value £5; the manor of Frytton with lands there in the tenure of Nicholas Garnyshe, of the clear yearly value of £20, and of a capital messuage in Frytton in tenure of Richard Fryer, gent., value £10 [marginal note that Fryer secured its discharge, see Easter 'Recorda' 44 Eliz.]; of divers lands in Frytton in tenure of Thos. Sayer of yearly value of 30s; lands in Frytton; in tenure of Ric. Stanton of yearly value of 20s; an enclosure (40 acres) in Hemhall in tenure of John Randall of yearly value of £7; enclosure in Hardwick (9 acres) in tenure of Wm. Sayer, yearly value 20s; 3 ac. land in Mornyngthorp in tenure of Wm. Johnson yearly value 5s; 4 ac. land in Stratton St. Mary in tenure of Thos. Gleane yearly value 13s. 4d.; annual rent in Mornyngthorpe, 36s.; 3 ac. land in Alborough in tenure of Wm. Ward, 5s; enclosure in Hardwick in tenure of Wm. Smith 20s; divers lands in Mornyngthorpe called Thorpehall £5; manor of Snoryng in tenure of Henry Clare, Esq., £40; rectory of Surlyngham, £5; rectory of Swandeston, £5.

He had no other lands in Norfolk either 29 July 11 Eliz. or since.

Inq. at Norwich 2 Oct. 43 Eliz. [i. e. 1601]

[evidently a supplementary inquiry]

Jurors say that the said Ralph held on 29 July 11 Eliz. the priory and Manor of Carrowe, of clear yearly value of £30.

Admon. Act. Book.   P. C. C. fo. 118.

5 May 1602

Commission granted to Barbara Shelton relict and to Robert Shelton son of John Shelton late of Bermingham Co. Warwick, to administer the goods and credits of the said deceased, in the person of Anthony Dalton notary public.

———

Chancery Inquisition post mortem (Series 2) 293 No. 54.
Essex. Writ of diem clausit extremum on *Humphrey Shelton* Esq., 12 May 2 Jas. I [1604].
Inq. at Stratford, Langthorne, 3 July 2 Jas. I [1604].

He was seised of the Manor of Ongar formerly Battells manor and a messuage and lands in High Ongar, Standford Rivers and Stapleford Tawney, and by indenture 4 June 11 Eliz. [   ] under the style of Humphrey Shelton of London Esq., enrolled in Chancery, he conveyed the same to Robert Hare of London gent. and afterwards viz. by indenture 14 June 11 Eliz. [1569] the said Robt. Hare, in consideration of £1000, re-granted the premises to Humphrey and to his wife Frances for their lives, with remainder to William Shelton gent. son of the said Humphrey and Frances, in fee simple.

Frances died at High Ongar.

Humphrey survived her, and died 1 May last [1604].

William Shelton his said son and heir was aged 30 at his father's death, and survives at High Ongar.

Feet of Fines Norfolk. Easter 5 Jas. I [1607].

Final Concord   Easter in one month 5 Jas. I
        between

Robert Gardener, knight, and William Poley, knight
        querent, and

Ralph Shelton esq., deforciant,
        of

the manors of 'Shelton alias Shelton Overhalle and Nether-
halle Snoryngs magna Snoring[es] and Shursford alias
Shursford Sheltons'; and of 100 messuages, 100 gardens,
1,000 ac. land, 200 ac. meadow, 1000 ac. pasture, 100 ac.
wood, 200 ac. heath, 200 ac. moor, and the rent of 10 librates
[i. e. pounds per year], in Shelton, Hardwick, Moorning-
thorpp, Stratton St. Mary's, Stratton St. Michael's, Fritton,
Hemphall, Denton, Alborough, Starston, Pulham, St.
Mary's, Pulham Market, Reddenhalle, Tyvett[es]halle,
Snoring Magna, Snoring Parva, Thursford, Eastebarsham,
Westebarsham, Walsingham Magna, Walsingham Parva,
Hindringham, Barney and Kettleston and the advowsons
of the churches of Shelton Hardwick Snoringe Magna and
Thursford;

Which Ralph Shelton acknowledged to be the right of the
said Robert;

Warranty from Ralph and his heirs to the said Robert
and William and the heirs of Robert, forever;

Robert and William gave £1,400.

Abstract of
Will of '*Ralphe*' *Sheldon* of St. Lawrence Evesham.
            Date of will 18 June 1619

Date of probate 5 July 1621
P. C. C. 66 Dale.

P. C. C. 66 Dale.

18 June 1619

Will of *"Ralphe"* *Sheldon* of St. Lawrence in the town of Evesham Co. Worcester.

My soul into the hands of Almighty God who of his endless goodness gave me being.

To be buried in St. Lawrence Church in Evesham in the north chapel above the seat wherein I usually sit there at God's service in the south side of the said chapel between the two pillars there, for my burial in which place and for my seat placed where now it is as long as my said seat and place of burial shall there remain, towards my now dwelling house for the use of my heirs being owners of my said house for their place at divine service and place of burial and for other more especial and charitable respects, I do give to 6 poor people that shall live in the alms house over against my now dwelling house, the allowance that now I give them every Sabbath to remain for ever and to each of them a coat every Christmas day, for the buying of which I bequeath £3 yearly for ever, to be paid out of my tithes of Honyborne as long as the alms house shall stand as it now is.

To "Miriall" Sheldon my wife £30 yearly to be paid out of my money and the rent thereof, for her life if there be not the like provision made unto her by me in my life time.

To my said wife, the use of my household goods and plate during her life, without waste, and if my wife marry or deny the poor the allowance and money formerly bequeathed to them, then she shall enjoy the said household goods no longer, but they shall pass to my heirs whom I likewise for ever charge with the said legacy given by me to the poor.

To Anne Sheldon my mother and her assigns if she survives me £20 to be paid within one year after my decease, and if she survive me not then the £20 shall be paid to them to whom my household goods shall pass.

To Sheldon Powell and Samuel Powell my brother Powell's sons (in case I have no heirs of my body), £200 to be paid within one year after my decease.

To Sheldon Stevens and Anne Stevens my brother Steven's children (in case I have no heirs of my body), £100 to be divided between them, to be paid within one year after my decease.

To my servants being with me at the time of my decease 20s. each, to be paid within one month after my decease.

To those people who attend me at my last sickness all my wearing apparel.

To my cousin Elizabeth Sheldon now living in the house with me, aged about 10 years and to her heirs and assigns for ever, in case I have no heirs of my body, all my lands, leases, plate and household goods whatsoever, also the remainder of my money unbequeathed, provided always that if the said Elizabeth Sheldon [   ] happen to die without heirs of her body then Sheldon Powell and Samuel Powell aforesaid, their heirs and assigns for ever shall enjoy the said lands, leases and extents, and if they die without heirs of their bodies then the said lands etc. shall fall to Sheldon Stevens and Anne Stevens aforesaid and to their heirs and assigns for ever.

For my burial in the place I have appointed £10.

To the poor at the time of my burial £10 to be distributed by my executors.

I appoint my friends Thomas Combes Esq. and John Kite gent. executors of this will and my cousin Frances Sheldon of Aberton and my brother Powell overseers.

Witnessed by: William Powell, Thomas Norman.

Codicil nuncupative.

About Michaelmass 1620.

To my brother William Powell my gray gelding or my gelding.

Witnessed by: Meriel Sheldon, Thomas Curteis [   ], Jones and others.

Commission issued to Meriel Sheldon relict to administer the goods of the deceased 5 July 1621 upon the executors renouncing.

Chan. Inq. p. m. (Ser. 2) 546 No. 124

on the death of Henry Shelton late of Shelton Esq. Inquisition dated 9 June 12 Chas. I.

He was seised of the manors* of Shelton Netherhall and Shelton Overhall Co. Norf. and of the advowson of Shelton church and of various messuages and land in Shelton (described).

He died so seised 17 Oct. last.

Maurice Shelton gent. is his *only* son and heir, and was aged 9 years 9 months when Henry S. died.

* Held of the Earl of Arundel as of Forncett Manor.

Abstract of

Will of *Thomas Shilton*

Date of will 4 July 1625
Date of probate 2 April 1627
P. C. C. 36 Skynner.
[Abstract]

P. C. C. 36 Skynner.
Battavia   4 July 1625

Will of *Thomas Shilton* [no description]

Sick and weak of body.

Soul to Almighty God hoping by faith in Jesus Christ to have free remission for all my sins.

To my wife "Elcibeth" Shilton dwelling in Wedgbery Co. Stafford £10.

To "Jeferie" Rodgers 40s.

To Thomas Shilton my son all such wages as shall be due to me from the "honorable Comp."

To my said son all legacies as are or shall be consigned to me or mine.

To William Paling my sword and all debts due to me "from any resident in Battavia or in the said rodes."

To 'Christefar' Teffeney and "Jon." Hunscott all goods that are in my chest equally to be divided in case of the death of my wife and child that then their parts be equally divided between Thomas Byram and Richard Shilton, the one dwelling at Wedgbery Co. Stafford the other in Ronly.

I ordain my son Thomas Shilton my executor and "Jeffrey" Rodgers and "Christifar" Teffeny my overseers.

Witnessed by:—Clement Norton, William Borne, the mark of Ellicas Hoyle.

2 April 1627 a commission was issued to Elizabeth Shilton, relict of the said Thomas Shilton in parts beyond the
seas deceased, to administer the goods of the said deceased
during the minority of Thomas Shilton his son, and executor
named in the will.

P. C. C. 28 Evelyn

William Shelton quarter-gunner "lying sick and weak
but not like to recover" aboard the good ship William being
in the East Indies, 20 Nov. 1639.

To Ralph Nicholdson chirurgion of the ship one cheese
and to his mate one cheese the remainder of a jar of sugar
and a cap.

Various bequests to shipmates:

Brother John Shelton 3s which John Collins oweth me.

Brother John Shelton living in Shadwell residue of goods.

Mother, Anne Shelton £20 out of the money which my
brother knoweth of, or if she be dead same to my sister
Joane Hall.

Piece of blue cloth etc. to be sold and the money paid to
my brother to pay unto my 'Cozen Blackwell' for the
tobacco which he brought me down to Gravesand when the
ship was going forth.

Pr. 1 Feb. 1640-1 by the brother John Shelton (altered
from Shilton) on renunciation of letters of administration
granted to a certain John Shilton Dec. 1640.

P. C. C. Will 155 Essex.

Samson Shelton of St. Bride's London: 25 Oct. 1648 out
of his 'goods, lands and leases' bequeaths to his only
brother John Shelton £100 within 1 year, if then living, 2

half-sisters 'Katharine and Bridget' Shelton £50; the Company of Watchmakers £50, the interest whereof to the neediest and poorest of the Company for ever;

William Proudelove, 20s.

Personal goods, leases and lands of inheritance to wife for life, beseeching her if she have a son to call him 'by my name Christian and surname namely Samson Shelton', he to inherit at her death, or else testator's heirs.

Overseers, loving father Mr. John Por-tar (sic) and my friend Mr. Thos. Lownes, 20s. for rings.

Witn. John Banister, Theo. Lownes, John Porter, Wm. Proudlove.

Pr. 2 Nov. 1648 by the widow Issabella Shelton.

Cal. of Committee for Compounding

p. 2240—*Richard Shelton* of Perton, Tettenhall Parish, Co. Staff. 9 Ap. 1650.

Compounds for delinquency in adhering to the forces raised against Parliament. Is discovered by Lady Moore.

24 Ap. 1650

Fine at 1/6, £40, 3s., 4d.

Rye. Norfolk Families.

794.

Henry Shelton b. 1577 went to the Low Countries in 1603, many years a captain in the States Army. By his wife Elizabeth d. of Thomas Jermyn of Debden he had (inter alia)

Maurice Shelton of Barningham Suff. b. 1625, d. 1666,

who by Elizabeth d. of Sir Robt. Kemp of Gissing had (inter alia)

Maurice Shelton, s. and h. of Barningham in Suff. m. Martha Appleton and died 1680.

1734—Shelton, Thomas—Bucks—of St. Martins in the Fields Middx. Brother Thomas North. No other relations mentioned.

1738—Skelton, Thomas. Middx. 21 *Brodrepp.

1738—Shelton, Thomas. Middx. 78 **Brodrepp.

* Mentions mother Eleanor Skelton, niece Mary dau. of Mathias Skelton her brother Thomas. No mention of wife and children; of St. Luke Middx.

**Of St. James Westminster. Dau. Dorothy wife of John Rawleigh. Daughter wife of Stephen Popham. No wife mentioned.

Search for *James Shelton of Bermuda* died 1668.

Wills and Administrations—1668-1678.

1674—Shelton, James. Admon. June. of St. Leonard Shoreditch. Wife Eleanor, son Edward Shelton. (No *will* only adm.)

Arch. London 1668-1687 Wills and Administrations. Only Shelton entries :—

Shelton Elizabeth widow St. Botolph Aldersgate. Will 10 Oct. 1685—AB. 14/124.

Shelton William St. Botolph Aldgate Renon 17 Nov. 1687 —AB. 14/265.

Comm. London 1668-1679. Wills and Administrations. Only Shelton entries :—

1670—Shelton Isacus—Admon. Dec. 89.

1670—Skeldon Radolphus—Will Feb. 98.

Consistory of London 1668-1680. Wills and Administrations. No Shelton entries.

P. C. C. Wills 1597-1649. No Sir John *but:*—1624 Sheldon, John, husbandman, Porton, par. of Tetenhall, Staffs. 33 Byrde; 1645 Sheldon, John, of Packwood, Co. Warwick, 131 Rivers.

Arch. London 1597-1620 Wills and Administrations. No John Shelton, only the following Shelton wills and administrations:—

1606—Shelton, Thomas, St. Andrew Holborn, will 6 Dec., A.B. 4/317 P.

1609—Shelton, Jane, spinster, St. Andrew Holborn, admon. 4 Oct., A.B. 4/369 A.

1609—Shelton, Thomas, St. Andrew Holborn, admon. 1 Nov., A.B. 4/371 A and A/C.

1609—Sheppard, alias Shelton, Margery, St. Andrew Holborn, admon. 8 Nov., A.B. 4/371A.

1613—Skelton, Thomas, St. Botolph Aldgate, admon. 14 Feb., A.B. 5/39 A.

1614—Skelton, Sara, widow, St. Botolph Aldgate, will 23 June, A.B. 5/41 P.

Comm. London 1597-1603-1607 Wills and Administrations. No Shelton entries.

Consistory London 1597-1620 Wills and Administrations.

Arch. Middx. Calendar begins 1608.

MISCELLANEOUS NOTES

Miscellaneous notes from the "Harleian Society Publications", the "Gentleman's Magazine", Stanleys "Westminster Abbey" and the Regs. of Cambridge and Oxford.

"At Ghent—Wm. Sheldon of Sheldon Hall Warwicks. Sept. 1780" Vol. 50 p. 445—G. M.

"In Germany in the Hanoverian Service, Capt. Edward Sheldon, bro. to Ralph of 'Weston' Warwicks in 1780." G. M. vol. 50 p. 589.

"At Bath Thomas Sheldon Esq. of 'Abberton' Worcesters. Aug. 26, 1804." G. M. v. 74 p. 886.

"Robert Sheldon of Bermingham Farm, Warwicks," died at 'Kingham' Oxfords on Jan. 6, 1810, aged 70. Mr. Robert Barnes, his brother-in-law died the same day." G. M. vol. 80, p. 284.

"Louisa, 2nd. dau. of Ralph Sheldon Esq. M. P. married Robt. Fellowes Jr. Esq. of 'Sharisham,' Norf. in 1815". G. M. vol. 86, p. 82.

"John Dolben, husband of Catherine, dau. of Ralph Shelton, was a student at Christ Church College and famed for his valor at Marston Moor and at York and for keeping up the service of the Church of England at Oxford; he is buried at York, d. 1686; his daughter Catherine is buried in St. Benedict's Chapel, Westminster Abbey." p. 524, Stanley's Westminster Abbey.

"Lease of Mansions and Rectory of 'Paddington' given by Archb. of Cant. to Joseph and Daniel Shelton his nephews; Jos. was Sir Joseph, Lord Mayor of London; he died in 1681 and Daniel inherited the estates of the Archbishop." H. Soc., vol. 65, p. 88.

"Dr. Wm. Jones of 'Hatton Gardens' Nov. 11, 1738 to the widow of Mr. Richard Shelton 'Maidstone' Kent; fortune of 40,000 lbs." G. M. vol. 29, p. 293. This Richard Shelton was buried in Thurnham Church, Kent.

"Rev. Mr. Shelton, app. Chaplain to Maidstone prison 1809 (ecc. app.). G. M. vol. 79, p. 813.

"Thos. Shelton app. Capt. of Marines 4-5-1755 of Kent; he was promoted to Col. and died in 1779." G. M. vol. 25 and 29.

"John Shelton app. Vic. of Aldersgate, St. Botolphis, Oct. 16, 1762." G. M. vol. 32, p. 505.

"John Charlton Esq. of 'Boxley' near Maidstone, died in 1770." G. M. vol. 40, p. 346.

"A 21 year lease of the Church and rectory of St. Mary of the Abbey of Chertsey, was granted to Thomas Shelton in 1566."

"Rev. Mr. Charlton, Fell. of Clare, Camb., died at Dorkin, Surry, Sept. 1736." G. M. vol. 6, p. 552.

"Wm. Shelton, Esq. of 'Mitcham' Surry, descendant of a very prominent family, died Feb. 1752." G. M. vol. 22, p. 192.

"John Charlton or Carleton of 'Walton-on-Thames' was a son of John Shelton called 'John of Land' Lincolnshire, and grandson of Thos. of 'Sutton' Kent; Thos. was a brother of Wm. of 'Abberton Manor' Worcesters."

"John married Joyce Welbeck of Kent; their son John married Eliz. Danyell, of W. Molesley, Surry, and their s. & h. married Joyce. John and Eliz. had another son, Geo. Gerard, Dean of Peterborough, and 2 daughters". H. Soc. Visit. of Surry.

"Thomas Sheldon of Worcester, Gent. Oriel Coll. Nov. 23, 1581; aged 15."

"Antony Sheldon, son of Wm. of 'Broadway' Mat. Oriel Coll. 1642; aged 17."

"Wm. of 'Broadway' was a son of Anthony Shelton, bro. of Ralph of 'Beoley'. Anthony's other sons were George, Ch. Ch. Coll. 1581, *and Sir Dudley*, Ch. Ch. Coll. 1591."

"Edward Sheldon of Worcesters. Gent. mat. Oxford Nov. 19, 1621; aged 18, as of Grays' Inn Oct. 1620" as of Stratton Gloucesters; son of Edward of "Beoley" Esq. b. Apr. 23, 1599, d. in London 3-27-1687, bro. of Ralph, later of *Steeple Barton* Oxfordshire.

"John Shelden of Worcesters. Magdalen Coll. Gent., mat. Dec. 1577; aged 17; at Lincoln's Inn 1581."

"John Shelden of Worcesters. Gent. mat. Oriel Coll. Mch. 1584; aged 15."

"Ralph Sheldon of Worcesters. Gent. Arm. Gloucester Hall. Reg'd Jan. 17, 1600-1, aged 7, of Steeple Barton, Oxon. son of Edward (the Monk) of 'Beoley'."

"Richard Sheldon, son of Richard of 'Bewdley' Worcesters. Ch. Ch., 1707; aged 17; Rector in Ellington, Norfolk and Dittisham, Devons. 1721-23."

"Edward, son of Thomas of 'Wolverhampton' Staffords. mat. Pembroke Coll. Ox. Apr. 8, 1693; aged 18."

"John Shelton, Fellow at Queen's, 1674 (Staffs.) bro. of Rich. d. 1682 *sons* of *John* of W. Bromwich, later of Warwicks." Cam. Reg.

"Thos. Shelton, Gent. mat. Oxford Nov. 11, 1650; B. A. 7-31-1652, M. A. fr. Magdalen Coll. May 1, 1655; nephew to *Holland* M. P."

"Sam'l. Skelton (spelled also *Shelton*) Clare 1608; s. of Wm. 1563, bap. Coningsby, Lincolns. 1592. B. A. & M. A. 1615. Chap. to Earl of Lincoln 1622; sailed for New England May 4, 1629. Installed as pastor of Ch. in Salem, Mass. Aug. 6, 1629; married Susannah Travis Apr. 27, 1619, at 'Sempringham' d. Salem Aug. 2, 1634, Bro. of *George* 1595." Camb. Reg.

"Geo. Shelton, St. Johns, 1595 (son of Wm. 1563) b. E. Barwith, Lincolns. 1578; M. A. fr. Clare, 1602; ordained Deacon and Priest of Lincolns. 1602; Rector of Coningsby 1602-36; d. 1636, bro. of *Sam'l*. 1608 and father of *Wm.* 1627."

"Wm. Skelton (also *Shelton*) St. John's 1563; *father* of *Sam'l*. 1608 and *Geo*. 1595; Rector of Coningsby 1582 to 1602; B. A. & M. A. d. 1602."

"Wm. Shelton of 'Brentwood' Essex, Jesus Coll. 1650 d. 1699; father of Wm. Shelton 1683 Jesus Coll., s. of Wm. Shelton 1650 (Rector of St. James, Colchester, Essex) died in College and buried in Chapel there 11-24-1686."

"Geo. Shelton, s. of John of Worcester (City) Gent. Worcester Coll. mat. 6-24-1779, aged 17; B. A. 1783; M. A. 1786; Minor Canon Worcester Cathedral, d. 1812."

"John Shelton, s. of John of St. Helen's Worcester Co. Gent. Worcester Coll. mat. Oct. 12, 1790, aged 18; B. A. 1795, minor Canon of Westminster Abbey and Rector of Child's Wickham, Gloucesters. d. 2-16-1828. Bro. of above *George*."

"Nicholas Shelton of 'Landilt' Cornwall, had son Thomas (Reg. at Christ Ch. Camb. as *Charlton*) who matriculated 1636; he was born at 'Sandyacres' Derbyshire in 1619 and died in 1690, aged 71; he was the father of Thos. Charlton

Fell. of St. John, Camb. 1659; born at 'Chilwell' Notts., adm. to Gray's Inn May 1662, d. 1701." Derby's Visit. Thos. was high sheriff of Nottinghamshire.

The Nicholas Shelton (above) married Elizabeth Wodehouse and his son Thos. married Susannah Shelton; prob. a cousin.

"James Skelton of London, St. John's College mat. Dec. 15, 1620, aged 20, of Merchant Taylor's School 1613, as son of Robert late of Southwark, dec'd; James b. July 21, 1600." Ox. Reg.

"Geo. Shelton, Trinity 1724-25 of Westminster, s. & h. of Richard of St. James; adm. Inner Temple 1-21-1726." Camb. Reg.

"John Shelton, Clare. licensed to teach at Long Medford, Suffolk, B. A. 1584-85."

"John Shelton, adm. age 16, Pembroke 1617, son of Edmund of London, mat. 1618, scholar, B. A. & M. A. of Norfolk and Suffolk."

"Peter Shelton, Trinity, of Carlton Rd. Norfolk, Proctor 1391-92, Treas. of Chichester, d. 1436; Commissary of Alexander, Bishop of Norwich. 1408." Camb. Reg.

"Theophilus Shelton, Clare. 1707, son of Theo. Sr. of 'Wakefield' Yorks, Fellow of Magdalen 1712."

"Sam'l. Skelton (also *Shelton*) Queen's 1612 of London; B. A. & M. A. 1619."

"John Shelton, Lieut. 1st Bat. 9th foot Roy. Eng. wounded severely, arm amputated; Dec. 1813, d. 1814." G. M. V. 83, p. 607.

"Lieut. Shelton 2nd. Bat. 28th foot wounded in battle 1812." G. M. vol. 81, p. 162.

"Sam'l. Shelton killed in an accident at Melton Mowbray 1809, aged 11." Vol. 79, p. 1236.

"Mrs. Shelton relict of A. J. Shelton Esq. of Pop Castle, Cumb. Aug. 1812."

"May 1817, on Nov. 3rd at Jamaica (Serge Island Estate) Fred'k Rich'd, eldest son of the late Robert Shelton Esq. of Kennington."

"Suddenly Mr. Richard Shelton one of the loyal Nottingham Inf. Mch. 1799." Vol. 69, p. 259 G. M.

"Mr. Wm. Shelton of 'Seaton' to Miss Ogden of Coldicott, Rutland Co. Apr. 1798." G. M. V. 68, p. 53.

"At 'Seaton' Rutland Co., Mr. J. Shelton aged 75, May 1797." G. M. vol. 67, p. 439.

"Anne, dau. of Thos. Shelton, Knt. and his 1st wife, married Richard Josselyn son of Sir Thos. Josselyn and Alice Shelton, dau. of Sir John Shelton and Margaret Parker. The Josselyn's are of Hide Hall-Hertfs."

"Thos. Shelton Esq. elected Clk. of the Peace of the City of London, 1801." Vol. 71, p. 1204, G. M.

"Henry Shelton, Brig. Gen'l. to be Col. of Ft. 1745."

"Henry Shelton Esq. d. 1743 and left a great fortune to his son Col. Henry Shelton." Vol. 13, p. 163. G. M.

"Henry Shelton pro. to Lieut. Gen'l. in 1747. He was made Maj. General of His Maj. Forces; he foll. the fortunes of James II and was an excellent Officer and Gallant Gentleman; he died in Paris while in exile." Vol. 17, p. 497, G. M.

"Mr. John Shelton of Canterbury, to Miss Holmes." G. M. V. 68, p. 353.

"James Shelton, Gent. died at Richmond, Va. Apr. 7, 1735."

"Ralph Shelton, Gent. d. June 1684, aged 61."

"Capt. J. W. Shelton of the 28th foot, wounded in battle June 18, 1815."

"Mrs. Shelton of 'Morcot' Rutland Co., aged 74, d. Feb. 20, 1803." G. M. v. 73, p. 385.

"Sir Chas. Cornwallis and Lady Anne Shelton wid. of Sir Ralph Shelton had a dau. Dorothy who married Wm. Fitz."

"Wm. Sheldon Esq. of Gray's Inn, to Miss Hester Cooper of Thornhaugh Str. Bedford Square, Feb. 22, 1809."

"In her 79th yr. wife of Mr. Sheldon of Bristol, May 1811."

"Mr. Shelton Sr. Surgeon, d. before 5-15-1783." G. M. vol. 79, p. 277-604-515.

"John *Shelton* Esq. in Queen's Square, Bath, d. 1766. His son Dr. *Charlton* married Miss Wright in 1759." G. M. vol. 36, p. 4398.

"At Kilkenny Castle, Ireland, Wm. Skelton Esq. e. s. of Robert *Shelton* Esq. of the 'Strand' London, March 27, 1813."

"At his Lordship's house in George St. Hanover Sq. Mary, Visc. Carlton, dau. of Andrew Matthew Esq. 3-13-1810. She was married to Hugh, Visc. Carlton, July 15, 1795; no issue, she was his 2nd wife."

Daniel Shelton, Gent. of Clifford's Inn, 40, and Helen Chatfield of St. Sepulchres, 22 dau. of Richard Chatfield, Gent. of same, at St. Sepulchres Aug. 24, 1641. P. 260, vol. · 26, H. Soc.

"Edward Shelton of the Inner Temple London Esq. and Anne Johnson of Ilford, Co. Essex, wid. at St. Andrew's

Holborn or St. Bartholomew the Less London, Apr. 9, 1661." P. 283, vol. 26, H. Soc.

"Sam'l Skelton of Christ Church London and Anne Wakefield, wid. of George, at St. Leonards, Foster Lane, London, Feb. 12, 1615." P. 39, v. 26, H. Soc.

"Benj. Skelton of Fobbing, Co. Essex and Eliz. Thompson, orphan at St. Stephen's, Coleman Str. London, Nov. 26, 1617." P. 55, v. 26, H. Soc.

. "Jane Skelton of W. Hanningsfield, s. d. 19, dau. of John Skelton, Gent. of same to Walter Lukin Gent., of Mashbury, Co. Essex Bach. 30, at St. Bennett's Paul's Wharf London, Feb. 10, 1623." P. 135, v. 26, H. Soc.

"Richard Shelton married Jane Hollingworth, wid., Gen. Lic. May 9, 1560 by the Bishop of London, in London." P. 21, v. 25, H. Soc.

"Anne Shelton married Edmund Stannton of Wyckham (Anne of Stamford Rivers) Gen. Lic. May 4, 1571 London." P. 48, v. 25, H. Soc.

"Lady Anne Shelton and Gawin Caren, Jan. 28, 1530, in London." P. 8, v. 25, H. Soc.

"Constance Shelton married Roger Brawnche of W. Horndon, Essex, Gent. Aug. 6, 1579, Gen. Lic." P. 89, v. 25, H. Soc.

"Frances Shelton, wid. of Hanwell, Middlesex, Gen. Lic. Jan. 3, 1588 to John Astwycke, City of London, Gent." P. 175, v. 25, H. Soc.

"Joyce *Shelton* of St. Peter's ad Vincula in Tower of London, wid. of Shelton of same, to Wm. Gower of All Hallows Stayning, London, Feb. 8, 1603." P. 282, v. 25.

"Richard Shelton, Gent. of St. Botolph Aldsgate, bache-

lor, 28, to Anne Smythe of Hackney, Middlesex, 21, dau. of
Bartholomew Smythe, Gent. at Hackney, March 15, 1612.''
P. 19, v. 26, H. Soc.

Some Shelton marriages in England:

"Dorothy Shelton, wid. of John, dec'd of St. James,
Clerkenwell, 30, to John Evans, Gent., of St. Andrews, Holborn, bachelor, 30, Feb. 16, 1627.'' P. 192, v. 26, H. Soc.

"At St. James, Clerkenwell, Sam'l Skilton of St.
Martin's, Ludgate, London, to Elisha Lane, at St. Botolph,
Aldersgate, London, Dec. 31, 1624.'' P. 148, v. 26, H. Soc.

"Wm. Shelton of St. Michael, Wood Str. London, and
Anne Smith, dau. of Hugh Smith, decd., at St. Michael's,
3-9-1618.'' P. 71, v. 26, H. Soc.

"Eliz. Shelton, wid. of Ellis Shelton to Francis Atkinson
of St. Clement Danes, Middlesex, at St. James or St.
Botolphs, Bishopgate, London.'' P. 162, v. 26, H. Soc.

"Jane Shelton, wid. of Thomas Shelton, late of St. Margaret's Westminster to George Martyn of the City of
London, at St. Andrew's in the Wardrobe, London, May 6,
1611.'' P. 2, v. 26, H. Soc.

"Thomas Shelton of St. Mary Woolnoth, London, and
Dorothy Swinburne, wid. of Henry Swinburne, of same, at
Stepney, Middlesex, May 12, 1613.'' P. 21, v. 26, H. Soc.

"Mary Skelson, dau. of — Skelson, dec'd. of Leicester
Co., at St. Trinity the Less, London, to Richard Alanby of
Waltham Cross, Herfs. Jan. 11, 1611.'' P. 8, v. 26, H. Soc.

"Mary Shelton, sp., age 19, of St. Paul's Churchyard,
London, and John Ryres of Brandisburg, S. Hampton, Esq.
Bach. 23, consent of mother, Mrs. Needham, Oct. 2, 1671 at
St. Dunstan's East.'' (Mary Shelton, dau. of Mrs. Need-
ham and her 1st husband, Sir John Shelton, of W. Brom-

wich, Staffordshire; both are buried in Westminster Abbey.)

"Miss Shelton, only dau. of Rev. Charles Shelton, of The Borough to Mr. Thos. Nott of Cornhill Abbey, 1788." Vol. 59, p. 276, Gent. Mag.

"Mary Shelton of Westminster and Edmund Daundy, at St. Margaret's, London." H. Soc., v. 32, p. 18.

"Lisle Hackett Esq. of 'Moxhall' Warwickshire, bach., 23, to Martha Shelton, Ch. Ch. London, parents dead, at St. Olive Jewry, London, July 13, 1688." H. S., vol. 24, p. 188.

From "Collins Peerage":

"Wm. 2nd Ld. Petre was one of the Knights of the Shire of Essex; in the 39th of Eliz. 1597, he married Catherine, 2nd dau. of Edw. Somerset, Earl of Worcester. His 2nd dau. Elizabeth mar. Wm. Shelton of *'Beoley Manor'* Esq. by whom she had Ralph Shelton, the great antiquary and herald, called 'The Great Sheldon'." Ralph's mother was a Lady of Honor of Queen Elizabeth's and the Queen was Godmother to Elizabeth's daughter Elizabeth.

This also from "Collins Peerage":

"Sir Constantine Phipps, Knighted in 1710, and appointed Lord High Chancellor of Ireland, died Oct. 30, 1728; issue one son, William who married Feb. 26, 1718, Lady Catherine Annesley, only dau. and heir of James, Earl of Anglesea, by his wife, Lady Catherine Darnley, dau. of King James II. Her first husband was John Sheffield, Duke of Buckingham; she was the mother of the last Duke of that family.

"Lady Catherine's dau. Catherine Annesley married 1st William Phipps (son of Sir Constantine) on Feb. 1st, 1730; after his death she married John Shelton of Croyden in Surry, and lived until Jan. 8, 1736. She is buried at Croyden. She left a dau. Catherine Phipps and a son Constantine Phipps, who was created 1st Lord Mulgrave, of 'New Ross' in Wexford Co., at St. James Palace, Aug. 8 and at Dublin, Sept. 3rd, 1767.

"William Phipps invented the diving bell, and was created a Knight by James II and appointed Governor of Massachusetts where he remained until his death Feb. 18, 1694. He is buried in the Parish Church of St. Mary Woolwoth in London, where a large monument was erected by his widow."

"Robert of London (Charlton) Arm, was father of *Sir Job,* Magdalen College 1632, aged 17, baronet 1686, d. 1697, father of Wm. (1666). Sir Job, knighted 1662, M. P. for Ludlow 1659-1678; Speaker of the House of Commons, Feb. 1673, created baronet 1686, d. 1697. Robert, prob. son of Sir John Shelton, b. 1559, and brother of Alice Shelton. The 2nd wife of this Sir John Shelton was Elizabeth Cromwell, whom he married in 1597.

"Lady Anne Shelton, sister of Charles Brandon, Duke of Suffolk, and widow of Sir John Shelton of Cornwall or Devonshire, married Sir Gawen Carew, of "Wood," Jan. 28, 1530, in London. The tomb of Lady Anne, is in Exeter Cathedral; the will of Sir Gawen is dated 1585.

"Eliz., dau. of John Shelton, Esq. 'of Leywood,' Cornwall or Devonshire, married Sir Peirs Courtney."

"Fred'k Granville of 'Ivy Bridge' Devonshire, married Isabel, b. 1810, dau. of Edw. Sheldon, of 'Brailes' Worcesters.

"Jane, dau. of John and Joyce of 'Walton-on-Thames', (called Charlton and Carlton in the record) later of 'Brightwell' Oxon, married Erasmus Gaynesford, (of

'Crowhurst') son of John Gaynesford; a sister of *John,* married a Crowe of 'Brasted' Kent. Joyce, wife of John Carlton (Shelton) was Joyce Welbeck of Kent.

"Joseph Shelton, s. John, of 'Salford' Co. Warwick p. p. St. Edmund Hall, matric. 26 March 1705, aged 23; student of Inner Temple 1696 (as son and heir of John, of 'West Bromwich' Co. Staffords Vicar of Salford (Priors) 1721, see Foster's Inns of Court Reg.''

"William Shelton, B. A. fr. Jesus College, Cambridge, 1653-54, M. A. 1657; incorporated 20 Sept. 1660. Vicar of Great Burstal 1662 and of Colchester St. James, 1670, and of Stisted (all Essex) 1691-1700. See Foster's *Graduati Cantab* etc.''

"John Shelton the poet studied at Oxford; Rector of Diss, Norfolk; wrote against the *Monks* and *Dominicans;* took sanctuary at Westminster; died 26 June, 1529, buried in the chancel of St. Margaret's, Westminster. See 'Ath.' 1.49; and Lansdowne M. S. 979 F. 76.'' This was the John called Skelton, Poet Laureate of England.

"John Shelton, of Cumberland, Gent., Queen's Coll. matric. 4 April, 1617, aged 17." Ox. Reg.

"Elizabeth, d. and heir of Wm. *Shilston* Esq., was the 2nd wife of Sir John Whiddon, Knt. Justice of the Kings Bench. Elizabeth was dau. of William Shilston (heir) and Alice, dau. and heir of James Upcott. Wm. was the heir of his father Wm. Shilston and his wife Constance, heir of Thomas Wraye, of 'Wrey' in Devonshire." Vol. 6, H. Soc., p. 355.

The above were *Shelton* marriages and estates.

"John Skelton, Gent. of Cumberland, Queen's Coll. Mat. Apr. 4, 1617, aged 17." Oxf. Reg.

"*John Skelton,* Queen's Coll. 1594, s. and h. of Launcelot, of Armathwaite Castle, and Catherine, dau. of Thomas Dalston, of Dalston Hall, Cumberland Co., married 1st Julia Musgrave, dau. of Christy Esq. of Edenhall; 2nd Barbara Fletcher of Cockermouth; d. 1652; father of John (1635) Marmaduke (1638) and Richard (1618); bro. to Sir Richard *Shelton,* King's Council and Sol. Gen." Ox. Reg.

"Thos. Shelton, son of Thos. Shelton, b. 1-11-1631, of St. James Parish, Clerkenwell, Middlesex."

"Eliz. dau. of Thos. Shelton, bap. 1-24-1631."

"Christofour *Selton,* son of Thos. *Shelton,* bap. Aug. 7, 1635."

"Sarah, dau. of Thos. Shelton, bap. May 4, 1633."

"Eliz. d. of Thos. Shelton, buried 1-25-1632. Hallow's Honey Lane, London." (All of the same Parish.)

The Army lists are full of Shelton Lieutenants, Captains, Majors, Colonels, etc., under the various spellings of the name. The following letter was a reply to a letter of the author of this History to the Registrars of Oxford and Cambridge, asking why such ridiculous entries (those of one man under two or three names) had been allowed to stand without correction or explanation for over two hundred years:

The Registry of the University Cambridge

30 July 1930

Madam,

In reply to your letter of July 6 I fear that I can only refer you once more to the work of J. & J. A. Venn. I share your regret that English parochial and academical records of the past should be in such a sorry state, but the mischief is done, and cannot now be repaired.

Yours sincerely,
E. Harrison,
Registrary.

Mrs. A. E. Whitaker.

.

HISTORY OF BEOLEY AND BEOLEY MANOR
From the Victorian History of England
Worcester, Vol. 4, p. 15

HE following description of Beoley is given: "Beoley, on the border of Warwickshire, which bounds it on the South and East, was one of the Manors purchased by the 'Earl of Warwick' and is described as "fyrst and worthyest; a Castle, Church and Manor, wanting nothing to add to its greatness".

Two Sheldon monuments divide the Shelton Chapel from the chancel of the Church. This former home of the Sheldons was destroyed during the Civil War of the 17th century; the present house was built after the Restoration. In 1549 John Nevill, Lord Latimer, sold "Beoley Manor" to William Sheldon who had acquired other land in Beoley in 1544, which had belonged to Alcester Monastery. This William married Mary Willington, eldest dau. and co-heir of Wm. of Barcheson, Warwickshire. Their son Ralph married Anne Throckmorton, dau. of Sir Rob't. Throckmorton, May 16, 1557-8. William settled "Beoley Manor" on this son Ralph and died at his estate, Skilts Studley, Warwickshire, Dec. 24, 1570. The Sheldons held land in Beoley as early as the reign of Edward IV, when William, a son of John[1] of Rowley Regis, Staffordshire, established himself

---

(1) John Shelton of "Rowley Regis" was a brother of Ralph Shelton (b. 1429, knighted in 1488, d. 1497). John died in 1517; the line runs thus; Wm. Shelton: d. 1420 and Catherine Baret d. 1456, had a son and heir John Shelton who married Margaret dau. of Sir Robert Brus (Bruce). They had

BEOLEY CHURCH FROM THE SOUTHEAST, IN WORCESTERSHIRE, ENGLAND

at Balsford Hall in Beoley; he also bought from Joane and Edward Benet, in 1488, Bentleys Place; when this Wm. died in 1517, he bequeathed Balsford Hall to *his brother Ralph Shelton.* The Wm. who bought Beoley Manor in 1549, was a son of *this* Ralph; he was buried with great pomp at Beoley, where a splendid monument was erected by his son and heir Ralph Shelton.

In the library of the College of Arms is the illuminated burial Certificate of *William Shelton.* His son Ralph who died in 1613, settled "Beoley Manor" on his son *Edward Shelton,* "then his *brother Wm.,* and then heirs of his *father* William Shelton.

Edward married Elizabeth Markham and died in 1643; he was succeeded by his son Wm. who married Elizabeth Petre, dau. of Wm., 2nd Lord Petre.

As a devoted Royalist Wm. suffered very heavily, his home being burned and the estate confiscated. In 1650 Treason Trustees transferred it to John Williams and George Day, who were holding it with Wm. Shelton and his sons, Ralph and George in 1653, in which year the Manor was discharged from sequestration; it remained in the possession of George Day until the Restoration. *Wm. Shelton* died in 1659 and in 1660 George and Ann Day restored "Beoley Manor" to *Richard Shelton,* to have him return it to *Wm.'s* son and successor *Ralph Shelton.* Of *this* Ralph, Nash wrote that he was of such remarkable integrity, character and hospitality, that he was known as the "Great Sheldon"; he was a learned antiquarian and

John Shelton (of 'Abberton Manor', Worcester and of 'Rowley Regis' Staffords.) and Ralph (who d. in 1497) who married 1st Joane, 2nd Margaret, dau. of Robert Clare.

a munificent patron of learning; he purchased and bequeathed to the College of Arms, the manuscript of Augustine Vincent, Windsor Herald; his own principal achievement being a "Catalog of the Nobility of England since the Norman Conquest, according to their several creations by every Particular King, with all arms finely emblazoned."

He was recorded as a member of the contemplated "Order of the Royal Oak" for this work and was licensed to travel abroad for his health; he left with 6 servants but died in 1684. He had no children and his brother *Edward* was a Benedictine Monk at Donay, and refused to have anything to do with secular affairs, so Ralph bequeathed his estates to his next *male heir* Ralph *Shelton* of *"Steeple Barton"*, Oxon, *Oxfordshire*.

Ralph made a conveyance of this Manor in 1708 and died in 1720; he was succeeded by his *son Edward,* at whose death in 1736 the Manor passed into the possession of *Edward's son Wm.;* in 1770, Wm. and his son and heir, *Ralph* barred the entail, made at the time of Wm.'s marriage; in 1780, *Ralph* succeeded his father and in 1788 he sold "Beoley Manor" to Thos. Holmes. In the same year Charles Shelton one of six *younger sons* of Wm., released the Manor from payments due him. Ralph's 4 daughters' shields of Arms, Savage, Pollard, Brayne and Plowden and Shields of 9 daughters of Edward Shelton and Elizabeth Markham, Russell, Fowler, Clare, Flower, Standen, Peshall, Trentham, Meyney and Sulliard, all impaling *Shelton* are in the Church with the *Shelton* tombs at "Beoley". See photos of Church opposite pages 68 and 70.

Edward (son of the Ralph who died in 1613) died in

INTERIOR VIEW OF BEOLEY CHURCH, WHERE ARE MANY MAGNIFICENT TOMBS OF THE SHELTONS—KNOWN AS SHELDONS

1643; his dau. Frances d. s. p. 1631, a plate states, which was placed there by Frances' brother, the Wm. who married Elizabeth Petre and died in 1659 in his 70th year; his wife Elizabeth died in 1656. Ralph Shelton survived his only son *Thomas,* who died in 1593, leaving two daughters.

In 1576 Ralph and Wm. Childe granted a "Capital Messuage" of land at *Broadway* to *Anthony Shelton,* brother of Ralph, who died in 1584, his son *Wm.* succeeding to the "Broadway" estate.

In 1595 Ralph settled the Manor on *this* Wm. Shelton, who held "Broadway" until his death in 1626 when *his* son *Wm.* succeeded him.

In 1678 this Manor was still held by the *Sheltons,* but was sold after the death of above Wm. in 1680.

Ralph had a sister Jane, who married Nicholas Blaby and had a son Ralph who is recorded as a gr-son of John Blaby.

The Ralph Shelton (who died 1546) also held the "Manor of Flyford Flavell" which passed to a younger son *Baldwin Shelton* of "Broadway", the transaction reading: "In 1549 by *Wm. Shelton* of 'Weston' and 'Beoley' Manors, by reason of minority of *Baldwin Shelton.*"

In 1560, Ralph, son of Baldwin Shelton and his wife Mary, settled the Manor on their son *Thomas Shelton,* with reversion to heirs of Ralph. Thos. died in 1593, leaving daughters Elizabeth and Mary and widow Elizabeth, who married Charles Kettleby; her daughter Elizabeth married John Keighley; in 1618, they and their husbands conveyed the Manor to Wm. Sambache, husband of the other daughter, Mary Shelton.

"DITCHFORD MANOR" — WORCESTERS.

Vol. 4, p. 260-269

The *Wm. Shelton* who died in 1649 owned Ditchford Manor; it was forfeited to the Parliamentary Trustees, but later was recovered by *Ralph Shelton,* son and heir of above Wm., who, during his life, settled it upon trustees for the use of *Joseph Shelton* and his wife Margaret and their heirs. (This Joseph was Lord Mayor of London.)

In 1681, Sir Joseph made a settlement by which trustees were to hold the Manor, after the death of Joseph's wife, Margaret, for use of his *brother Daniel,* and Daniel's son *Gilbert Shelton.* (This Daniel was nephew and heir of Gilbert [called "Sheldon"] Archbishop of Canterbury.) A portrait of this Archbishop was in the gallery of Sir Peter Lely in 1807. Sir Joseph left legacies of 3000 lbs. to each of his daughters Elizabeth and Ann. Gilbert succeeded to the Manor in 1696 and in his will, 1721, he bequeathed the Manor to his wife, Elizabeth, to be sold after her death for his daughters, Judith, wife of Paul Jodrell and Mary, wife of Wm. Craddock.

ABBERTON MANOR — WORCESTERS.

Vol. 4, p. 260-269

On Jan. 16, 1544 this Manor was granted to Wm. and Frances *Sheldon;* Ralph *Shelton* was the previous owner; he held "Abberton" in 1540 and had been preceded as owner by his *brother Wm.* who d. s. p. in 1517, and is entered in the "Visitations" as "Wm. *Sheldon* of Abberton." John *Shelton,* father of Wm. and Ralph (called *Sheldon*) was also "seated at Abberton"; he was later John Shelton of "Rowley Regis" Staffordshire. Wm. and Frances *above grantees* were sons of Ralph, *brother* of the

Wm. who died in 1517. The Manor was settled on *Francis* and his wife Mary and their children: Wm., Thos., Francis and Lucy. Wm. Shelton (the other grantee of 1544) died Dec. 24, 1570, when his nephew Wm. son of Francis, was of full age and residing at "Abberton"; he was succeeded by his son Francis in 1608, who, with his wife Elizabeth, still owned it from 1625 to 1699 or 1700, when Francis died and was succeeded by his son Francis, who died in 1711.

"Abberton" was held in 1776 by Thos. *Shelton* and in 1798 by "Thos. *Shelton* and wife Margaret". In 1798 it was sold to John Hardcastle.

"Strawley Manor", Worcester.
Wm. Shelton of "Beoley" owned this Manor in 1558.

"Strenham Manor", Worcester.

In 1557 Thos. Russell (Knt., 1549) settled the "Bishopric of Worcester", on his wife Frances, dau. of Sir Roger Cholmley, and in 1572, he settled "Strenham Manor" on his son John Russell, who married a daughter of Ralph *Shelton* of "Beoley Manor".

Sir Thos. died Apr. 9, 1574 and was succeeded by his son John, later Sir John, whose lands were attainted but were restored before the death of Sir John in 1593.

The William Shelton, who died in 1617, made Ralph, son of Ralph Shelton and Amy Wodehouse, his heir.

SHELTONS IN IRELAND

OHN SHELTON, son of Sir Thomas Shelton, Gentleman Porter of the Tower of London" and 3rd son of Sir John Shelton and Lady Anne Boleyn, was Lord Mayor of Dublin in 1537. He married a Miss Hodge. His will is dated Oct. 21, 1573; in it he mentions a Taylor whose "wife Clarah Humphrey" admin. the remainder of the estate of John Shelton July 17, 1577. It also mentions "a son Nicholas Taylor."

Thomas Shelton, son of Sir John, married Katherine, daughter of Bartholemew Ball and his wife, Mary Bermingham, and sister of Nicholas Ball (Mayor of Dublin in 1583 —M.P. 1585—will dated 1610), and Walter Ball, another mayor of Dublin.

Nicholas Ball's daughter, Jane, married Richard Usher and her sister, Margaret, married Robert Usher.

Thomas Shelton and Katherine Ball had a son, Sir John Shelton, Mayor of Dublin in 1604, who married Rose (she was buried Dec. 26, 1601), daughter of Robert Usher of "Santry" and his wife, Margaret, daughter of Nicholas Ball. Gennet (probably Jeanette), a sister of this Sir John Shelton, married Francis Taylor, second son of Robert[1] Taylor and Joan Edgeworth. The second wife of above John Shelton was Mary, daughter of Mathew Handcock, Mayor of Dublin. By his first wife, Rose Usher, Sir John had a son, Thomas Shelton, living in 1608, when his father died. By his second wife, Mary Handcock, Sir John had a

(1) Robert was the second son of "Taylor of Erverdes" and his wife, Amy Segrave, daughter of Walter Seagrave, Mayor of Dublin and Eleanor Ball, daughter of Bartholomew Ball.

son, Christopher Shelton, a very young child when his father died, March 23, 1608.

Eleanor, daughter of Robert Usher and his wife, Margaret Ball, married Walter Ball, another Mayor of Dublin 1572 to 1581; he died Dec. 8, 1598. John Shelton witnessed his will. Walter was a brother of Katherine Shelton, wife of Thomas. His daughter, Rose, married Rev. Luke Challoner, and their daughter, Phoebe, married Archbishop James Usher, Primate of Ireland. Walter Ball's e. s., Robert, was elected to take the place of Sir John Shelton, who resigned as mayor in 1604 because he refused to take the oath of supremacy. He was again alderman when he died in 1608.

Richard, Sr., eldest of the "Ushers of Santry", died Aug. 18, 1625; his wife, Jane Ball, July 26, 1641, leaving four children, John, Rose and Mary, who were single in 1641, and Eleanor, who married Lindick Nottingham.

Another son of Sir John Shelton and Miss Hodge, Henry Shelton, who was Alderman and High Sheriff of Dublin in 1579, married Margaret Shelton, daughter of "John Shelton of Shambo and Bolies". Henry Shelton and Margaret (she was buried 7/13/1603) had issue: (1) William Shelton of Dublin who married Bequet Conrad; (2) John Shelton; (3) Thomas Shelton; (4) Peter Shelton; (5) George Shelton; (6) Launcelot Shelton; and (7) Edward Shelton. I have no record of the daughters, if there were any. After death of Henry his widow married John Nangell; also spelled Nangle in the Dublin Records.

Launcelot Shelton, born in 1566, is on record as "of Armathwaite Castle, Cumberland" and is entered at Oxford as "Launcelot Carleton".

Peter Shelton married 3 times; by his second wife, Mary Leigh, he had a son and heir, Thomas, born 1567, who married Jane, daughter of Seth Holme "of Huntington". They had a son, Seth (living in 1612) who married Mary, daughter of Israel Ford "of Hadley"; their son and heir, William, born in 1608, married and had a son, "Henry Shelton of Osmanthorpe", Mayor of Leeds, Yorkshire.

These records were sent to me from the official files of "The Castle", Dublin. The Yorkshire branch of this family appear in most of the English records as *Skelton*. I was fortunate to secure this data before the Sinn Fein uprising when the Castle was burned, and many records destroyed.

Two other sons of the Sir John Shelton, former mayor of Dublin in 1537 who died in 1573, are carried on the records at "The Castle", Dublin, as Sir James Schylton and John Schylton; there is no further data for Sir James but John married Matilda Fleming; his will reads: Will of John Schylton, Gent., Feb. 12, 1589. In it is mentioned his kinsman Christopher Shelton.

There is a will of Christopher Shelton of Dublin, Gentleman, dated 30 June 1650; in it is mentioned his kinsman *Francis Taylor* so this must have been the son of the Sir John who died in 1607/08.

Another Shelton chart, sent me from Dublin, is as follows:

A dau. of Shelton = ... married Leonard Drew, Esq., second son of Barry Drew of Drew's Court Co. Limerick, Esq. She had sons Shelton (or Sheldon) and Leonard Drew. Her brother John Shelton of Co. Limerick, Esq., Capt. in the Royal Dragoons, d. at Ghent while serving under the Duke of Marlborough. His heir was Robert Shel-

ton of "Rossmore House" Co. Limerick, Esq., J. P., who =
Margaret—dau. of Giles Powell of Hounds Court Co. Cork,
Esq. They had son and heir John Shelton of "Rossmore
House" Co. Limerick, Esq., J. P., who married Elizabeth,
second dau. of John Willington of Co. Tipperary, Esq.
They had two daughters, Alicia, who married John Chap-
man of Castle Mitchell, Esq., and Mary, who married
Thomas Hayes of Sunbury, Middlesex, Esq., and a son
and heir

John Willington Shelton of Rossmore House, Esq., Capt.
and J. P. born 10 Aug. 1791, who married Mary, eldest dau.
of John Richards of Blackdown House, Hampshire, Esq.
They had John Willington Shelton, Lieut. and Rev. Grant-
ley Willington Shelton in holy orders at Rossmore House.
(I do not know why the "Esq." is put after the County,
instead of the man's name, but I am quoting it from the
chart sent to me.)

FUNERAL ENTRIES

Rose daughter of Rob: Usher, wife to John Shelton, of Dublin, alderman
Mayor, was buried the 26 of December, 1601.

———

Margaret Nangle, former wife of Henry Shelton, sometime Alderman of
Dublin, buried 13 July 1603. She was a daughter of John Shelton of Shambo
and ye Bolies.

———

John Shelton, of Dublin, alderman mayor, deceased ye 23 March 1608,
and lefte issue by his first wife (Rose, daughter of Robte. Usher of Santrisse)
Thomas Shelton, and by his second wi: (Mary, daughter of Matthew Handcock, alderman mayor of Dublin) Christofer Shelton, a younge childe.

———

Arms of Shelton impaling Chamberlain.
This shows that a Mr. Shelton married a Miss Chamberlain.
Funeral entry made between 1607 and 1611, for Mr. Shelton.

———

Henry Shelton, of Dublin, Merchant, buryed the 26th day of November,
1596; he had to wyfe . . . . . . Margaret, by whom he had issue.

Margaret Nangell buryed St. Mikan's Church the 23rd of July, 1603. She was twice married; by her first husband, Henry Shelton, Merchant, she had issue, William, John, Thomas, Edward, Peter, George and Laurence Shelton. (Other records give Launcelot.)

To Peter Shelton, son of Henry and Margaret Shelton, was re-issued the arms used by Sir Ralph Shelton at the Dunstable Tournament and later used by Sir John Shelton, husband of Lady Anne Boleyn and later still, by the Virginia Sheltons.

Of the Usher family John was Alderman of Dublin in 1581 when he was appointed Commissioner of Ecclesiastical Causes. Rose—daughter of Walter Ball, Mayor of Dublin, married the Rev. Luke Challoner and their daughter Phoebe married Archbishop James Usher, Primate of all Ireland. Robert, eldest son of Walter Ball and brother of Rose Challoner was elected Mayor of Dublin to take the place of Thomas Shelton's son Sir, *John Shelton,* elected in 1604 and who resigned and was elected Alderman which office he held at his death in 1607/08.

A copy of the will of John Shelton of "Mitcham" Surry, is on record at "The Castle" Dublin showing that he owned land in both England and Ireland.

LIST OF FREEHOLDERS OF THE COUNTY OF LIMERICK

Giles Shelton, Lismaveen.
John Shelton, Groghteen.
Robert Shelton, Ross.

LEET'S DIRECTORY OF IRELAND, 1814

Rev. Thomas Shelton, Eagles-nest, Mount Nugent, Co. Cavan.
J. Shelton, Esq., Ross, Charleville, Co. Limerick.

"ALUMNI DUBLINENSES"

George Augustus Frederick Shelton, Pensioner (Mr. Turpin), July 3, 1837, aged 15; son of John Willington, Magistratus Com. Limerick; born Kingston-on-Thames. B. A. *Vern.* and M. B. *Aest.* 1842.

John Shelton, Pensioner (Mr. Turpin), July 4, 1836, aged 16; son of John, Militaris; born Middlesex.

ADMINISTRATIONS PREROGATIVE

Administration of the goods of John Shelton, of Dublin, Alderman, deceased intestate, was granted to Mary Taylor, widow, for her son, Edward Taylor, the next of kin. 14th January, 1658.

ROLL OF FREEMEN OF THE CITY OF DUBLIN

Admitted Freeman of the City of Dublin, Johes Shelton (son of Thomas Shelton, Merchant), by birth, *Easter, in the 26th year of the Reign of Queen Elizabeth.*

Admitted Freeman of the City of Dublin, Johes Shelton, Junior (son of Henry Shelton, Merchant, deceased) by birth, *Easter, in the 40th year of the Reign of Queen Elizabeth.*

Admitted Freeman of the City of Dublin, Willus Shelton, Merchant (son of Henry Shelton, deceased), by birth, *Christmas, in the 40th year of the Reign of Queen Elizabeth.*

Admitted Freeman of the City of Dublin, Edwardus Shelton, Merchant (son of Henry Shelton, late of Dublin, Alderman, deceased), by birth, *Easter, in the first year of the Reign of James I.*

Admitted Freeman of the City of Dublin, Thomas Shelton, Merchant (son of John Shelton, Alderman), by birth, *Christmas, in the fourth year of the Reign of James I.*

Admitted Freeman of the City of Dublin, Petrus Shelton (son of Henry Shelton, deceased), by birth, *Easter, in the 5th year of the Reign of James I.*

Admitted Freeman of the City of Dublin, Lawrencius Shelton, Merchant (son of Henry Shelton, Alderman), by birth, *Easter, in the 14th year of the Reign of James I.*

Admitted Freeman of the City of Dublin, Robertus Shelton (son of Edward Shelton, Merchant), by birth, *Christmas, in the 10th year of the Reign of Charles I.*

Admitted Freeman of the City of Dublin, John Shelton, Calcear (son of

William Shelton, Merchant, deceased), by birth, *Midsummer, in the 11th year of the Reign of Charles I.*

Admitted Freeman of the City of Dublin, Maria Shelton, virgo (daughter of Edward Shelton, Merchant), by birth, *Midsummer, in the 12th year of the Reign of Charles I.*

Admitted Freeman of the City of Dublin, Willus Shelton, Calcear (son of William Shelton, Merchant, deceased), by birth, *Midsummer, in the 12th year of the Reign of Charles I.*

Admitted Freeman of the City of Dublin, Martin Shelton, Shoemaker ('son of John Shelton, Shoemaker, deceased), by birth, *Midsummer 1659.*

Admitted Freeman of the City of Dublin, Maria Shelton, spinster (daughter of William Shelton, Shoemaker), by birth, *Christmas 1661.*

Admitted Freeman of the City of Dublin, Alexander Shelton, Chiro., by special grace, *Midsummer 1670.*

Admitted Freeman of the City of Dublin, Patric. Shelton, Joyn. (son of William Shelton, Shoemaker), by birth, *Easter 1672.*

DUBLIN CONSISTORIAL GRANT BOOKS

Katherine Shelton and Rowland Thorneborough 1639
Jane Shelton, *alias* Williams, widow, and Thomas Hollis 1642
Henry Shelton, Dublin (Will) 1674
John Shelton, Dublin, Shoemaker (Will) 1642
Laurence Shelton, Dublin (Will) 1628
Mary Shelton and Robert Gill 1668
Robert Shelton, Dublin (Will) 1725
Thomas Shelton (Will) 1636
William Shelton, New Street, Dublin, Blacksmith (Intestacy) 1642
William Shelton, Schoolhouse-lane, Dublin, Gentleman (Intestacy) 1669

PREROGATIVE MARRIAGE LICENSES

William Shelton, of Robertstown, Co. Meath, Gent., and Maria Sumner, of Orchardstown, said County. 22nd February, 1663.

Robert Moor, of St. Mary's, Dublin, Distillator, and Mary Shelton, of St. Catherine's, Dublin, spinster. 4th January, 1733.

MAGAZINES

John Shelton, of Ross, Co. Galway, and Eliza Willington, 2nd daughter of John Willington, of Killoshane, Co. Tipperary. August 1789.

Lieut. McKenzie to Miss Shelton, 1799.

WILLS OF THE DIOCESE OF LIMERICK

John Shelton, Gentleman, of Ross, Co. Limerick, 1734.

THE FIRST SHELTONS IN AMERICA

 HAVE found no indication that Sir Ralph Shelton ever came to America, but his son, "James Shelton, Gentleman", came with his kinsman, Lord Delaware,[1] arriving in Virginia in June, 1610. (English records "Stiths" and "Smiths", History of Virginia, "Alexander Brown's Genesis of the U. S.", and "Record of the London Company" by Kingsbury). One record gives him as Captain; in the London records, he is given of "Canterbury".

James Shelton was a resident of Jamestown in 1620 (Smith, Vol. 2, p. 549), a member of the Courts of 1619 and 1624 (Brown, "Genesis of U. S.,;" "Records of the

(1) The second Charter for Virginia was signed and sealed May 23, 1609; there were seven ships; Sir Thomas Gates, first named in His Majesty's Patent of Grants in Virginia, was wrecked on the shores of Bermuda. His ship was the "Sea Venture"; the other six ships proceeded to Virginia. It is probable that James Shelton was with those wrecked at Bermuda, and was sufficiently interested to go back there to colonize. There was to be no division of land in the Colonies for seven years, and the divisions were to be decided by commissioners. Lord de la Warr died at sea, June 7, 1818, while he was on his way to take over control of the Virginia Colony. He was Thomas the 3rd. Lord de la Warr, born in 1577; he married 11-25-96—Cecily—dau. of Sir Thomas Shirley and from them descends the present Lord de la Warr.

Thomas was a member of the Council for the Va. Co. of 1609 and 1st Gov. and Capt. Gen'l for life by appt. of Feb. 28, *1610*. It was his arrival with supplies at Jamestown, in June 1610, that saved the disheartened Colonists from abandoning their venture. He went back to England in 1611 and published his "Relation of the Condition of affairs in the New Colony." Returning to Va. in April 1618 he died at sea; and was buried June 7, 1618. Alex. Brown in his "History" states that "if any man can be called the Founder of Virginia, I believe he is that man." Thomas was the son of the 2nd Lord de la Warr and his wife Anne Knollys. His brothers Francis, John and Nathaniel West came with him, and became Governors of Virginia.

London Company''), and is given in the ''Partial list of
families in America entitled to bear arms''. (William and
Mary Quarterly, old series, Vol. 1, Bk. 2, p. 59)[1]

The Sheltons owned their own ships and did a large
business with Bermuda. There are many records of births,
marriages and deaths there, where they had large tracts of
land. The Governor of Bermuda, Captain Wodehouse, was
a kinsman of Sir Ralph Shelton, Sr. John Shelton, son of
James (1) is given on list of ship owners and merchants
who made large sales of commodities to the Virginia
planters, and Stephen of Accomac, called ''Charlton'', was
a part owner of John's ship.

As soon as trade was opened between Bermuda and Virginia, James Shelton moved to Bermuda, where he had
large grants of land, and died there in 1668; his wife's name
was Ann, as his son, William, names ''my mother, Ann
Shelton'', in his last will. In the earliest records, the Shelton name is spelled Felton, Melton, Sheldon, Sealton, Sher-

---

(1) "The original of the James Shelton coat of arms was last in the
custody of Mr. Brock of the Virginia Historical Society, Richmond, Virginia.
It was photographed by "Davis of Richmond" who had an office on "Church
Hill." The original was found by Mr. Stannard and the list was published
by him in the "Critic". It is given in Volume 1, William and Mary College
Quarterly, and is the same as that used by Sir Ralph Shelton."

Francis Griswold who has taken the Shelton family to write a novel
(The Tides of Malvern) about, states that "James and his wife, Ann Hebert,
came to South Carolina from Bermuda (where he had gone as heir to his
father, James (1) of Virginia and Bermuda) in 1674; if this is correct, the
first wife of James, Jr., Eleanor, died in Bermuda. I wrote Mr. Griswold to
verify his data and he wrote that he was so intrigued by the Shelton history
that he had woven his story around it. He stated that up to the arrival of
James and his family, the story was proven fact—from there on, it is fiction;
the home he writes of in Warwickshire, England, as "Malvern Hall", is his
own ancestral home in that shire, instead of "Sheldon Hall".

ton, Carlton, Carleton, Carelton, Charlton, Chilton, Shilston, Yelton, Shilton, Chelton, Skylton, Skelton, etc.

The John Shelton who bought "Carotoman" in Lancaster
Co. Va., "Currioman." in Westmoreland Co. Va. and built
"Rural Plains" in Hanover Co. Va. was a son of James
Shelton of York Co. Va. who was a son of Thomas Shelton,
son of the first James Shelton, Gentleman of Va. and Ber-
muda. Thomas died in Cecil Co., Md., in 1684. See will.[1]

James was eldest son and heir. One early grant to John

October 24th, 1683.

(1) IN THE NAME OF GOD, AMEN: I, Thomas Shelton, of Bohemia River,
in Cecil County, in the province of Maryland, Planter, being sick and week in
body but of perfect sense and memory, do make and declare this my last Will
and Testament, in writing, in manner and form following:—

First:—I recommend my soule into the hands of Almighty God, my maker,
hoping through the merits of Jesus Christ, my Redeemer, to inherit life ever-
lasting—and my body to the earth from whence it came, to be buried in
decent burial according to discression of my Executor or Executrix or Executors or Executrices hereinafter named.

And as for my worldly Estate wherewith God hath endowed. First—my
debts being paid and my funeral expenses discharged, I give unto my son
James, *Mayne Oouzen*, and to his heirs or assigns forever, saveing and provided allwais that Miss Penelopa Woods is to have a maintenance out of my
Estate during her lifetime.

ITEM: I give and bequeath unto my daughter Elizabeth Whitton one cow
and a calf by her side to be payed unto the said Elizabeth Whitton two years
after my decease. Lastly, I nominate constitute ordain and appoint my trusted
and well beloved friend Elwood Ladamore to be my sole and only Executor of
this my last Will and Testament. In Witness Whereof, I have hereunto set
my hand and seale the day and year above written.

His

THOMAS   X   SHELTON   (SEAL)

mark

Signed, sealed, published and acknowledged in ye presence and hearing of—

William Evans

Richard Robts.

Proved May 4th, 1684.

Examined by David Smith, Regr. 3½ sides.

Shelton is *especially* badly written, and is copied as Whetson, but can easily be read Shelton, and the *land belonged to Shetlons.*

On the vestry book of St. Paul's Hanover Co. Va. John Shelton signs as Vestryman and Reader in 1705. In this same register the land of James Shelton and Richard Shelton are ordered processioned, "Meriweather Shelton, Gentleman" is given as Warden of the Parish, and the names of Robert Shelton and the widow Shelton, appear frequently. Even here in two records I found John Shelton's name wrong and in *Georgia* I found the *same* misspelling "Snelson" for Thomas, James and John. Evidently carelessness in writing or copying the records.

Twenty years ago, when I started my work on the family history, I would not have accepted *anyone's* word that all these people were descendants of one family, but I have proven them to be so by the official English records, the rosters of Cambridge, Oxford and Dublin Universities, by the early land grants (tracing the land held by men under their various names to Shelton land), and by the first two census lists in Virginia, as well as by the wills, court records, family bibles, papers of executors of estates, etc., both in England, Ireland and in America.

Many "Chilton Genealogies" have been published in different books, but all of them I have seen claim the "Currioman[1] Westmoreland County, Virginia, estate bought in

(1) Part of "Currioman" was one of the original grants of James Shelton (1) in America, who had a grant on the S. S. of the Potomac, October 16, 1650. This grant was very probably taken up by Thomas Shelton his son who died in Cecil County, Maryland, in 1684. Another grant to this Thomas was as follows: "Land of Thomas Shelton in Adam Thorogood's grant on Ches. Bay Lower Co. of New Norfolk upon Chisopeian, beginning at first

1652, as the property of the first Chilton in Virginia''. *Part* of this plantation was the original grant of Colonel Thomas Speaks, September 16, 1651. He willed the 900 acres of which it consisted at that time to Dr. Thomas Gerrard, a member of the Council for Maryland, who was banished from the colony for taking part in the rebellion of Josiah Fendall. This part of ''Currioman'' was bought from *John Gerrard,* a nephew of the above Dr. Thomas Gerrard, by John *Shelton* who built, in 1670, ''Rural Plains'', Hanover County (then New Kent County) Virginia. John owned thousands of acres of land in various counties in Virginia and Maryland. He died in 1706, and his will was filed in Westmoreland County, Virginia, where he owned more than 2000 acres in the Currioman Estate alone. The records give him as John *Chilton* but the name was always pronounced *Shelton.* This John was executor

creek of that river and running to a broad creek that shooteth behind a long point of land, westerly, into etc. ———.'' This grant was for 900 acres— 6/24/1635. On Feb. 6, 1638, another grant of 200 acres adjoining was made to ''Thomas Shelton and wife Hannah''. There is a description of the ''*Carotman*'' Lancaster Co. estate in ''Colonial Churches of Virginia''. This also belonged to the Sheltons. A map of this great estate is in the clerk's office at Lancaster Court House. It contained 1800 acres, stretching along the banks of the Carotoman River, and far into the country, including the present sites of Kilmarnock and Irvington. A close-set row of cedar trees ran on both sides of a straight road for three miles from the house on the Rappahannock to the Church.''

The first Christ Church in Lancaster Co., Va., was built on the present site, on part of John *Shelton's* land, in *1672.* The present church was built by Robert Carter, called King Carter in *1732;* his will is dated Aug. 26, 1728, but he did not die until 1732, at which time the church was not finished. John Shelton sold the plantation to Robert Carter in 1703.

Meade in his history of Churches in Virginia states that the *Sheltons* have always been staunch friends of the Church of England. All branches of the family seem to have been active in church affairs.

of the estate of John Ethell in Westmoreland County, Virginia, in 1698. In this record, the name is spelled *Chelton*.

William Shelton, youngest son of John of "Rural Plains", was presiding Justice of York County, Virginia, and High Sheriff in 1717-1725. He married Hannah, daughter of Captain Anthony Armistead, in Elizabeth City County, Virginia, December 10, 1698. "Currioman" was inherited by the eldest son of John and his father settled "Rural Plains" in Hanover County, Virginia, on William who was succeeded by his son, John, who married Eleanor Parks, and whose daughter, Sarah, married Patrick Henry in 1754.

The eldest son of John Shelton of "Currioman" Westmoreland Co. Va. and of "Rural Plains" Hanover Co. Va. who died in 1706 was "Captain John Chelton" of "Belleview" on the Potomac. This place was later owned by Thomas Ludwell Lee. *This* John died in *1726*, and his tomb stone has recently been restored at "Currioman". It says, "Aged about 60". If this is correct, he must have been born about 1666. This Captain John married first, Lettice Ball, by whom he had two sons, no daughters. John and Captain Thomas were the sons. In 1704, as *John Chilton, Jr.,* and in 1709 as *John Chilton* (his father having died in 1706), *Capt. John Chelton* added 900 acres to "Currioman". After the death of his wife, he married Mary Watts, widow of Richard Watts. She had a number of children, but none by John Shelton. From the records, I judge she had been married three times as in her will, she speaks of "a son, James Bowcock", and her "children by Richard Watts".

The will of this Captain John (1726) mentions "land on Chopawomsic Creek in Stafford County, Virginia" to his son, John, and "the Westmoreland County, Virginia", property to his elder son, "Captain Thomas". From this *Captain Thomas and his wife, Jemima Cook,* descended the *Chiltons* of "Rockhill", Fauquier Co., and from *his* brother, *John,* descend the *Sheltons* of Caroline, Stafford and Spott-sylvania Counties, Virginia. In 1747, "John Chilton of Caroline County", son of Captain John who died in 1726, sued his brother, Captain Thomas, for recovery of part of the estate, claiming that their father, Captain John, had only "an estate tail" in the property and slaves.

"Maidstone", one of the so called William *"Chilton"* estates in Westmoreland County, Virginia, was named after the home of Richard Shelton in Kent, England, and one of the Sheltons had the living of the Church there. I have the record of this "Richard Shelton of Maidstone, England", whose widow, with a fortune of £40,000 was about to marry again. Another plantation of the John Shelton, who died in 1706, was "Carotoman" in Lancaster County, Virginia. This plantation, he sold in 1703 to Robert "King" Carter. John bought the estate November 11, 1672, from William Clapham.

The Virginia historical markers at Christ Church, Lan-caster County, Virginia, state that "Carotoman" was built on the grant of John Carter, father of Robert. This is, of course, another error. Both men happen to be ancestors of the writer of this history, as Robert Carter's grand-daughter, Elizabeth Hill Carter, married the writer's great-great-great grandfather, Colonel William Byrd, III. The transfer deed for Carotoman is recorded December 8, 1703, Volume IX, page 74, Lancaster County Records.

Daniel Shelton, supposed to be a brother of John of

Lancaster County, is on record in York County, Virginia, and in North Carolina in the 1670's and 1680's. In some records, he is given as a son of the Archbishop of Canterbury which is, of course, another error. The *Daniel Shelton,* nephew and heir of the Archbishop, lived and died in England. In 1685, according to Connecticut history, which agrees with all family tradition, Daniel Shelton, brother of John, (d. 1706), was shipwrecked on the coast of Connecticut and became one of the leading citizens of the state. He married the granddaughter of Governor Thomas Welles. His descendants are given in my "Genealogy" published in 1927.

William Shelton, son of James (1) of Virginia and Bermuda, made his will on board his own ship, "The William", in the East Indies, November 20, 1639. He names his "mother, Ann", a "brother, John Shelton living in Shadwell" as executors, and a "sister, Joane Hall". In December, 1640, there is recorded the renunciation of the administration on this estate of William Shelton by John Shelton (the record states "name changed from Shilton"). This will is filed in London, England.

FIRST THOMAS SHELTON IN AMERICA

T has been impossible, as yet, to trace the entire *second* generation of Sheltons in America, but the *grandsons* of the first James are legion and, of course, with their descendants, are entitled to the family history. In my "Genealogy", I assume John of "Rural Plains" to be the son of James (2). He is on record in St. Paul's Church, Hanover County, and in an old book at "Rural Plains" as "son of James Shelton", but *this* James proves to have been a *grandson* of the first James (1610); he was the son of Thomas Shelton, and a grandson of James (1). This Thomas must have been born in England earlier than 1610, as I understand he would have had to be eighteen years old to obtain a land grant. He came from Bermuda in "The Hopewell" in 1628 with Captain Thorogood, and was one of those taking up part of the 5350 acre grant to Captain Thorogood in Lower Norfolk County, Virginia, June 20, 1635.

Henry Wood, who came in "The John and Dorothy" in 1634, had part of this same grant and, evidently, Thomas married a sister or daughter of this Henry Wood, as a sister-in-law, Penelope Wood, is mentioned in the will of Thomas in 1684. This Thomas Shelton, *or his son, Thomas,* (the Maryland records give no date) was "Attorney for the Provincial Courts of Maryland." He was among the head-rights of Edw. Williams in "The Potomack Freshets", in 1658. I have a copy of a deed for land sold by John Collett of Accomac in 1665 to Thomas Shelton. This land was in Baltimore County, Maryland, and he also had part of a

2700 acre Virginia grant in New Kent County, November 9, 1665; the will of Thomas is filed in Cecil County, Maryland, in 1684. In it, he mentions a daughter, "Elizabeth Whitton", and leaves his estate and his home "Maynecouzen" to "his son James and his heirs". No wife is mentioned, but in an early deed, his "wife, Hannah" is named; she evidently predeceased him. (See will p. 83.)

In 1638, February 20, Richard Shelton, a son of James (I) had a grant in Isle of Wight County, Virginia, and his son, John Shelton (a grandson of the above James) was living in Isle of Wight County, Virginia, in the late 1600's. His wife's name was Susannah. He died in 1701, and his will was proved in 1704. He had sons: John (who had a son, William), James, William and Thomas (d. 1730-1), and daughters: Ann, Mary and Sarah, and a grandson, John. Thomas's wife, Sarah, was evidently named Briggs as there is a deed from James and Sarah Briggs to Thomas Shelton, November, 1715. The John Shelton, grandson, was attorney for Ann Randall and George Symes in 1796, Isle of Wight County, Virginia. The first named John must have been the "John Shelton aged 39 in 1688", who is on record in York County, Virginia, and whom I thought to be the John who built "Rural Plains". I have never been able to find the surname of this *last-named* John's wife. He named "wife, Jane", in his will (1706), but he may have been married more than once. The Randolph records and "Lee of Virginia" give a marriage of "John Shelton, grandson of Sir Ralph Shelton" to "Ann, daughter of Peyton Randolph and his wife, Helen Maxwell McCauley Southall." No date is given in either record, but the writers could have figured out from the position of Peyton on the Randolph family tree that this John could not have been the *grandson of Sir* Ralph Shelton but was a *fifth great grandson*. This John was later the Colonel John of "Rural Plains". His will has never been published as far as I can find, but it, and his Bible and prayer book have recently been located in possession of a descendant, and prove that he was married three times; only his last marriage (to Ann Southall) has ever been given in Virginia history. There were no children by his marriage to Ann Randolph; at least, none are mentioned in his Bible or will. His second wife, whom he married September 29, 1773, was Nancy Williamson. By her, he had Robert, Walter Parks, and Eleanor Shelton. After the death of Nancy, he married on January 7, 1784, Anne Southall, by whom he had six children.

The Maryland records are spelled Shelton, Sheldon, Skelton, Chelton, Chilton, Carlton, Carleton, and Charleton and several very weird spellings. In the Bibles and on the tombstones, the names of members of the same family are spelled three different ways.

"Fr. Shelton" sold his part of a 2100 acre tract in Accomac County to John Fludd in 1638, and also had a share in a large tract in James City County. (This could be *Mr.* Shelton instead of *Fr.,* and mean Thomas or James (1)— James had a grant on S. S. Potomack Oct. 16, 1650. The eldest son, James evidently stayed in Bermuda or England. There is no trace of him—no early records and the *gr. son James* would not be old enough to *buy land.* I can find no other Sheltons, Chiltons, Charltons or Skeltons this early; Thomas Shelton also had part of a 1600 acre tract in Westmoreland County, Virginia, 12/12/1654, and a part of the 1,000 acre Valentine patent in the same county, 6/16/1654.

This Thomas *Shelton* (The Bermuda record reads *Shel-*

ton, the American record has been *published* as *Melton*)
came from Bermuda in "The Hopewell" with Captain
Adam Thorogood, in 1628. In 1635, 1638, and 1665, he had
large grants in Virginia and Maryland and probably many
others in other years. Stephen, Dennis and Henry *Charlton*
had land in Accomac in 1637 and 1638; according to the
court records and wills in Virginia and Maryland, these
men, together with the following, were all of one family,
descendants of James (1) who had part of the 9000 acre
grant in Northampton County, Virginia, of Captain John
Savage, Oct. 2, 1664; Stephen *Charlton,* who had 1000 acres
in August, 1650, on Watchepamqua Creek, Northumberland
County, Virginia (son of Thomas, d. 1684), and probably
the Stephen whose daughter was Mary Scarborough), John
and George *Chilton* and their brother Stephen *Chelton.*

Symon *Shelton*—headright of Thomas Lullaman on Chop-
awansic Creek in 1658

Wm. Sheldon—headright (Charles Ratcliffe) Aug. 16, 1664

James Sheldon*—headright (Capt. John Savage) Oct. 18,
1664

John Charlton—headright (Mrs. Ann Toft) Nov. 17, 1664

Job Skelton—headright (Col. Edmund Scarborough) Feb.
16, 1665/6

Charles Calvert, Lord Baltimore, married "Margaret,
daughter of Thomas Charlton (Shelton) of Northumberland County, Virginia", and Col. Edmund Scarborough
married Mary Charlton (Shelton)—erroneously given in
Maryland records as a daughter of "Stephen Charlton and
his wife, Mary of Accomac". This Stephen, evidently a
brother of Thomas (d. 1684), was joint owner of the Vir-

---

* This must have been the James (1) who died in Bermuda in 1668.

ginia Ship "Captain John Stone", in 1634. He is given in the records as "Captain Stephen Charlton of Nuswattox, Northampton County, Virginia". He died January 1654/5. His will mentions two wives.

Stephen was born in England, in 1602. He could not have been the father of Mary Scarborough who was born in 1610. The will names "Bridget Severn" (widow) and "Anne West" (widow) and two daughters: Bridget who married Capt. Isaac Foxcraft, and Elizabeth who married John Gitting.[1] He mentioned no sons, and neither of these daughters left issue. Tabitha Scarborough married John Custis, Sr., and Matilda Scarborough married Colonel John West; both were daughters of Colonel Edmund Scarborough and his wife, Mary Charlton (Shelton).

Shephen Charlton's (Shelton) wife, Anne, was the widow

(1) In 1673, Maryland was the Gretna Green of Virginia. Scarborough and Calvert ran the boundary line in 1663 and selected an avenue of oaks to mark the division; these were known as "The Marriage Trees" as many Accomac couples crossed the boundary to be married.

Elizabeth eloped with John Gitting, but was married on the Virginia side of the Bay; she was only 12 years old. This elopement is described in "Social Life of Virginia in the 17th Century" (p. 239); in it, Elizabeth is referred to as "a great heiress, and member of one of the most distinguished families on the Eastern Shore". Elizabeth died a very short time after her marriage, and her husband tried to claim possession of the Glebe lands which consisted of 1600 acres of the best land in the country.

This land was left to Hungar Parish by Stephen, father of Elizabeth; he was one of the first vestrymen of this parish and was one of the earliest justices of Accomac. In 1644, he was in command of one of the two districts of the Peninsula for protection against the Indians.

In 1646, his home was the meeting place of the Court; in 1645, he was one of two men who owned a horse on the Eastern shore. In 1650, when Col. Norwood and his men were ship-wrecked, they were taken to Stephen's home, and he personally outfitted all of them and furnished them with supplies. His land, situated on Church Neck, is still known as "The Glebe Land".

of Anthony West, and they were the parents of Colonel
John West and the Katherine West who married Charles
Scarborough.

Lady Baltimore's father was the Thomas ''Chilton''
(also spelled Shelton and Charlton) son of Stephen (d.
1718) and Elizabeth Chilton of Lancaster County, Virginia,
and grandson of the Thomas Shelton who died in Cecil Co.,
Md., in 1684. Thomas bought land in Northumberland
County, Virginia, in 1691; his wife's name was Margaret,
and his daughter, Margaret was born in 1683; Lord Baltimore, her husband, died in 1714.

This may have been the Thomas ''Chilton'' who married
Sarah Chinn, daughter of John Chinn, Sr., in Lancaster
County, Virginia, before 1691. If so, he was married twice.

A Stephen ''Chilton'' was a Vestryman at St. Peter's in
New Kent County, Virginia (where many of the Sheltons
were members), in 1684/6/7. This probably was the Stephen
Chilton (son of Thomas Shelton who died in 1684) who also
owned land in St. Mary's County, Maryland, in 1666. In
the grant to John Shelton in Northumberland County, Virginia, April 9, 1663, the name is very indistinct; it *looks* like
''Whetson'' in the records, but the land is ''Shelton'' land,
inherited by Sheltons.

Thomas Shelton (d. 1684) had brothers: Stephen, John,
William, Richard, George, James, Ralph, Robert and, probably, others. Stephen was the Captain Stephen who died
in 1654. William died at sea in 1640. John died in Bermuda
in 1691. James, the eldest brother, lived in Warwickshire,
England; he, with his wife Eleanor, and son Edward, went
to Bermuda as heir of his father, James Shelton, in 1674;
his father had died in 1668. Ralph lived either in England

or Bermuda, presumably as he is on record in both of these countries and I can find no trace of him in Virginia or Maryland.[1]

The Peter who married Susannah Jaxon (Jackson) in 1684, was a nephew or cousin of John "Shelton" who died in 1706, probably the son or gr. son of Ralph Shelton, as the name comes down in each generation for 200 years or more. (Christ Church, Middlesex County, Virginia, record). Thomas (d. 1684) had sons (besides James, his heir) : John, Stephen, George, Thomas and William. James was the eldest son, and heir; John owned his own ships, and Thomas was a ship's surgeon. These are all I have been able to trace.

A Ralph, son of William Shelton and Hannah Armistead, died in 1766. They also had sons: James and Richard Shelton, who died before 1780. Stephen (whose will is filed in Lancaster County in 1780) (son of Thomas, d. 1684), who had 1000 acres on Watchepowqa Creek, Northumberland County, Virginia, had a nephew, Robert Shelton, who bought land from William King of Lancaster County, Virginia, in 1689. The John who built "Rural Plains" and died in 1706 had a grant of land in Northumberland County, Virginia, April 9, 1663, so he must have been born earlier

---

(1) The Maryland records for these men are spelled Shelton, Chelton, Chilton, Charlton, Carleton, etc. This cannot be explained except by the absolute disregard of spelling in those days and their having taken it for granted that "everybody knows the Sheltons", as an old gentleman answered me when I asked why those living all their lives in Virginia and Maryland had not corrected the numberless errors made by the historians and county clerks. This may have been true in the early days in England and America, but it has certainly wrought a great injustice to the posterity of this illustrious house, by making them ignorant of their splendid family history. In Elizabeth City County, Surry and York Counties, the Shelton and Sheldon is used interchangeably, and a few of the records are Skelton and Chilton.

than 1649, the date given in my "Genealogy", which was taken from York County records, but evidently referred to another John; I think *this* John was a son of Richard of Isle of Wight Co., Va.

In Stafford County, Virginia, the family of James Shelton, son of John and Ann of Caroline and Stafford Counties, Virginia, appears on the record of Overwharton Parish as "Yelton". This James married Isabel Hinson in 1743, November 13, and the birth of four of their children is given: Charles, b. 1746; James, b. 1749; Mary, b. 1752; and Ann, b. 1755.

In Lancaster County, Virginia, the Chilton spelling predominates, but *deeds and wills signed Shelton are filed Chilton.*

John, brother of James of Stafford County, Virginia, was John Shelton, later of Spottsylvania County, Virginia, who married Susan (called Sukie in the records) Hord. Their son, Richard *Shelton,* was living on the land left by John *Chilton* (d. 1726) of Westmoreland County, Virginia, *to his "son, John".* The *Charlton* records in old Bruton Church, Williamsburg, Va., should read *Shelton,* also those of Accomac County and Maryland. Ann, widow of George Charlton (Shelton) is buried just in front of the door of old Bruton Church and the "Charlton Inn" in Williamsburg belonged to Richard *Shelton.*

From Bible records, deeds and wills, Stephen, George, William, John, Henry, Thomas, James, Job, Symon, etc., called Chelton, Charlton, Chilton, Sheldon, Skelton, were all brothers or cousins.

The first family *really bearing the name of Skelton* to come into Virginia, came from New Jersey in the early

1800's. They settled in Powhattan County, and from them descend the late Mr. John Skelton Williams and his brother, Mr. Edmund Randolph Williams of Richmond, Virginia. If this line was worked back to England, I have no doubt that they, too, would be proven to be *Sheltons.*

The Bible of George W. Shelton (Chelton in these Maryland records) is in possession of Mrs. James L. Dorsey, Marion Station, Somerset Co., Md. (April 1929); Mrs. Dorsey was Addie R. Shelton, youngest child of Fleety James *Chelton* descended from Stephen *Shelton* of Lancaster Co., Va., through his marriage with Judith Fleet. The following records are from Geo. W. Shelton's Bible:

Fleety James Chelton was the son of Fleety C. *Shelton* and his wife, Frances. Fleety C. was born Oct. 12, 1782 and d. May 22, 1853 in Somerset Co., Md. His wife, Frances, was born March 15, 1789 and died March 18, 1856. Children besides Fleety James were: Ellen Francis mar. a Nevitt—settled in Ohio and d. 6/9/1877. Nancy S. mar. a Crosswell, b. 9/20/1825, d. 8/4/1874. John W., b. 1827, d. July 7, 1856, aged 29. George mar.————

William mar. and had twin sons, Winfield Scott and Zachary Taylor and settled in Washington, D. C. Sarah mar. Boni Claroo of the Diplomatic Service and also settled in Washington. Fleety James Chelton was b. in Somerset Co., Md., in 1820 and died in same Co. in 1879; he mar. Leah Anne Adams, b. in 1825, d. 1918, in same Co.; Geo. W. Chelton, their son, was b. in same Co. Apr. 9, 1851 and died in Baltimore Apr 7, 1915. His wife was Sally Cullin, b. Mar. 7, 1862 in Somerset Co., Md., and died in Baltimore, Md., Feb. 22, 1924. They were married in Somerset Co., Md., Aug. 2, 1876 and moved to Baltimore in 1900. Descendants of these Sheltons live in Fairmount, Md. Fleety C. Chelton was a member of the old Kingston Episcopal Church in Somerset Co., and is buried in the church yard there. Geo. W. Chelton had a brother James Francis who died in Johns Hopkins Hospital about 1910. This Geo. had an aunt Nancy. Fleety James Chelton is buried in St. Paul's Churchyard in the same Co. Both bible and tombs bear several spellings of the surname Shelton and Chelton.

BERMUDA

HAVE not been successful in obtaining all of the Bermuda data, but I have records of James who died May, 1668; Ralph, Richard, George, Edward, James, William, Samuel, Robert, Joseph, John, Guy, Thomas and Stephen. Most of these, with Henry and an occasional Peter, have been names in every generation and every branch of the Shelton family since 800, and have continued to the present time. Many of the above lived in Bermuda and died there. Whether this second generation will ever be entirely straightened out, is doubtful as so many records have been lost or destroyed. But I shall feel amply repaid for my years of hard work, if I have been able to bring out the history from the obscurity in which it has rested for six generations, and give the Shelton family the place in the sun to which its lineage entitles it, and to establish the facts about the *wives* of *Thomas Jefferson* and *Patrick Henry.*

I have found descendants of dozens of the Virginia Sheltons in Missouri, where they have taken active part in the history of this great state as members of the Legislature, judges, lawyers, physicians, teachers, clergymen and writers. Dr. Lewis Shelton, a Baptist minister, used to get quinine from Dr. Sappington, one of the first physicians in Missouri, and carry it in his saddle bags to his parishioners on his circuit. Many hundreds of Missourians are descendants of the Virginia Sheltons, and, under the names of Chilton, Carleton, Skelton, Sheldon and Charlton, many Sheltons have held high office and rendered distinguished service in England as well as in various States in America. In every instance in which I have traced the Shelton family, I have found the descendants "carrying on" in a manner worthy of their ancestors, who served their country and community in peace as in war.

Another apparent error made in Virginia history is that Alexander Whitaker, the second minister in Virginia, who came in 1611, died without issue. This is based on the fact that no marriage record has been found. I had not traced this line back, but after the publication of my book, I received ten letters from people in widely separated parts of the United States, all stating that they "were descendants of Alexander Whitaker, but whenever they tried to prove it, they ran up against the brick wall of Virginia historians who claimed that 'he left no descendants'." Surely, all of these families cannot be wrong. Alexander Whitaker was drowned at the age of 31. In that day of early marriages, it would have been most improbable for him *not* to have married. The Communion Cup he used to administer Communion to Pocahontas is still in the possession of one of his descendants, and the font in which the Princess was baptized by Alexander Whitaker, is in old St. John's Church, Richmond, Virginia.

THOMAS JEFFERSON'S WIFE

OW, to clarify the record of the wife of Thomas Jefferson. She was Martha (called Patty) Wales, daughter of John Wales of "The Forest", Charles City County, Virginia. She married Bathurst Shelton, son of Dr. James Shelton and Jane Meriwether in 1766. Dr. James was a son of James Shelton (brother of John of "Rural Plains") and his wife, Mary Bathurst. Bathurst Shelton died in 1768, leaving one son, John Shelton, who is *supposed* to have died without issue. Bathurst Shelton and Thomas Jefferson had been rivals at William and Mary for the hand of Patty Wales (see "The Youth of Jefferson"). After the death of Bathurst, his widow married Jefferson. Ann Wales, sister of Patty, married Henry, son of Sir William Skipwith. Some histories state that Henry married the widow of Bathurst Shelton; this is, of course, another error of Virginia historians. (See photo and marriage bond facing pages 101 and 102.)

In the signature of Bathurst Shelton, the "H" in his first and last names is identical as it is in the signature of Meriwether Shelton. James also used this old English "H" that looked like a "K". The early records in the land office at Richmond of James Shelton have been changed since my "Genealogy" was published in 1927. A large "K" has been made over the "H" in black ink. This is pure vandalism, as no one is supposed to even have a pen to make notes in this office, and the authorities were amazed (as was Governor Pollard who was in the library office at the time I discovered it) when I called their attention to the change of name. This James Shelton was the eldest son of William and Hannah Armistead, and a brother of John, of "Rural Plains". He married Mary Bathurst and had grants of land in Henrico County alone of over 7,000 acres in 1723-6, and was one of the commissioners called in a Court in Goochland County, June 25, 1733, and is on record in St. James Parish, Goochland County, as "James Shelton, Gentleman, of Goochland and Essex Counties". He was appointed to supervise the rebuilding of the old Capitol at Williamsburg, but he died in 1753 and his son, Reuben, who married Elizabeth Lomax, was appointed to complete it. The death of James is announced in a letter from Francis Jardon to Captain Hugh Crawford in 1753: "Your good friend, James Shelton, died recently". His wife had died in 1751, according to the "Diary of John Blair". This James was the grandfather of the Sarah Shelton who married Thomas Jones and whose sister, Lucy, married Robert Gilliam.

It was a *Shelton,* not *Chelton* who collaborated with Blair in writing "The Present State of Virginia".

Here are two documents copied from the reams of data in my possession, which should speak for themselves:

"At a court in Goochland County, September 16, 1771, on motion of Meriwether *Shelton,* Gentleman, by William Fleming * * * * * are appointed to lay off and allot Martha *Shelton,* widow and relict of Bathurst *Shelton,* her dower in her deceased husband's lands, commonly known by the name of "Elk Island", etc." (D. B. 10, pg. 169). These lands are specified in the so-called *Skelton* wills.

In Albemarle County, Virginia, is the record of a transfer from "E. Smith to Meriwether *Shelton* of the County of

Know all men by these presents that we Thomas Jefferson and Francis Eppes are held and firmly bound to our sovereign lord the king his heirs and successors in the sum of fifty pounds current money of Virginia, to the paiment of which well and truly to be made we bind ourselves jointly and severally, our joint and several heirs executors and administrators in witness whereof we have hereto set our hands and seals this twenty third day of December in the year of our lord one thousand seven hundred and seventy one

The condition of the above obligation is such that if there be no lawful cause to obstruct a marriage intended to be had and solemnized between the above bound Thomas Jefferson and Martha Shelton of the county of Charles city, widow, for which a licence is desired, then this obligation is to be null and void; otherwise to remain in full force.

MARRIAGE BOND OF THOMAS JEFFERSON AND MARTHA SHELTON

Hanover'', April 17, 1775. The name *Shelton* is repeated several times (B. 8, page 39).

"CURRIOMAN"

N ACCOUNT of the curious laws of entail, it has been impossible for me to trace the various members of the Shelton family who have owned the "Currioman" estate in Westmoreland Co., Va.

I think it must have been part of the original grant of our first James Shelton, Gentleman, who moved to Bermuda and died there in 1668. His sons took up these grants and Thomas whose will is given on p. 83 and who died in Cecil Co. Md. in 1684, owned part of this land. That part probably came down to Thomas' gr-son John Shelton who died in 1706 and who owned "Currioman" and built "Rural Plains" Hanover Co. Va. This John left "Currioman" to his eldest son, Capt. John of "Belleview" on the Potomac, who added to the estate at least *twice;* each time he bought 900 acres. At the time of the death of John 1706 the estate consisted of *more* than 2000 acres. The son Capt. John, who died in 1726, left "Currioman" to his son Capt. Thos. who married Jemima Cook. The court suit brought by his brother John in 1647, shows that Capt. Thos. had only what was called a "tail right" to "Currioman".

I have not been able to find how this suit was settled, but the estate evidently reverted to the heirs of John who died in 1706. Probably through William and his son John of "Rural Plains" husband of Eleanor Parks whose 2nd eldest son Col. Thomas was in possession when he died about 1791/92; as the plat on the Court House books shows the estate broken up into shares or lots, evidently the entail had been broken. Unfortunately, the shares are only numbered and no record could be *found* showing which child got which part of the estate. Some day all of these missing records in the "Northern Neck" of Virginia may be recovered, and the various knots untangled, we can only live in hope. (See plat facing pages 104 and 105.)

EXPLANATION OF ARTICLE IN
WM. AND MARY MAGAZINE
July, 1929

HE controversy over the Sheldons, Skeltons, Chiltons, and Sheltons of Virginia all being one family, has been quite amusing. I have been accused of being a "headhunter", of "appropriating distinguished members of other families to establish a family tree of my own", to have "faked" the coat of arms, and many other foolish charges. To each of the disgruntled ladies and gentlemen, I simply reply, "Go to the records and be convinced for yourself". To read their articles, one who did not know that they were wrong, would be convinced that they knew the facts.

In *January, 1928,* Dr. Swem of William and Mary College, Williamsburg, Virginia, wrote and *offered* me ten pages in his Quarterly for a "History of the Shelton Family". Shortly after this, Mr. R. D. Gilliam of Petersburg, Virginia, started a controversy in the Richmond, Virginia papers about the Skelton famliy. Whether or not this influenced Dr. Swem, I do not know, but when my article was published *in July, 1929,* it was so apparently mixed up and contradictory, and such a large part of my data was omitted, that I was amazed and humiliated.

I had sent all new information as it came in, to Dr. Swem, together with forty notes from the English magazines, and photostats of the coat of arms, and deeds of Meriwether and Bathurst Shelton, and the marriage bond of Thomas Jefferson and Martha Shelton. In the book plates of Reuben and Meriwether Shelton, who were brothers and lived at

"Spring Garden", Hanover County, Virginia, the name of Reuben is plainly Shelton, while that of Meriwether looks like Skelton, but the "h" in his given name is identical with the "h" in his surname.

Had all these records been published, there could have been no further uncertainty, but three of the pages *offered* me were given to Mr. Gilliam, and all of his deeds, etc., (even family portraits) were published, and mine omitted. This left people in greater confusion than ever. The article was not submitted to me for proof reading and I did not know of its publication (*eighteen* months after it had been sent to Dr. Swem) until letters of inquiry commenced to arrive.

Later, Dr. Swem wrote me that Mrs. Anne Chilton McDonnell of Norfolk, Virginia, had sent in an article claiming I was entirely wrong about the *Chiltons* being *Sheltons*. He asked me if I cared to send in an article controverting hers, for publication in the Quarterly; as I did not wish to be again made ridiculous, I declined with thanks. Mrs. McDonnell claimed that the John Chilton of "Rock Spring", Fauquier County, was the Captain John killed at "Brandywine" in 1777. I have a record of the B. W. of land for service as Captain, by this John, signed by his "eldest son and heir, Thomas", and another, signed by his "son, Captain John". The Captain John of "Rock Springs" was a descendant of Captain Thomas and Jemima Cook. That Captain Thomas was the son of John and his wife, Lettice Ball, of "Belleview", later of "Currioman", Westmoreland County, Virginia. The Captain John of Fauquier County was born in 1739, and his sons were *Thomas, born 1769,* George and Joseph. The war records of the three Captains John Shelton have been dreadfully scrambled.

The Captain John of Fauquier County was in the *3rd* Virginia Regiment and *served from March 26, 1776.* Captain John of "Rural Plains", father-in-law of Patrick Henry, was an old man and did not enlist until *January 1, 1777.* He was a Captain of Cavalry and was killed at "Brandywine". As he was killed in action, the full quota of land allowed to his rank, 4000 acres, was allotted to his heirs. One warrant was signed by Thomas, "eldest son and heir", and another by his son, "Captain John", in 1783. This Captain John, in 1777, was in Colonel Alexander Spottswood's *2nd* Virginia Regiment. In 1783, he was given a B. W. for three years service as Captain in the Virginia line. *Thomas,* the son of Captain John Shelton (called Chilton in the records) and Letitia Blackwell of Fauquier County, Virginia, was not born until *1769.* There was no "son, John". Unfortunately, all of the war and pension records are spelled *Chilton,* and it has, of course, caused endless confusion. I have photostats of the official records made at the State Library in Richmond, Virginia. Here are some of the many:

Military Certificates, Book I, page 223, No. 1249: "I certify that Captain John Chilton of the Virginia line was killed at 'Brandywine', September 11, 1777, and that his representative is entitled to the land which the law allowed to that rank of officer.

(signed) William Davis"

On the same page is the following: "A warrant for 4,000 acres issued to Colonel Thomas Chilton, eldest son and heir and legal representative of Captain John Chilton, above, was delivered June 27, 1783."

Another entry follows: "B. W. of Lieutenant Jos. Holt, 1838; note of officers in the Virginia Continental Line who settled with the State Auditors for short service, yet were allowed full bounty land by executives. Captain John Chilton's heirs settled from *January 1, 1777* to *September 11, 1777*, received in 1783, 4,000 acres of land."

Another record is signed by "son, Captain John". (See photostats in back of book.)

When I published my "Genealogy" in 1927, I knew that the records were badly mixed but I thought, of course, there *were* Chilton, Chelton, Charlton, Sheldon, Skelton, etc., families other than those whose records were confused with *Shelton* records. Since the controversy arose, however, I have gone exhaustively into the records both in England and America. The findings are so absolutely indisputable that it is again necessary to publish the *facts*.

Many of these "Chilton" descendants came to Missouri. I have affidavits stating that the "name was always *called Shelton* and they never could understand *why*."

Van Tromp, son of Mark Anthony Chilton (Shelton, a descendant of the Captain John from Fauquier County who served in the 3rd Virginia Regiment in the Revolution) and Eloise Blackwell, came to Missouri from Fauquier County, Virginia. He married Susan Hampton, a niece of General Wade Hampton of South Carolina. Members of their family tell me that this Mrs. Chilton always resented very keenly the name being called Shelton, and said, as they were "all well educated people, it was the silliest thing she ever heard of to spell it one way and pronounce it another".

So, again, to all doubting Thomases, I say, "Investigate the records for your own satisfaction. I ask no one to take my word for proof."

Both Mr. George Norbury MacKenzie and Stella Pickett Hardy, quoted by Mrs. McDonnell in her article in the William and Mary Quarterly, are probably very honest in the statements they make in regard to the *Chilton* family. The only trouble is that neither of them secured the data of *all* families using the various spellings of Chilton, Chelton, Shelton, Sheldon, Charlton, Skelton, etc., in England and in the early days in Virginia, as I have done to verify my statements. And they did not go back far enough, or they would have found the descent from a common ancestor, much nearer than Adam.

Mrs. McDonnell quotes "Shaw's Notes on Kent",[1] page 186, and states that "in 1654, three sons of John and Catherine Chilton of "Chilston", Thomas, John and Mark, were in Virginia". Thomas was Thomas Shelton (ancestor of the writer of this history) whose will is filed in Cecil County, Maryland, in 1684. In my own branch of the family —and I have the Bibles back more than 200 years—the name has always been spelled and pronounced Shelton. I also have the records of direct descendants of Mark, who have been *Sheltons* always; although the court records in London and Pittsylvania Counties, Virginia, are spelled

(1) William de Shelton, who was given a large grant in Kent, held the "Manor of Chilton" (Shelton), in the time of Edward I, and it remained in his possession until the 31st year of Edward's reign, when, at William's death, it passed to his descendants, remaining in the family until the 4th year of Edward III. (Hasting's History of Kent, vol. 3, p. 680). William Shelton also owned, at his death, the Manor of Ash, near Sandwich. Charles (spelled Skelton in the records) Shelton, "Lieutenant-General in the French service and Grand Croix of St. Louis, married Barbara Leonard, daughter of Ann, Countess Leonard, who died May 16, 1722, and the Earl of Sussex of Clevening Manor. The Church and Manor of Charlton (also called Chilton), Kent, was surrendered to the crown with the possessions of the Monastery of St. Savior's of Bermondsey, at its dissolution June 1, 29th year of Henry VIII. It remained part of the "Royal Demesne" and was granted to the "See of Canterbury" by Henry; many years later, James I granted it to Adam Newton. Charlton is in the diocese of Rochester and deanery of Dartford.

*Chelto*n and *Chilton,* the descendants living today, with whom I have been in correspondence, are and have always been *Sheltons.*

In my letter to Miss Hardy, quoted by Mrs. McDonnell, I only referred her to the official records. I did not dream of asking her, or anyone else, to accept my word without verification. I am purposely avoiding the unkind criticism so freely handed out by Mr. Gilliam and Mrs. McDonnell, as I most thoroughly appreciate their chagrin. And, I know that they, and Miss Hardy who has been a genealogist for years, *thought* that they were right, so I will not accuse them of the various things of which they accused me. I share with Mrs. McDonnell ''a saving sense of humor'', which *''we Sheltons''* have always possessed; and, Mrs. McDonnell has never professed, to my knowledge, to be a genealogist. However, she did not read my article in William and Mary very carefully or, even as mixed up as it is, she would not have misquoted me so many times. No statement was made that ''the War Department records would be changed''. This would not be possible as the records belong to the various states. My article says that the then Secretary of War, Mr. Dwight Davis, had written me that an explanation of the confusion of names would ''be attached to the official records of these men so as to assist all future enquirers'', and to save the expenditure of much money and years of hard work to other searchers for *facts.*

I am seeking no glory, only making an honest effort to correct errors which have been published and republished so many times that they have been accepted as truth. I felt that I must hand down to *my* descendants our true family history. I am more than willing to leave my reputation for veracity in the hands of the honest seekers after facts, who will take the time and trouble to verify my data. I have waited patiently for each new historian to give the facts in this book. Either they are publishing from the early incorrect records, or they are afraid of starting a controversy by publishing what they *must* have discovered if they had made *personal* research for data.

Wilstach, in three volumes on "Tidewater Virginia", "Tidewater Maryland", and "Potomac Landings", makes only two references to this family by *any* of its names. One reference is made to "Lady Margaret" of "My Lady's Manor", the wife of Charles Calvert (the Lord Baltimore who died in 1714), and one to "Captain Chelton's place", "next to Stratford." This, of course, refers to "Currioman", the grants of which are all a matter of record, as are the early grants in Maryland and in "The Potomeck Freshets".

No other mention of the family under its various spellings is given by any historian that I have ever discovered, in spite of the fact that they held more land than probably any other family in that entire part of the country. No historian could *conscientiously* search the records without coming across the scrambled condition of the names of the various branches of this family. Probably none of them had a personal interest in untangling them, as I have done, and when I consider the years of work I have devoted to it, and the amount of money expended, I am not surprised at their failing to make the effort; if they *have* discovered the fact of the families all being one, they have hesitated about making such a statement for fear of the upheaval that would be sure to follow.

It is not necessary for me to pick up a family tree, as I have the family bibles for 200 years, and my grandfather, having been born and reared in Virginia, knew all of the Shelton connections, and much of the family history. It was not until I went to the library, out of curiosity to look up a history of Patrick Henry, after reading a stupidly inaccurate magazine article, that I found the ridiculous statements that had been published and republished, so I set to work to get the facts, and discovered the mess the records were in.

The enlistment in January, 1776, of the author's great, great great grandfather, Thomas Shelton, is given in the official manuscript in the Virginia State Library. It is also given in "Saunders' Early Settlers of Alabama", and has always been a matter of family knowledge. The Virginia histories state that "he settled in Lancaster County, Virginia", and his bible gives my grandfather's (John Gilmore Shelton) birth in Lancaster County, Virginia.

Although Thomas enlisted in the Revolution from this county, the land given him on his marriage, and on which he lived, might have been either Westmoreland, Northumberland or Lancaster, as his family had large plantations in each of these counties; I can find no *will* in any of these counties, but there is an inventory and distribution of Col. Thos. Chilton of Currioman in 1792, at the court house in Montross, Westmoreland County, Virginia.

The Thomas Shelton whose wife was Katherine Payne at the time his will is on record, in 1806, probably was a grandson of Col. Thomas. There are several court records concerning this man. He left sons: John Payne Shelton and Thomas Burton Shelton. If this is the son of the author's Colonel Thomas, Katherine Payne must have been his second or third wife as they were married in 1790, when Thomas had grown children. I shall greatly appreciate information from any descendant of this Thomas Shelton.

On May 10, 1782, a pay check was sent to "Colonel Thomas Shelton" by Samuel Ford. This record is Shelton; he is carried on the auditor's accounts as Captain, Lieutenant-Colonel and Colonel *Thomas Chilton,* and receipts under this spelling, as eldest son and heir of Captain John Shelton of "Rural Plains", Hanover County, Virginia. June 27, *1783.* He is given as Thomas *Shelton* in the Washington manuscripts, and his gr. son, Jesse *Shelton,* is given in April, 1777, as Lieutenant, "Albemarle Guards, Colonel Francis Taylor's Regiment". Colonel Thomas was one of the patriots of Westmoreland County, Virginia, who signed the first public protest against British misrule in the American Colonies in June, 1776. His name is on the tablet in the Court House at Montross. Two sons (of either this Col. Thomas, or the other Captain Thomas "Chilton"), William and Charles, also signed. They may have been sons of the Captain Thomas, husband of Jemima Cook, who died in 1764/5, and whose will was proved September 4, 1765; he was born in 1699. Both of these Thomases had sons, William and Charles.

OLD SHELTON HOMES IN VIRGINIA

IT IS distressing that so few remnants of the old homes in the "Neck of Virginia" remain. Of "Carotoman", only a fragment existed, when I last visited it, and only a part of a wall and chimney and a pile of old brick where the house stood, remained at "Currioman". There is no trace of "Millenbeck", and the gravestones are buried under several feet of underbrush, and many of them have been washed away. A small frame house on the place was shown the author as "Millenbeck" (in 1932), but this was evidently the home of an overseer or employee on the place. It was quite old, and probably was on the original place. At "Belmont", Mrs. Cordelia Ball Gilmour's home, the same conditions exist. An old frame house, with an interesting old chimney, is occupied and shown as "Belmont". The real "Belmont" was a large, handsome residence and stood more in the center of the old estate and on a hill, as it overlooked the Rappahannock River to whose banks the original estate extended; now, the highway cuts it into two parts. I could find no trace of "Belleview" or "Bellevue" (the records spell it both ways) the home of John Shelton, whose first wife was Lettice Ball, and which, later, belonged to Thomas Ludwell Lee. I could not even find the location. The records read "Belleview on the Potomac". "Belle Isle", where Cordelia Ball Gilmour lived after her second marriage to Rawleigh Downman, and where she died, is still in very fair condition, and one can visualize something of its former beauty. The lovely hand carved mantles, stairs, the beautiful floors, etc., have all been sold "to a Northerner, one of the DuPonts," I was told by Captain

Somers, the owner at the time I visited it, and the grave-yard is in a dreadfully neglected condition. I could find no trace of Mrs. Gilmour Downman's grave, nor could Mr. Downman of Richmond and Fredericksburg, Virginia, the owner of the graveyard which was reserved when the estate was sold, give me any idea as to where she was buried. Her son and grandson both died without issue, and the gr-father of the writer, John Gilmour Shelton, was the legal heir to these two estates, Millenbeck and Belmont.

It is a tragedy, of course, and makes one's heart ache at the devastation and poverty in one of the garden spots of early Virginia, "Sic transit gloria mundi".

Within the last few years, some old family deeds have come into my possession, one of which is a Gilmour Deed witnessed by *Florinda Ball*. This changed entirely what I honestly had believed to be my own lineage.

We were brought up on the knowledge that the mother and father of my grandfather (John Gilmour [he later used the 'Gilmore' spelling] Shelton, born in Lancaster Co., Virginia, March 1, 1802, according to his bible) had died in his infancy, and that his *Aunt* Cordelia Ball Gilmour was his legal guardian. As stated before, I have never been able to verify any of this in Lancaster Court House. The records simply could not be found. All published records I have found give "Cordelia Ball" as " 'only child and heiress of Dr. William Ball (6) of Millenbeck,' " so I had to *assume* that my great grandmother was a Miss Gilmour, as grandfather had named his eldest daughter Mary Gilmour and one of his sons John Gilmour.

After reading the deeds referred to, I determined to make another trip to the Lancaster Court House; the results and conditions were the same I had encountered on my previous investigations. I finally decided to go through all of the files in the archives department of the State Library. This was a herculean task as the records are not indexed in any way — alphabetically, chronologically or even in the centuries—the 1600's would be the next papers to 1800's, etc. However, I made several valuable and helpful discoveries.

I found the will of Dr. William Ball (6) of Millenbeck; it was dated June 17, 1785 and proved July 22, 1785. In it, he mentions "wife, Catherine" and daughters Cordelia *and Florinda*. It is witnessed by William Shelton. (Lancaster Wills, Box 207—Fo. 88—Archives Div. Va. State Library.)

I also found the will of Mrs. Lettice Lee Ball, mother of Dr. William; she also mentions "grand-daughter *Florinda*, daughter of my deceased son, Dr. William Ball" and "grandson, William Ball—daughter Mary Graham, grand-daughters Mary Bland Ball and Letty Ball". This is dated Oct. 16, 1788, and proved Dec. 15, 1788. Another deed I have, dated Jan. 1, 1798, is signed by *Florinda* Ball and in 1799, on Dec. 24th, there is another signature of hers. Jesse Shelton, single, bought his "Poplar Neck" plantation, of 390 acres, in Lancaster County, paying 937 lbs. for it; it adjoined the land of Cordelia Ball and her husband, John M. Gilmour. This deed is dated Dec. 24, 1799 and is recorded July 21, 1800. I am convinced now, that Jesse Shelton married Florinda *Ball* (and not a Gilmour) in 1800 or 1801. (See deeds at back of book.)

This is confirmed by a family incident that I had never been able to explain to my own satisfaction. In my mother's young girl-hood, a lawyer by the name of Webb, connected in some way with the Sheltons of the Northern Neck, came to St. Louis to tell my grandfather that Mrs. Gilmour's (Cordelia Ball, his aunt) son and grandson had died and that he, my grandfather, was the legal heir to Mrs. Cordelia Ball Gilmour Downman's two estates, "Millenbeck" and "Belmont". At that time, my grandfather was a very wealthy man, and he refused to go back to Lancaster County to establish his claim. I had never understood how he *could* have been heir, if his mother was a sister of Cordelia's *husband*, John Gilmour. But, if she was a sister of Cordelia, as I now *am* sure, he *would* be the *legal* heir.[1]

(1) The tradition has come down in my branch of the family of descent from Pocahontas and also a Huguenot line, but I have not discovered it unless it is through the Bland line, or the wife of Wm. Ball (6) Catherine, whose surname I have not been able to find.

My membership in the Huguenot Society of South Carolina, is from John Alden and Priscilla Molyneux ("Mullins" as our historians insist on calling *her*) through the Campbell Noble Edson etc., lines.

In tax lists of Lancaster Co., Va., Jesse (1) is listed up to 1801. In 1803 and 1804 he is listed Jesse Shelton (3), showing wife and child. In the late 1700's he owned the ferry run between his land in Lancaster Co. and Urbanna.

The will of a Jesse Chilton of Lancaster Co. (not the son of Col. Thomas, who d. 1791-2) is dated May 28, 1793 and proved Jan. 19, 1795, W. B. 28, p. 9. He had Jesse Jr., Alice, Ann and Cyrus. Jesse Jr. died, or rather his will is dated Feb. 11, 1811 and proved May 21, 1811. Jesse Shelton, son of Thos. (later Lt. Col.) and Gr-son of Thos., Col., Westmoreland Milita (d. 1791-2) joined the Albemarle Guards, Col. Francis Taylor's Reg., in 1777.

The early Lancaster County, Virginia, records are in a very disgraceful condition in the *loft* of the old Court House at Lancaster; they are not accessible to the public, and are covered with filth and vermin, and are rapidly becoming beyond preservation. Loose leaves of inestimable value to all who are interested in our true American history, are scattered all over the loft. Fumigation and classification of these records is the first work to be done, and I have personally urged the necessity for it on three governors of Virginia, but have been told in each instance that there are no State funds available for work of this kind. What a crime and disgrace to allow the history of our country to be destroyed in this shiftless manner.

The same condition exists in *many* of the old Court Houses in Virginia, though some use cellars and vacant rooms to hide the records in, instead of lofts.

Our patriotic organizations have done fine work in the volumes they have preserved, but these are the books *in use* at the various court houses; the most valuable records to posterity have never been uncovered. Although my name does not appear on these preserved books, I take pride in the knowledge that it was I who brought this condition to the attention of the patriotic organizations and by constantly hammering on the necessity of immediate action, finally got them started on this work. I hope, before I pass on, to see the complete preservation of what is left of the records of our early American history.

MISCELLANEOUS NOTES

OHN SHELTON of Hanover County, Virginia, had a grant of 800 acres in St. George's Parish, Spottsylvania County, in the fork of the Rappahannock River, May 30, 1726. In 1826, this land was sold by the author's grandfather, John Gilmour Shelton, after his estate had been turned over to him. This land was near, or adjoined the 1,000 acres of land granted to Ambrose Grayson, October 13, 1727.

Thomas Shelton, son of Thomas (d. 1684), is on record in York County, Virginia, as twenty-three years of age in 1657.

John Shelton, in Captain Francis (one record says Captain *William* Taylor) Taylor's Company of Colonel Alexander Spottswood's Regiment in July, 1777. (Later Captain John of ''Rural Plains'', brother-in-law of Patrick Henry.)

In roll of Captain *Francis* Taylor's Company, Second Virginia Regiment, 3/17/1776; *Thomas Shelton* is given as Corporal. He enlisted 1/29/1776.

Lt.-Col. Thomas Chilton, warrant for pay for officers and men of Westmoreland Militia, called on duty June 15, 1779. Auditor's account 1780, pg. 23, ''Virginia State troops in the Revolution'' pd. to Thos. Chilton for a rifle for Capt. Triplett's Company.

Warrant to Hudson Muse, Esq., for 23 lbs. for use of Captain *Thomas Chilton*, account of payroll and forage for his company of Westmoreland Militia, October 8, 1776. (Journal of Council of State of Virginia, Vol. 1, p. 182.)

November 1, 1777, Captain *Thomas Shelton* was recommended for Lieutenant-Colonel. This recommendation was approved by the Governor at the Court in the Spring of 1778. (signed) W. M. Scott.''

''Westmoreland County Militia''. Thos. Chilton, Lt.-Col., John Lane, Major, James Triplett, Capt., Court of Aug. 25, 1778.

Colonel Thomas Chilton warrant for supplies for his Company in Westmoreland, November 26, 1781. (Auditor's Account No. 9, pp. 21-308, 1779-80.)

All of above are records of Thomas Shelton, second eldest son of John and Eleanor Parks Shelton''.

On recommendation of Court of Westmoreland County, it is ordered that a Com. be issued to Thomas Chilton, Gentleman, app. him Sheriff of Westmoreland County, December 7, 1776. (Son of above Colonel Thomas) J. of C. of S. Vol. 1, p. 268.

Meriwether Shelton, Gentleman, com, as Sheriff of Hanover County. (Vol. 1, p. 210, C. J.)

WAR DEPARTMENT RECORDS

"Colonial and Revolution Soldiers and B. W." (Bounty Warrants)

Warrant issued to *William Shelton* for cost of hiring two horses to assist an express from Congress to Williamsburg, October 31, 1776. (C. J. V. 1, p. 222)

Warrant for 5 lbs. to *Peter Shelton* for rifles supplied to Captain Dabney's Company of Militia Men, November 28, 1776. (Vol. I, p. 255, C. J.)

Captain *John Chilton* (brother-in-law of Patrick Henry) June 4, 1784. (War. 4, p. 32.) This was John Shelton of Hanover County, in Colonel Alexander Spottswood's Regiment, Second Virginia.

William Chilton, Aud. Account XXII, p. 70. H. D. 1834. R. C. Saf. 274.

Jesse *Shelton,* Albemarle Guards, Colonel Francis Taylor's Regiment, April 1777 (W. D. 2-351) Grandson of the Colonel Thomas, spelled Chilton in records, and son of Thomas, later Lt.-Col. in the War of 1812.

David *Shelton* served as matross in the Reg. artillery for three years previous to December 20, 1779, and obtained an exchange from Colonel Carrington. (B. W. 1783, signed in Richmond September 11, 1783.) (Brother of John of ''Rural Plains''.)

Joseph Shelton, Sgt. Inf. pay rec'd by J. Hawkins September 2, 1783. (War. 4-346.)

Colonel Joseph Shelton of Goochland (S. of W. 1835. Pen 2-142) Rec'd Pension September 6, 1833, to begin March 4, 1831, when he was 73 years old.

Claim of Estate of *John Chilton,* Captain, settled from January 1, 1777 to September 11, 1777. Heirs rec'd in 1783, 4,000 acres of land. (This was the father-in-law of Patrick Henry, the John Shelton who was killed at Brandywine.)

In 1783, the heirs of Captain John Chilton killed at Brandywine, received 4,000 acres of land. Heirs of his son, Captain John Chilton, ask additional pension, Feb. 13, 1834, and on March 17, 1838, Edward G. Marshall, as attorney for heirs of Captain John Chilton, appeals for additional land for service of said Captain John.

CHILTON, JOHN (Capt.) acc't com. safety, 1775-6 B. W. R. C.

CHILTON, JOHN (Capt.) Fauquier acc't com. 1775-6 p. 82.

CHILTON, JOHN (Capt.) Third Virginia Regiment (C. J. 1776-7, p. 35) (Heitman, 123)

The last three entries are Captain John of Fauquier, descendant of Captain Thomas Shelton and Jemima Cook.

Chilton, John, Captain. War. 4, 32, June 4, 1784 (son of John *Shelton* and Eleanor Parks.)

John Shelton, War. 5, 180, report says Colonel Thomas Shelton received pay by Samuel Ford, May 10, 1783. (These are John *Shelton* of Hanover County and Thomas called *Chilton* (his *brother*) in Westmoreland County.)

Shelton, Joseph. War. 4, 356.

Shelton, Stephen, C. J., 1783-4-5, p. 121. Infantry, living 8/18/1783, War. 4, 345.

Shelton, Thomas. Infantry. Jan. 5, 1785, B. W. Saf. 274 (Son of Colonel Chilton (Shelton) of Westmoreland Co.)

CHILTON, Captain, Acct. Com. Sfty, 1775-6, e 4.

CHILTON, Captain, Third Virginia Regiment, Acct. C's, 1775-6, 2-74.

CHILTON, Captain, Culpepper Battle, Acct. C. S., 1775-6, 61. (These are Captain John of Fauquier County.)

CHILTON, Andrew (Lancaster County) s of W. 1835; Pensions 2-76, B. W.

CHILTON, Captain Charles, Auditor's Account XV. 584, October 21, 1783. Either son of Col. Thomas who died about 1791 at ''Currioman'', or the son of Captain Thomas and Jemima Cook. Both had a son, Charles, that this date could apply to. I am inclined to believe this is the son of the author's Col. Thomas, as the sons of Captain Thomas and Jemima Cook had moved to other counties. His name is on a tablet of a roll of Patriots of Westmoreland County, Virginia, 1776, at Montross.

Chilton, Henry, Saf. 274.

Chilton, John, R. C.

Chilton, Newman, B. W., War. 5-53.

Chilton, Stephen (Culpepper) B. W., War. 5-53.

Chilton, William, H. D., 1834, Doc. 35-4-R.C. Saf., 274, Auditor's Account, XXII, p. 70.

Charlton (New Kent County) Auditor's Account, 1779, 210.

Charlton, Francis (Montgomery County), S. of W. 1835, Pension 2, 173.

Charlton, George, B. W.

Charlton, William, War. 4, 150.

Lieutenant Colonel Thomas Chilton, Commander Fifth Brigade, War of 1812, Honorable Discharge, April 15, 1814. (Grandson of John and Eleanor Parks Shelton of Hanover County, Virginia, son of Col. Thomas[1] of Westmoreland County. (See photostats of service records in back of book.)

(1) I have not been able to find the will of Col. Thomas Shelton (Chilton) of Westmoreland County, Virginia, but there is a record of an inventory of his estate in Montross at the County Court House in 1791; and later "Division of Estate" Aug. 28 and Dec. 9, 1782; this must be an error in copying and mean 1792, as Col. Thomas received his army pay May 10, 1783; and the inventory is listed 1791, years after he died. Evidently the entail has become broken on the Currioman estate; there is a fine drawing on the books (Bk. 6 pgs. 220-4) showing extent of this estate in 1782 (prob. 1792), but unfortunately, the shares are only marked in lot numbers, so the names of his children do not appear in the distribution. His wife's name is given as "Isabella" and he appoints his son, Charles, as executor for his infant son, "Orrick." This must have been a recent marriage, as Col. Thos. was the second eldest son of John of Rural Plains and must have been quite old in 1791.

The date of death is borne out in the tax lists, Col. Thomas was executor of a Turbeville Estate on lists of 1786 and 1787. Tax on "Estate of Orrick

Shelton" appears on lists of 1792, 1793, 1794 and on up to 1803. I did not check further than this. (See plat facing pages 104-105.)

In 1802, Orrick's Estate is taxed for 31 slaves. The son, Thomas, evidently settled on one of the Lancaster County plantations after the death of his father, as he appeared on the tax lists of that County from 1792 as far as I checked the lists, to about 1803. He also appears in many Court records in these years, but always as Thomas Shelton. In the war of 1812, he was Lt. Col. of his father's old Reg. the Westmoreland Co. Militia.

In 1791, he bought the Rappahannock River plantation of 60 acres, of George Chitwood. His son, Jesse, witnessed this deed. In 1794, he bought an additional 10 acres from John Arms and was guardian for John's son, Walter Arms, July 21, 1794.

This Thomas Shelton = Elizabeth Webb, Aug. 6, 1777, in Pr. Geo. Co., Md.

Jesse Shelton, *brother* of Col. Thomas, (2) died before 1795; the inventory of his estate was signed by Thomas Shelton, Jan. 9, 1795. Thomas, Jr.'s son, Jesse died in the early 1800's. There are so many Jesse's that the records are very confusing. One called Jesse Shelton was actually Jesse Hopson, but was called Shelton for his step-father. The Jesse who died in 1795, also had a son Jesse Jr., all of these appear in the records of Lancaster Co., Va., in the Archives Division of the State Library at Richmond.

RECORD OF COLONIAL SOLDIERS

Charlton, James, D. W. 408, September 10, 1774. Captain John Lewis' Company of Volunteers from Botetourt County.

Shelton, Ralph, H. S. 7-201.

Shelton, Thomas, Colonel, Washington MMS. p. 1460, son of John and Eleanor Parks Shelton.

Skelton, John, Washington MMS., 5-4 (father of above Thomas).

Skelton, William, H. S., 7-224 (Lunenburg County) R. C., 1834.

John Chilton of Westmoreland County served on the galley "Fly" (enlisted under John Thomas) from 1777 for over three years, until "The Fly" was sunk in 1780 at the siege of York. (Recorded 6/30/1818). Claim refused on ground that said Chilton served in the State Navy and not in the Continental service. (Born 1755, son of Colonel Thomas Shelton.) John's will was proved Sept. 14, 1812, and final settlement made in 1821. Milly Chilton Robinson and Robert Forrester, are named as nephew and niece.

Virginia Militia in the Revolution, Dec. No. 131. Record of David Shepherdson gives a *Thomas Shelton*, Lieutenant in Captain Anthony Winston's Company in 1780. (Son of Colonel Thomas, spelled Chilton in the records. Later, he was made Lieutenant-Colonel.[1])

Grants in old Rappahannock County, Virginia. Grantor, Edward Sheldon and Shildon on record in this county from 1664 to 1686. (Edward Shelton, spelled Chilton by historians, Attorney General of Virginia and Bermuda, grandson of first James Shelton in Virginia, later of Bermuda.)

Shelton, John, Bk. 1677-82, p. 173, June 19, 1678.

Shilton, Thomas, Bk. 1682-88, p. 111, Witness 5/3/1684.

Shelton, Thomas, Book 1683, p. 1683-86, p. 145, March 4, 1685/6.

After selling "Carotoman" to Robert Carter in 1703, John Shelton, Sr., must have lived at "Rural Plains" with his son, William, as he was a Reader in St. Paul's Church, Hanover County, in 1703. His son, John, Jr., probably lived at "Currioman" as John, Sr., was buried there in 1706, and his son, Captain John in 1726. His son, William,

(1) In "Sidelights on Maryland History" by Richardson, in a list of Colonial Militia 1732-1748 are the names of Stephen Chilton, Capt. 3rd Troop. Col. Geo. Plater and Mark Chilton, Trooper, same Co.

Hennings Statutes and Crozier's Col. Militia give Peter Shelton (Chelton) Middlesex Co. Nov. 23, 1687. Ralph Shelton, Amelia Co., 1758; Wm. Shelton, Lunenberg Co., 1758, and Eliphas Shelton in Henry Co., 1782. In the History of Maryland, Vol. 6, Charles Shelton (Chilton) was one of the delegates from Maryland to ratify the Constitution Sept. 17, 1788.

was dead before 1734 when William's son, John, released
Allen Howard as guardian of his estate.

At Tappahonnock Court House, Essex County, Virginia,
are the following early records. There are no *Skelton*
records there.

	D. Bk.	Page
April 24, 1678—John Shelton—witness.....	6	39
November 7, 1684—William Sheldon, Pltff. vs. Jones........................	0-1	75
March 4, 1688—Thomas. Shelton, Deft., Col. Loyde...........................	0-1	210
January 7, 1708—Ralph Shelton—Devisee of Thos. Meriwether		
January 7, 1708—Ralph Shelton—witness to will of Thos. Meriwether D. & C........	13	186
January 31, 1701—Thos. Shelton, Witness		
November 10, 1702—Thos. Shelton, Witness D. & W..............................	10	104-121

THE SHELTON TAVERN, HANOVER COUNTY, VIRGINIA, BUILT ON A GRANT OF JOHN SHELTON'S IN 1725. THIS VIEW IS THE ORIGINAL FRONT OF THE TAVERN, BUT IS NOW THE BACK, AS THE OLD CREEK ROAD HAS BEEN ABANDONED.

HANOVER COURT HOUSE AND THE
SHELTON TAVERN, HANOVER, VA.

HE land on which the Shelton Inn and Hanover County Court House stand, was originally Shelton land. The Inn has again been opened to the public; it is on the new National Road to Washington, but the period of the building cannot be judged as it stands with the back of the building facing the highway. The original "Creek Road" was abandoned after the Court House was finished. (See photo, opposite page.)

In 1723, John Shelton of "Rural Plains", Hanover County, Virginia, had a grant from "the junction of the Pamunkey and South Anna Rivers to Beaver Dam", and on "both sides of Owen's Creek" in what are now Goochland, Hanover and Louisa Counties, Virginia. The land for the Court House was given by John Shelton in 1734, and the building was erected in 1735. The "Inn" antedates the Court House by ten years. Both buildings are in an excellent state of preservation. This was the John Shelton who finished writing the "Laws of Virginia", which had been commenced by his father-in-law, William Parks, the editor; in his will, he requested his "son-in-law, John Shelton", to complete the work. I can not find any record of the will or the death of this John Shelton's wife, Eleanor Parks, but she was living in 1764, when both signed a land transfer. Most of the records of this branch of the Shelton family were destroyed with the Hanover County records when Richmond was burned—the irony of fate. They were taken there "for safe-keeping"; had they been left in the old Hanover Court House, they would have been saved for posterity. (See photo on opposite page.)

The Virginia histories have scrambled up the Shelton families most dreadfully but this was, of course, caused by the various spellings of the name, and from the fact that so many records had been lost or destroyed.

HANOVER COUNTY COURT HOUSE, BUILT IN 1735 ON LAND DONATED BY JOHN SHELTON OF "RURAL PLAINS." HERE PATRICK HENRY ARGUED THE "PARSON'S CAUSE" THAT STARTED HIM ON THE ROAD TO FAME.

CHILDREN OF JOHN SHELTON (1) OF "RURAL PLAINS", HANOVER CO., VA.

Spelled Chilton in Lancaster Co., Va., Records

HE children living in 1706 (when his will was proved) of John Shelton (called Chilton) who built "Rural Plains" in 1670 were John, presumably the eldest son as he was left the home plantation "Currioman"; William, Thomas, Mary, Sarah and Elizabeth. John married Lettice Ball first, and later, Mary Watts. William married Hannah Armistead. Thomas (data given later on in this history.) Mary married John Sharp of Lancaster County. Elizabeth married Bryan Graves and Sarah married, first, Richard Gissage. She was widowed before September 30, 1703, when she married Joseph Bickley of King William County, Virginia, son of Sir Francis Bickley of Norfolk, England. Joseph died before his father and William, son of Joseph and Sarah Shelton Gissage, inherited the title and estates of his grandfather. He lived in Louisa County, Virginia. Sarah is always referred to in the records as Sarah Shelton, and her son by Richard Gissage, Ralph, took his mother's name, Shelton. He was born in 1698. In 1722, he married Mary Pollard and from them descend the line of Col. Richard Shelton of Amherst County, Virginia.

Thomas, the youngest son of John (d. 1706) married Winifred King in 1723 and died in 1738. He left a son, Thomas, and probably other children. John, husband of Lettice Lee, called "Captain John of Belleview", (later of Currioman) had Captain Thomas (probably his eldest son, as Currioman was left to him) who married Jemima Cook, and John Shelton, later of Caroline and Stafford Counties, Virginia.

William Shelton and Hannah Armistead had a daughter, who married a Trueheart, and sons: David, Joseph, Samuel, William and Captain John of "Rural Plains", all living (except Joseph and Captain John) in 1780, when Joseph's will was proved. Two sons: Ralph and Richard had died previously. Captain John married Eleanor, daughter of Colonel William Parks, the first editor in Maryland, and Virginia, and Thomas was their second eldest son; the eldest son was James—on whom John settled the "Red House", Louisa Co., Va., plantation. This Captain John's daughter, Sarah Shelton (sister of Col. Thomas) married Patrick Henry in 1754; not "at four o'clock in the morning, coming home from a dance" and "by a Justice of the Peace", as some of our historians tell us, but in the parlor of old "Rural Plains", the house still occupied by the Sheltons, having descended from father to son for eight generations. It has never been out of possession of the male line of the family, and never been remodelled, although it has been under shell fire in many battles. This is a record, I believe, unequalled by any other house in America. The brick for the outer walls was brought from England; that for the inner walls was made on the place.

The first time I had the honor of being the house guest of Mr. and Mrs. William Robert Shelton at "Rural Plains" was in 1926, when I slept in a bed brought over from England more than 300 years ago, by the family. The swords and helmets worn by the Sheltons in the Revolution and in the War of 1812, are preserved there with great pride. The elder Captain John, father-in-law of Patrick Henry, was a

"RURAL PLAINS," ATLEE, HANOVER COUNTY, VIRGINIA. (Built by John Shelton [d. 1706] in 1670. The room to the left as one enters is the old parlor in which Sarah Shelton, d. of John [3] Shelton of Rural Plains, was married to Patrick Henry!)

Captain of Cavalry and was killed at "Brandywine". His son, Captain (later *called* Colonel) John, marched with Patrick Henry to Williamsburg to protest to the Governor against the removal of the powder from the old magazine. The Sheltons have volunteered and served in every war in England and America. Six sons of Crispen Shelton and his wife Letitia *or* Lettice, fought in the American Revolution. They have been patriots always. Thomas, second son of Captain John, Sr., and Eleanor Parks, was a Colonel of the Westmoreland Militia in the American Revolution, and his son, Thomas Shelton, held the title of Lieutenant-Colonel of the same regiment in the War of 1812. Thomas, Sr., was on the muster roll of forces in the army on October 25, 1754, commanded by Hon. Col. John Starkey, Esq., "in Captain Hick's own Company"; he re-enlisted from Lancaster County, Virginia, in Captain Taylor's 2nd Virginia Regiment, January 29, 1776. He had served as Corporal, Lieutenant and Captain by October 8, 1776. In 1777, he was "recommended for Lieutenant-Colonel" and this was "confirmed by the Governor at a Court of 1778". In 1778, he is given as Lieutenant-Colonel in a list of Field Officers in the 4th Regiment Light Dragoons and, in 1781, he was Colonel of the Westmoreland County, Virginia, Militia. (In the later records, Thomas's name is spelled Chilton.) He is mentioned in the Washington Manuscripts as Shelton. He was the great, great, great grandfather of the writer of this book. In 1783, he receipted as "eldest son and heir" (his elder brother James, was dead) for 4000 acres B. W. allowed to heirs of his father, "Captain John, killed at Brandywine"; The heirs were allowed the full quota for their father's rank as Captain, although he only served from January, 1777, until September 11, 1777, but was killed in action. (MMS in Virginia State Library.) In 1783, Colonel Thomas's brother, Captain John of "Rural Plains", was granted a B. W. for three years' service as Captain in the Virginia line. Unfortunately, the Revolutionary records give these men as *Chiltons,* and it has caused endless confusion. (See photostats at back of book.)

Instead of Sarah Shelton, the first wife of Patrick Henry, being "of low origin, the daughter of a poor farmer and tavern keeper", as some of our historians state, her father owned many thousand acres of land (see land-grants given in Misc. Notes at end of book), and dozens of slaves. When Sarah married, her father gave her 300 acres and six slaves. The tavern at Hanover Court House, Va., came into possession of John Shelton through his wife, to whom it was willed by her father, William Parks. As Patrick Henry was only 18 when he married, Sarah, who was only 16, John Shelton closed "Rural Plains" and moved to the "Inn", to enable Patrick to read his law and be in easy access to the court house. Six children were born in a very few years, and John Shelton supported the family until Patrick was able to take over the task. He had sold Sarah's land, and opened a store in Old Hanover Town. This failed, as did his earlier venture in business. If it had not been for the generosity of John Shelton, his father-in-law, America would never have heard of the "Tongue of Virginia". As to the Shelton origin, let history speak for it. The line goes back through Alfred the Great to Adam. This surely should satisfy the most ambitious descendants, and the family is descended from fourteen (some records say sixteen, but I have only fourteen traced) of the twenty-five Barons who were Sureties for Magna Carta (only seventeen of these men left issue), and from *at least* forty-

PATRICK HENRY, THE "TONGUE OF VIRGINIA,"
FROM THE PORTRAIT IN THE OLD COURT HOUSE
AT HANOVER TOWN, HANOVER CO., VIRGINIA

seven Knights of the Garter. The title of Knight was not hereditary, but was given for distinguished service. Several of each generation of Sheltons received it, from Sir Ralph the Crusader, and indeed several generations before him, to Sir Ralph of Warwickshire, England, knighted at Theobald's in 1607, whose son was founder of the American line.

A history of the Sheltons of Norfolk, England, with photographs of old and new "Shelton Hall", St. Mary's Church, containing the tombs of the family for hundreds of years, the royal descendants, etc., are given in my "Genealogy", published in 1927. (See charts in center of this book.)

CHILDREN OF JOHN SHELTON (3) OF "RURAL PLAINS" AND HIS WIFE, ELEANOR PARKS

HE now known children of John Shelton and Eleanor Parks were: (1) James, (2) Colonel Thomas, (3) Robert, (4) William Parks, (5) David, (6) Eleanor, (7) Elizabeth, who married Robert Anderson, son of "Robert of Gold Mine", (9) Sarah, who married Patrick Henry, and (8) Captain John who inherited "Rural Plains"—he married three times.

(2) Colonel Thomas is supposed to have settled in Lancaster County, Virginia. He owned land there and also in Westmoreland and Northumberland Counties, and served in the Revolution in Regiments in both counties, and his descendant, the writer's grandfather, was born in Lancaster County; but I have not been able to clarify the record of Colonel Thomas without help from others of his descendants with whom, so far, I have been unable to get in touch, as the Chilton spelling is used in all of these counties for my first Col. Thomas Shelton.

1) James, eldest son of John of "Rural Plains", settled in Goochland County and, later, in Louisa County, Virginia. He was a member of the Grand Jury in Hanover County, Virginia, April 18, 1745, and was the first owner of "Red House", Louisa County, Virginia, which was built on the plantation of and given him by his father, John *Shelton* of Hanover County, Virginia.

(3) Robert—no record.

(4) William Parks, d. s. p. 1778.

(5) David enlisted from Hanover County, Virginia, for the Revolutionary War. He was at Valley Forge, and later

settled in Caswell County, North Carolina, and died there. He married first, (?) and second, Susannah Vaughan.

(6) Eleanor married Colonel McClanahan of the Seventh Virginia Regiment.

(7) Elizabeth married Robert Anderson, son of "Robert of Gold Mine".

(8) Sarah married Patrick Henry and the youngest son

(9) Captain (later called Colonel in the records) John, who inherited "Rural Plains".

JOHN SHELTON (4) OF "RURAL PLAINS", ATLEE, HANOVER CO., VA.

NLY one marriage of Colonel John Shelton, youngest son of John and Eleanor Parks Shelton, has ever been published. Newly discovered family records (including his bible and prayer book, and his will) prove that he was married three times.

By his first wife, Ann Randolph, there is no known issue, and no children by that marriage are mentioned in his will. The date of his first wife's death is not given.

In 1773, he married his second wife, Nancy Williamson, daughter of Robert and Susannah Williamson of Lunenburg County, Virginia. By this wife, he had Robert, born August 17, 1774; Walter Parks, born May 13, 1777, and Eleanor, born July 16, 1779. I have no further record of Eleanor, neither her marriage nor death are given in John's bible, nor is she mentioned in his will, in which he states that his son, Robert, had been provided for and leaves all of his land in Goochland to his son, Walter Parks Shelton. Eleanor probably died in infancy.

The "Buford" genealogy states that this Eleanor married Robert Anderson, but this is incorrect. It was her aunt, Elizabeth, who married Robert Anderson, as stated on page 135 of this history.

Nancy, the second wife of Colonel John Shelton, died about 1780, and on January 7, 1784, John married his third wife, Ann Southall, daughter of Turner and Martha Van der Vall Southall of Hanover County, Virginia. Their children were: (1) John Southall, born 1785, who married

Sarah Boyce; (2) Alexander Barrett, born September 16, 1787, d. s. p.; (3) Philip Turner, born April 6, 1791, d. s. p.; (4) Harriett, born February 13, 1794; (5) Polina, born March 3, 1796, d. s. p., and (6) Colonel Edwin, born June 5, 1798, youngest son, who inherited "Rural Plains".

Colonel John Shelton died October 31, 1798, and December 15, 1804, his widow married Peter Foster. There was no issue.

Colonel Edwin Shelton married Sarah Elizabeth Oliver (daughter of Isaac Oliver of Hanover County, Virginia, and his wife, Ann Alexander Austin Oliver) September 4, 1827. She died July 21, 1887, and Colonel Edwin died November 4, 1874. Their children were: (1) Harriett Ann, who married Dr. William Southall; (2) Mary Eliza, who married a Dr. Lumpkin; (3) Frances Foster, d. s. p.; (4) Dr. Edwin Turner (M. D.) who married Mary Sutton Hamlin; (5) Sarah Ellen, who married Turner H. Southall; (6) John Southall, d. s. p.; (7) Isabella, d. s. p.; (8) Emma Edwina, who married John B. Oliver; and (9) Walter Mitchell, youngest son, who inherited "Rural Plains" and married Bertie Winn, daughter of Colonel William Robert Winn and Susan Parke Goodall.

Walter Mitchell Shelton (born June 1, 1849—died 1932) and Bertie Winn, had the following children: (1) William Robert, born 1875, present owner of "Rural Plains", who married June 2, 1915, Maud Greenlee; they have two children: Mary Winn and William Robert; (2) Bertie Winn, single, living in Richmond. (3) Frances Edwina, single, living in Richmond. (4) Sarah Oliver, d. s. p., aged 17. (5) James (I have no record of him; he may have died in infancy. (6) Walter Mitchell living in North Carolina. (7)

Turner Southall, M. D. of Richmond. (8) Emma Parks, single, living in Richmond;

Dr. Turner Southall Shelton was a Lieutenant in the World War. He married in 1919, Miss Mae Hundley of Dinwiddie County, Virginia. They have two children, Mae Elizabeth and Eleanor Winn. Dr. Shelton is a prominent physician of Richmond, Virginia.

The children of John Southall Shelton (b. 1785) and Sarah Boyce were: (1) John, who married Amanda McRae. (2) James, no further record. (3) Alexander Barrett, born 1807 and died 1844, who married Sarah Elmira Royster (said to be the lost "Lenore" of Edgar Allen Poe); the records of St. John's Church, Richmond, give her as his second wife. I have no record of a first marriage; (4) Sarah and (5) Ellen, no further record, and (6) Southall Shelton, who married Page Fitzhugh and had Alexander Fitzhugh (born 1865 and died 1918) who married Emma Preston and had a son: Preston Fitzhugh Shelton of Richmond, Virginia, who married Julia Bland. His sister, Martha W. Shelton, married Jesse M. Strong.

After the death of Page Fitzhugh in 1867, Southall Shelton married Mrs. Laura A. Reed. No issue.

Alexander Barrett (3) Shelton and Sarah Elmira Royster had: Southall Shelton and Ann Elizabeth, born February 6, 1830, who married October 17, 1848, John Henry Leftwich. Their daughter, Jennie Lee, married Dr. Edwin Powell Wright, a dentist of Richmond, Virginia. Their daughter, Elizabeth Powell Wright, married December 5, 1914, Dr. Charles Brown Pearson of Richmond, Virginia; they had, in 1933, two children: Margaret Irving Pearson, born September 2, 1916, and Charles Brown Pearson, born November 16, 1921.

Dr. Edwin Turner Shelton and Mary Eliza Sutton Hamlin were married March 11, 1858. Dr. Shelton died November 2, 1882. His wife died June 24, 1887. Their children were (1) Sarah Rosebell, who married Thomas I. Southall, April 12, 1899. (2) Mary Oliver, who married Orville W. Shepherd, March 20, 1877. (3) Elvira, who married William H. Cosby, March 9, 1887. (4) Dr. Edwin (M. D.) who married Ella K. Hundley, October 15, 1890. (5) Harriett Elizabeth who married Archie Woodfolk Camp May 13, 1886, and (6) John Sutton, who married Minnie Blair Shelton, daughter of James Blair Shelton of Louisa County, Virginia, October 18, 1900.

Dr. Edwin Shelton and Ella K. Hundley had only one child, a son, Edwin Stuart Shelton, who was born May 3, 1894 and married September 3, 1921, Maud Marjory Tapscott, who was born July 10, 1899. They live in Richmond, Virginia, and have one child, Dorothy Stuart Shelton, born November 9, 1923.

Other children of Ann Elizabeth Shelton and John Henry Leftwich were (1) Louise, who married William Goodwin Coghill. (2) Harry Scott, who married Lila Norvell, and (3) John Bransford Leftwich, who married, first, Lelia Barnes, and, second, Delia Yarborough.

Robert Shelton (son of Colonel John of "Rural Plains" and his second wife, Nancy Williamson) was born in Hanover County, Virginia, in 1774. He married Alpha Vawter, November 2, 1790; I have no record of his descendants. He was given land in Lunenburg and Lancaster Counties, Virginia, which was settled on him before his father's death in 1798. The Hanover County records are from the bibles and prayer books, and wills of Col. John Shelton (son of John and Eleanor Parks Shelton) and of his youngest son, Colonel Edwin Shelton of "Rural Plains".

"RED HOUSE", LOUISA CO., VA.

APTAIN JOHN SHELTON, (3) SR., settled "Red House" plantation in Louisa County and Goochland County on his son, James[1] who was living in 1778, when he signed a bond for $3,000 for John Shelton (husband of Mary Payne) for Sheriff of Goochland County, Virginia. (James is said, by members of the family, to have married a Miss Blair.) The "Red House" plantation passed to William, eldest son of James, then to his eldest son, John, husband of Mary Payne. At John's death in 1828, it reverted to his brother, William, Sr., who had only two children: William (insane) and Ann who married Booth Woodson and had a life interest in the estate. Both William (insane) and Ann Woodson were dead by 1841, and the estate passed to William, Sr.'s brother, James Blair Shelton. He was dead by 1850 and William (called minor in the records, who married Maria Coles), son of John and Mary Payne Shelton, inherited. At William's (minor) death, it reverted, in 1859, to John Blair Shelton, only living son of James Blair Shelton.

The second son of John and Mary Payne was John Payne

(1) In the vestry book of St. Paul's Church, Hanover County, Virginia, the "lands of James Shelton are ordered processioned March 27, 1736. This James must have been the brother of John of "Rural Plains" as his son could not have been old enough to own land in his own name. In the "Register of Abingdon Parish Church, Vol. I, pg. 65, there is this note: "Mr. James Shelton departed this life Aug. 31, 1754". This also appears in the obituaries in the "Gentleman's Magazine" in London, England, except that "in Richmond, Virginia" is added to the notice, and "Gentleman" to the name. On the Abingdon Par. Reg. also appears this record: "John, son of Wm. and Isabell Shelton, b. Feb. 25, 1680, bapt. soon after," Vol. I, pg. 4.

Shelton, who married his cousin, Massie, daughter of Major Thomas Shelton of Louisa County, Virginia, and had: (1) George Payne Shelton, who married Ann E. Winston; (2) Elizabeth who married Dr. John Winston and had John Shelton Winston and William Jordan Winston; (3) Mary (Polly) who married her cousin, Nelson Shelton, and had a son, David, who went to Georgia; and (4) Nancy, called Ann, who married John L. Harris. A letter from a Mr. Robert Shelton, written in 1896, states that John and Mary Payne Shelton had a son, Peter, who had four sons: James D. (who had an only son, John), Thomas and two daughters: one who married Garland Anderson, and one, Ann, who married John S. Woodson. I find no mention of these in the will of this John Shelton. The eldest son and executor of the will of William Shelton, Minor, was Walter Coles Shelton, born 1813, who married Maryella, or Samuella (family statements differ) Mosby in October, 1836, and had Walter Coles Shelton (born 1849, living in 1932 in Palmyra, Virginia) who married, in 1879, Emma Green Clark. They had only one child, a son, an attorney in Palmyra, Virginia: William Shelton. He married Phyllis Watts Crawford of Louisa County, Virginia, and in 1935 they had three children; two sons, Samuel and William Shelton, and a baby born in 1934.

Children of William Shelton and Maria Coles:
Walter Coles Shelton—born December 17, 1813.
John Shelton—born July 6, 1815.
Alexander Shelton—born April 9, 1817.
George William Shelton—born April 19, 1819.
Edward Shelton—born February 5, 1821.
Mary Elizabeth Shelton—born March 31, 1823.
Indiana Shelton—born March 2, 1825 (d. Oct. 23, 1829).

Maria Louisa Shelton—born October 31, 1828.

Indiana Coles Shelton—born November 25, 1830.

Lavinia Ann Shelton—born February 22, 1833.

Jane Elvira Shelton—born June 21, 1835.

William Shelton was born in Goochland County, Virginia, September 6, 1788. He was married to Maria Coles (who was born July 1, 1795) on January 28, 1813. William died August 7, 1847, in Louisa County, Virginia, and Maria, his wife, died December 29, 1869.

Indiana Coles Shelton (called Nannie) married T. C. Leake and had Evelyn Archer Leake, who married B. W. Binford and had a daughter, Nannie Binford, who married George Warren Chappelear of the Department of Biology of the State Teacher's College at Harrisonburg, Virginia.

The above William Shelton who married Maria Coles, was the William, called Minor, in the Court records. I think that the woman who married John S. Woodson, referred to in letters of Robert Shelton, was Nancy Ann, daughter of William, Sr., of "Red House", who married John Shelton Woodson, and that the James D. was James Dabney, son of Major Thomas Shelton of Louisa County.

WILLIAM SHELTON OF "RED HOUSE", LOUISA CO., VA.

HE children of William Shelton, Sr. (who died in 1800 w-proved 1802), of "Red House", son of James and grandson of John and Eleanor Parks Shelton, were: (1) John, (2) William, Jr., (3) Robert (d. 1800), (4) James, (5) Elizabeth (Betsy), who married Peter Crawford, April 11, 1782 (their only child, Judge William Crawford, was living in 1896), (6) Jesse (d. by 1842), lived in Davidson and later in Stuart Counties, Tennessee), (7) Martha, who married a Lucas (no issue), (8) Susannah, who married Richard Farrar (their daughter Sophia was the mother of Shelton F. Leake), (9) Nancy Ann, who married John Shelton Woodson, and (10) Sarah (Sally), who married Mathew Grubbs (and had John "about to go West in 1831"; William, who was living in Benton, Mississippi, in 1848 and Elizabeth (Betsy), who married David Jones. Ann Woodson and Sarah Grubbs were both dead by 1848. Robert Shelton, who died in 1800, left three children, William, Jr., James and Elizabeth, who married a Halsall and had sons Robert and James. Wife's name is not mentioned in wills of either Robert or William.

Robert's sons William and James moved to Henry County, Virginia, before 1781, as James enlisted in the Revolution from Henry County in 1781. The histories of Henry County include a Nathan Shelton as a brother of Wm. and James, but the will of Robert names only two sons. The descendants of this James moved to Missouri. William, Jr. (2), died in Richmond, Virginia, November 15, 1850. *His* son Robert B. Shelton was executor of the estate. At this time Robert B. had three children: (1) William J., (2) Ann E., and (3) Dorothea P. Shelton. Jesse (6), (son of William, d. 1800) who went to Tennessee, had a son, Washington (1) G. Shelton, an attorney, a son Jesse, (2) Jr., a daughter, Priscilla (3) who married first a Harris (and had son, W. G. Harris) and second a Kemp. A son by this marriage, Henry Kemp, was a minor (orphan) in 1850 in Davidson County, Tennessee, and his guardian was Jesse Shelton Harris, very probably a brother of the above W. G. Harris.

In 1845, Jesse Shelton, Jr., of Davidson County, Tennessee, transferred or conveyed his equity in the estate of his grandfather, William Shelton, of Louisa County, Virginia, to Washington G. Shelton of Davidson County, Tennessee.[1] Jesse, Sr., had another daughter (4) Maria Shelton, who married G. W. McQuary and had a daughter Priscilla, who married George W. Hale of Davidson County, Tennessee, April 5, 1850. George and Priscilla Hale gave above W. G. Shelton a power of attorney to collect their share of the estate of William Shelton of Louisa County, Virginia, who died in 1800. Mrs. Lucinda and Mrs. Elizabeth Wharton and Mrs. Sam W. Seay were heirs of this William Shelton through Susannah Farrar. Lucinda Wharton left six children in Tennessee. John C. Farrar of Charleston, South

---

(1) There is a will of a Wm. Shelton, dated Nov. 4, 1852. Rec. Aug. 27, 1853, on the books of Davidson Co. Tenn. at Nashville, "Book 15, Wills, 1851-53." He mentions "son Jesse" and leaves him ½ of the land on which he (Wm.) lives, on the S. bank of the Cumberland River, "and $500.00 to complete his education" "Jesse" and Andrew I. Shelton are run together and it may be one name.

He mentions "a D. Herriot Crouch" leaves her "her house & land." Gr-son Wm. I. Crouch, gr-D. Louisa "D. Eliz. Marg. Hooper and Lucada," Avis Brown—Exec.—Proved Dec. term 1852.

Carolina, also had a claim in the William Shelton estate.

The division of Anne Shelton Woodson's estate was made November 11, 1843.

James Shelton, son of William of "Red House" (d. 1800), married a Miss Thompson, daughter of the Thompson of Thompson's crossing, and had as far as known, an *only* son, John Blair Shelton, who was born November 19, 1799, and died January 16, 1862. John Blair Shelton married first Mary Virginia Turner, by whom he had: (1) James Blair, born 1826, (2) Lucy, who married Major R. Courtenay of Richmond, Va., and (3) Elizabeth (Bettie) who married Joseph P. O'Ferrall, brother of Governor O'Ferrall of Virginia.

The second wife of John Blair Shelton was Emily C. Smith, daughter of Jesse and Lucy Smith. She died September 20, 1847, aged 37. The children by this marriage were: (1) Emily, who married first Dr. T. Guerrant (by whom she had three children) and second William Harris; (2) Lieutenant Robert J., killed in Civil War, July 24, 1864, aged 22 (I do not know whether or not he was married); (3) Catherine, who married Samuel Hill. Members of this family stated that Elizabeth was a child of the first wife. From John's will, it looks as though she was a full sister of Catherine and Emily. John's will mentions land in Richmond, Marion, Louisa and Goochland Counties in Virginia.

James Blair Shelton, John Blair's eldest son, by Mary Virginia Turner, born in 1826, married first, April 15, 1848, Frances Ann Sims, "daughter of Hezekiah Sims, deceased"; (her guardian Robert W. Kemp signed as security) second, July 30, 1874, Emma Snow Walton, d. of Mrs. Frances Walton. By his first wife, James Blair Shelton had: (1) Francis, who married Ann Meredith; (2) John William, who married Delia Bowles, a daughter of John Price Bowles; both John Wm. and his wife Delia were living on "Red House" plantation in 1932; (3) Dr. Robert Shelton (died 1931), who married Sally Walton; and (4) Virginia, who married Frank Monterio.

By his second wife, James Blair Shelton had: (1) James Lee, member of the Virginia State Legislature, who married Mrs. Lucilla Powers Guest of Richmond, Virginia; (2) Emma Blair, who married Dr. Connie Smith; (3) David Rice, who married Lillie Gibson; (4) Minnie Blair, who married first John Shelton, son of Dr. Edwin Shelton of "Rural Plains"; and second Ralph Sellman, of Bridgeport, Conn.; (5) Julia Cecelia, who married Stanford Young; (6) Cleveland, d. s. p.; (7) Gilmer R., who married Carrie Brooking; (8) Marvin Haley, who married Virginia Lacey; (9) Penelope (Nellie), who married Virgil Howard; (10) Katie Ray, who married Clem Ross; and (11) Marion, who married Linwood Dunn. Mr. and Mrs. Stanford Young live at Chesterfield, Virginia. They have two children, Gordon and Sarah Frances.

DAVID SHELTON, CALLED
"DAVID OF OLD TOWN"

AVID SHELTON (brother of the John who was the third owner of "Rural Plains", whose wife was Eleanor Parks) was called "David of Old Town"; he made his will in 1789, and it was proved in 1797. He mentions sons Thomas and Joseph, and daughters Elizabeth and Sarah. One of his wives was Massie Rice, and one was Elizabeth Winston; there is a great difference in the ages of Major Thomas and Col. Joseph, but a member of the family told me they were brothers, but the records look as though they must have been half brothers. The records of the Revolution in the Pension office state that a pension was granted to Colonel Joseph Shelton in 1833 to "take effect from 1831, when he was 73 years old." This would fix his birth about 1758. The family state that Major Thomas who was born in 1722, did not marry the first time until nearly the end of the Revolutionary War and that "he was nearly 60 years old at that time." Both he and Colonel Joseph served with Lafayette, the latter as a courier. Their sister Elizabeth married Joseph Watson in 1773, and had Joseph Shelton Watson, an attorney in Louisa County, Virginia, who died in Louisa County, Virginia, September 23, 1805, aged 26. I have no record of his marriage. Sarah, sister of Elizabeth Watson, was born October 10, 1763, and married October 23, 1780, Dr. Thomas Terrell. She died October 31, 1837, and her descendants were living in Sparta, Georgia, in 1929.[1]

Colonel Joseph Shelton, son of the David who died in

(1) FAMILY BIBLE RECORDS — TERRELL & SHELTON

Thomas Terrell, Son of William & Frances Wingfield Terrell, was born in Hanover County, Va., Jan. 3, 1761, d. Jan. 17, 1822 and his wife, Sarah Shelton Terrell, daughter of David and Massey Shelton, b. Oct. 10, 1763, d. Oct. 31, 1837, married Oct. 23, 1780.

Their Children

1. David Shelton Terrell, b. Aug. 19, 1781, d. Nov. 3, 1808
2. William Higgins Terrell, b. Apr. 12, 1783
3. Elizabeth Terrell, b. Mar. 23, 1785
4. Francis W. Terrell, b. Nov. 14, 1787, d. Mar. 14, 1832
5. Massey Rice Terrell, b. July 25, 1790
6. Mary H. Terrell, b. May 7, 1793
7. Thomas Waddy Terrell, b. Nov. 6, 1795
8. Absolum Terrell, b. June 15, 1798

Dr. Thomas Waddy Terrell, married Martha Everard Hamilton Raines, Sept. 28, 1820

Their Children

1. Sarah H. S. Terrell, b. July 16, 1821
2. Robert Raines Terrell, b. 1823
3. Cornelia A. Terrell
4. William Joseph Terrell, b. Oct. 16, 1828, d. July 16, 1899
5. John Henry Terrell
6. Thomas Waddy Terrell, Jr.

William J. Terrell, Son of Dr. L. W. Terrell and Martha Raines Terrell his wife, was born Oct. 1828, d. 1899 married Hattie Neblett, July 5, 1858

Their Children

1. Wm. J. Terrell, Jr., mar. Etta Songster
2. Thomas Waddy Terrell died in infancy
3. Everard Hamilton, Terrell, mar. d. Oct. 1933
4. Arthur Powe Terrell, mar. 1st Bessie Mullins; 2nd Grace Booker
5. Cornelia Terrell, died in infancy
6. Hattie Terrell, mar. Dr. Alfred Huntington Ketchum
7. Robert McCaskill Terrell, mar. Mary Spann
8. May Terrell, mar. Edward Duncan Blockshear
9. Pearl Terrell, mar. John Britt Daniel

1797 and his 2nd wife, Miss Winston,[1] married his cousin
Judith, daughter of Colonel Joseph Shelton of Nelson
County, Virginia, and their son Richard Shelton was born
in Louisa County, Virginia, in 1779. He moved to North
Carolina, where he married Frances Barnett, who had also
been born in Louisa County, Virginia. Their descendants
are given on page 226 of my "Genealogy".

Major Thomas married three times: first, Cecelia Dabney
in 1782, by whom he had (1) James Dabney (d. 1824), (2)
Joseph, (3) Dr. Thomas (d. about 1850), who lived at
"Shelfar Station", Louisa County, Virginia, and d. s. p.
and (4) Massie, who married John Payne Shelton, son of
John and Mary Payne Shelton of "Red House"; the second
wife of Major Thomas was Susannah Farrar, whom he
married in 1809 and who was living in 1824, and by whom
he had (1) Sarah Terrell, (2) Martha, (3) Mathew (d. 22
years of age—no record of marriage), (4) Elizabeth Watson, (5) Cecilia, and (6) David Rice, born November 13,
1814, owner of "Roseneath". Louisa County, Virginia, who
married twice; first, Victoria Kean, born January 8, 1815,
by whom he had (1) Martha (called Patsey), (2) Margaret,

(1) The records of David Shelton are confusing; he may have been married
three times but I have only two marriages in my records—one to Elizabeth
Winston and one to Massie Rice. The Terrell line claims descent through the
marriage of David and Massie Rice and the records from the Terrell bible
proves its claim. A David is mentioned in the administration papers of the
estate of William Shelton (died 1800, pro, 1802) in Louisa Co., Va. One
record states "about to leave for Georgia" the date is Nov. 26, 1845, from
Goochland Co. It is addressed "Polite attention of Col. Soloman Shelton"
and mentions claim of "Eliphaz Shelton" asking John Blair Shelton to "sell
or trade my (David's) portion of land, as I have no use for it." In 1850, on
Oct. 9 David signs receipt to John Blair Shelton for "1/5 of 1/6 of sale of
"Red House" negroes, this is written from Georgia. (This David was a son
of Nelson Shelton and Mary Shelton, d. of John Payne Shelton).

(3) Charles, (4) Sarah (Sally), (5) Elizabeth (Betsy), (6) Lucy, (7) Clara, and, (8) Eleanor. Lucy (6), born January 20, 1844, died November 28, 1920; married H. P. R. McCoy, October 11, 1872; he was born February 2, 1830 and died October 25, 1914. Their children were (1) Dr. William Kenneth McCoy, born 1873, who married Jean Page Morton; both living in Louisa County, Virginia in 1932; no issue. (2) Victoria Kean, who married a Mr. Mapp, and (3) Helen Mary, who married Dr. S. F. Hart. Both Doctor and Mrs. Hart were living in 1932 at ''Roseneath'', Louisa County, Virginia; and (4) Charles Daniel who married Martha Bibby.

David Rice Shelton died in 1880. His second wife was Martha Swann by whom he had (1) Caroline, who married a Mr. Brown of North Carolina; (2) Mary C., single in 1880, and (3) Eleanor A., who married Stephen W. Cole of North Carolina.

James D. Shelton's father, Major Thomas, married his third wife, a Miss Sarah Miller, after 1824 and died in 1826, aged 104.

Another Shelton home was ''Cornwallis Hill'', in Louisa Co., Va.

A David Rice Shelton, who had a son, David Raymond Shelton, living in Washington, D. C. in 1934, comes in on this line somewhere, but I could not get in touch with the son in Washington to get any data on his branch of the Shelton family.

The succession at ''Red House'', Louisa County, Virginia, was as follows: the land was part of a grant to John Shelton of Hanover County in 1723; it was given to his eldest son, James, (1) who married a Miss Blair. Next in order of succession was William Shelton, Sr., (2) son of James (1) John (3) eldest son of William, Sr. William, Jr. (4) second son of William, Sr. William (5) Insane—son of William, Jr. William (6) called William, minor, in court records, son of John Shelton and Mary Payne and John Blair Shelton (7) who willed it to his son, James Blair Shelton (8) in 1862. The descendants of James Blair Shelton are given on pages 146 and 147.

The author is printing the following miscellaneous items concerning the administration of the estate of *William Shelton, (prob. 1802, in Louisa Co., Va.)* in hope that it may help some of the descendants of William to prove their lines of descent.

Oct. 9th, 1850—David Shelton (Georgia) signs receipts to J. B. S. for 1/5 of 1/6 on John Shelton's part of sale of "Red House" negroes. 1/5 of Wm. S. (insane).

For sale of negro est. of Wm. S., Sr., $477.00 from est. of Wm. (insane) $150.30 (Legateel in both receipts).

David paid Will S. Fowler $395.00 to collect David's share in estate of Col. Jos. Shelton dec'd. David also signs as agent for John C. Farrar of Charleston, David R. Shelton, exec. of Mathew Shelton against Nelson F. Shelton and others—Louisa Co., 6-10-1855.

Wife of R. W. Pleasants a legatee of Wm. Shelton decd. June 21, 1850— Jno. Morris Exec.

Eliz. Winston signs in full for balance due her from both Wm's. estates 11-22-1850.

Mary P. Pleasants asks J. B. S. to pay her balance to son H. Clay Pleasants, 9-16-1850.

Walter C. Shelton, adm. of Wm. S. (minor) signs to J. B. S. as adm. of Wm. S., Sr., for 1/4 of the value of crops of "Red House" est. in 1847. 10-17-1850.

A. W. to James S. 6-21-1818.

George P. Shelton's interest in two Williams' estate to R. O. Isbell.

Harriet E. Harris assigns 11-19-1850; bal. of her interest in both estates to H. Clay Pleasant.

Sept. 23, 1850, Dr. G. W.—Harriet and Juliet A. sign 1-18-1851.

1855. Nelson P. Shelton married Polly S. Harris—legatee of the two Williams.

Juliet A. Harris receipts in full Dec. 5, 1850. Henry C. Pleasant's receipts in full Dec. 26, 1850.

W. C. Shelton signs for Wm. S., minor, fr. 1/4 of Red House crops due him for 1847. W. C. was Adm. for William, minor, who was a legatee of both Williams Oct. 17, 1850.

James Shelton, in 1834, had a general store in Louisa County.

David Shelton in Goochland, 11/26/1845, about to leave for Georgia— letter to Jno. B. "Polite Attention of Col. Solomon Shelton", mentions claim of Eliphaz and asks J. B. S. to sell or trade David's portion of land as he, David, had no use for it.

John B. Shelton's home, "Gum Springs", Louisa County, J. B. S. sold 53½ acres of land belonging to William S., insane, to Jno. Amos, May 1, 1850.

R. W. Pleasants deceased by 1850, had share in estate of William S. (the elder).

Sarah Grubbs, legatee of Ann Woodson, deceased before June 29, 1842. David R. Jones, Ex. for Sarah Grubbs.

Letter to J. B. S. calling him "cousin" from Walter C. Shelton delivered by Edward B. Shelton, asks for receipt for amount due his father's estate as committee: Oct. 18, 1850, date of letter.

David R. Shelton (alive in 1855) receipt signed to J. B. S. on that date.

J. C. Harris had a school in Louisa County in 1859 (from letters).

Richard Clough and Joseph Shelton, note to James Shelton, Nov. 17, 1814.

P. H. Jones signs for Thos. Poindexter, later sheriff of Louisa County, and com. administrator of Jesse Shelton, dec'd March 21, 1842.

William S. (minor) alive June 29, 1841, sends notice by Edward S. of his suit about to be filed; asks J. B. S. to sign the petition and states Thos. D. and wife have signed.

January 26, 1841, William S., minor, authorized J. B. S. to pay an order given J. B. S. by brother of William (minor).

George W. Harris, administrator of Ann Harris deceased, signs receipt June 1, 1844, for money received from Ann Woodson's estate from Jno. B. S., executor of James who was executor of William, Senior, deceased.

Receipt for Sara Grubbs (deceased) interest in estate of Ann Woodson 2/8/1841, signed by David R. James, administrator for Sarah Grubbs.

March 28, 1842. Norborn R. Farrar promises to pay J. B. S. costs of suit for contract; a deed made by Shelton Farrar to his wife, Sarah Farrar, in which he conveys to his wife all interest he may have in a suit of Shelton F. Leake (Supreme Court of Louisa County). Deed filed in Nelson County, 3-28-1842.

James (executor) living July 1, 1820.

Division of Ann Woodson's estate November 11, 1943. 1/7 part to heirs of Jesse Shelton. Heir of Ann Harris signs receipt for 1/5 part of her father's share of Ann Woodson's Estate November 11, 1843.

Jno. S. Woodson signs as administrator for John Shelton Woodson, Jr., for his full share of his grandfather's (William, Sr.) estate loaned to Ann Woodson for life—6-11-1844.

Letters of Administration granted to Robert B. Shelton on estate of William S. Henrico Ct. 3-4-1850.

Mrs. Lucinda Wharton and Mrs. Elizabeth Wharton and Mrs. Sam W. Seay, 1/8 and 1/5 share in Susanna Farrar's portion of William S., Sr., and William, insane; Lucinda Wharton left six children in Tennessee.

Elizabeth Kelso calls Ann Woodson, "Aunt Nancy" and William Shelton, "Brother William" in a note, July 23, 1830.

Nancy, a sister of James, executor of William—note to "Sister Sally", Nov. 7, 1827.

Sarah Grubbs heirs 1/7 of estate of Ann Woodson. Receipt from Ann Woodson to James Shelton, March 1, 1820.

Bouth Woodson signs for wife, Ann, in Goochland Court, October, 1823, to James S.

Robert B. Shelton gave order to Thomas Woodson for $135.00 to be paid out of his share of estate of William S. (insane) which fell to William Shelton, Jr., who conveyed it to Robert B. Shelton. Recorded in Louisa County.

Thomas Woodson's wife had interest in estate of William S. (insane) 11-25-1850.

Robert B. Shelton, in note dated Richmond, Jan. 12, 1852, to J. B. S., asks him to pay to Halsall the balance due him, Robert, for "my father's interest in his Uncle William Shelton's estate." Receipt signed Feb. 24, 1850, for this money says, "Wm. S., insane".

Dec. 4, 1810, Receipt from Ann Woodson to James Shelton.

D. R. Shelton signs receipt to J. B. S. Oct. 11, 1858, for cloth bought for J. B. S. in Richmond.

William Shelton, Chestnut Grove, Tennessee. Oct. 3rd, 1851. (J. B. S. sent him $500.00).

Elizabeth Winston, Legatee of William, insane. Receipt signed Oct. 1850.

J. Crawford and his nephews in Alabama, May 30, 1846.

Elizabeth Winston, niece of Ann Woodson.

William Grubbs calls them Uncle William and Aunt Nancy in asking for money due him from their estates. Living in Benton, Miss., April 11, 1848.

Garland Anderson, Legatee of William S., Sr. and William S. insane, September 23, 1850.

Sarah N. Brown, husband Jno. R. Brown, Legatee of William S. 2/26/1849,

Obion County, Tennessee, appointed Washington G. Shelton of Davidson County, Tennessee, attorney to look after their interest.

Stuart and Davidson County, Tennessee—Jesse L. Harris, son and heir of Priscilla Harris who was Priscilla Shelton, daughter of Jesse Shelton deceased of Davidson County, Tennessee, November 4, 1850.

Mary F. Shelton, a legatee of both Williams.

Mrs. Frank Shelton had daughter, Elizabeth who married Jno. B. Henry; 3 children: W. G., William and Margaret Henry.

Elizabeth died October, 1852, at "Chestnut Grove," estate of Wm. Shelton on the south bank of the Cumberland River, Davidson County, Tennessee.

Howell Harris, legatee of both Williams, 3/31/1852.

Vanburen Harris, Columbus Harris and Priscilla Harris, heirs of both from Henry—Live Port—(June 10, 1853)—Stuart County, Tennessee.

May 28, 1834, letter from James Shelton.

Robert Shelton of Richmond, October 18, 1850.

Shelton Farrar also a legatee of both Wm. Sheltons of Louisa Co., Va.

(These notes are all from the files of the administrator of Wm.'s estate John Blair Shelton.)

SOME HENRY CO., VA., SHELTONS

AMES SHELTON, son of Robert of Louisa County, and grandson of William Shelton of "Red House", with his brother, William, moved to Henry County, Virginia, before 1781; in that year, James is on record in the Revolution, serving under Gen. Green, as of Henry County. James also was a veteran of the War of 1812. He was sent to Norfolk on official business and died there during this war. His wife was Frances, youngest daughter of William Allen and his wife, Sarah Ann Smith.

After the death of Captain James Shelton, his wife married William Abingdon. Her children by James Shelton were: Pines Henderson, Nancy, Polly and James. The family of James and Frances Allen Shelton moved to St. Charles County, Missouri.

Pines Henderson Shelton represented this county in the State Legislature for years and later was State Senator for four years, until he moved to Texas; he came back to Missouri and settled in Henry County, Missouri. The first wife of Pines Henderson Shelton was Rebecca Carter; by her he had George James Shelton and Rebecca Shelton. His second wife was Mary Wyatt, by whom he had: James Lamartine Shelton (who married Janie Pomeroy and had three daughters: Mrs. Alvin Winsureid, Mrs. John Harris and Miss Lula Shelton of Windsor, Missouri) and a daughter, Freedonia, who married Pafner Greenwade. Pines' third wife was Mary O. Scales by whom he had: William A. Shelton, Banker of Windsor, Missouri, and Thomas Marvin who died and left a daughter, Mrs. Harper Stephens of Temple, Texas.

George James Shelton, son of Pines and his first wife, Rebecca Carter, married in Wentzville, Missouri, April 26, 1889, Ann Bailey Allen. Their children were: Mrs. Norman Campbell of Colorado Springs, Colorado; Alice Bobinreith and Miss Byrd Shelton of Kansas City, Missouri; Mrs. J. W. Dawson of Eldorado Springs, Missouri; Mrs. W. C. Lamping of Denver, Colorado; Mrs. Todd M. Pettigrew of Bronxville, New York, and James Lamar Shelton of Kansas City, Missouri. George James Shelton lived in Waco, Texas; he enlisted in the Confederate army from there and served four years; he died June 2, 1913; and was buried at Windsor, Missouri.

William and James Shelton are mentioned in executor's papers of their father, Robert, who died in 1800 (son of William Shelton of "Red House", Louisa County, Virginia), whose will was proved in 1802. William married Pattie Dillard, daughter of Colonel John Dillard, a pioneer of Henry County, Virginia. Their children were Peter (1) born Nov. 12, 1798, who married 3/21/1832, Magdalene Dupuy Watkins (daughter of John Watkins and wife— Miss Wilson) and had twelve children: (2) John, (3) George, (4) Ruth, (5) Polly, (6) Susan, and (7) Nathan who married Mary Hatcher and had four children: (1) Alfred who married Susan Shelton (2) Joseph, who married Narcissus Astrup; (3) Judith who married John Pickney Scales, and (4) James, who married Adeline Taylor and had (1) William Nathan, (2) George, (3) Lucy, (4) Martha, (5) Fanny, (6) Chester, (7) Benjamin and (8) Joseph.

William Nathan (1) married Martha Wells, daughter of John and Matilda Wells, and granddaughter of Baker

Wells. They had (1) Addie, who married Fred Doyle; (2) Mollie, who married T. J. Glenn, (3) Dean, who married George L. Price, (4) Annie, who married Thomas M. Fair, (5) Maggie, who married W. A. Stanford, (6) Daisy, who married Joseph Scales (son of Judith and John Pickney Scales), (7) James Taylor, who married Sally Loosing, and (8) William P., who married Beulah Basham.

Peter Shelton, born in Henry County, Virginia, Nov. 12, 1798 (son of William Shelton and Pattie Dillard) and Magdalene Dupuy Watkins who were married March 21, 1832, had (1) William Henderson, who married Nancy Jane Hylton; (2) Sarah Martin, who married Joseph Pannill; (3) John Watkins, who married Rhoda E. Howard; (4) Anne Wilson, who married James S. Martin; (5) Virginia Magdalene, who married Dr. R. R. Robertson; (6) Peter Fowler, who married Laura Howard (7) Mary Elizabeth, unmarried; (8) Ruth Stovall, who married Joseph G. Penn; (9) Susan Louisa, who married John Hill Mathews; (10) Thomas Meade, who married Fannie Clopton; (11) George Hunt, who died unmarried; and (12) James Buchanan, who married Miss Price.

The Hezekiah Shelton whose name is signed to a petition to the Court of Henry County in 1794—Eliphaz and Raleigh Shelton who signed an oath of allegiance in Henry County in March, 1779, do not belong to the branch of the Sheltons which is given here, but were evidently sons of the Ralph Shelton who died about 1789. Eliphaz was appointed Captain and marched with his company to the assistance of the force defending Guilford Court House, March 11, 1781. In the histories of Henry County, Virginia, a William Shelton, who married Peonia Critz, is said to be the founder of the Henry County, Virginia, Shelton family. I cannot find where he fits in, nor have I placed Eliphaz but think he was a gr-son of Ralph Shelton, b. in Middlesex Co., Va., in 1709, although he is mentioned in a letter to John B. Shelton of Louisa County, by David Rice of Georgia, in 1845, as having a claim on the estate of William Shelton, Sr. (1802).

DAVID SHELTON OF CASWELL CO., NORTH CAROLINA

DO not know the name of the first wife of David Shelton (son of John and Eleanor Parks Shelton). He must have been married in Hanover County where so many records were destroyed. He enlisted from Hanover County and fought at Valley Forge. In his will, filed in Caswell County, North Carolina, March 31, 1800, he names three children by his first wife as having been previously provided for. They were *John* and Agnes Shelton and Lucy Carney.

The will of a John Shelton is filed in Mecklenburg Co., Va., Nov. 18, 1777; he had a son, William, who died before his father; will proved 3/13/1769. In it, William mentions "wife, Mary" and "brother, Mark". John's will was probated July 13, 1778; he named his eldest son, Mark, as his heir; he also named a grandson, "William, son of Mark".

John, son of David Shelton of Caswell Co., N. C., was living in Stokes County, North Carolina, as late as 1785. The census of that year gives John (13) in family and John, Jr. (5), in family. The descendants of David Valentine Shelton state that he and John Shelton of Stokes Co., N. C., were half brothers.

David's second wife was Susannah Vaughan; after the death of David, she married Godfrey Crowder. By Susannah, David had (1) Elizabeth; (2) James; (3) David Valentine; (4) Nancy; and (5) Henry, the youngest son, who inherited the home plantation on Shelton Creek, which was part of a grant to John Shelton of "Rural Plains", Hanover County, Virginia, in 1756. Later, this land became part of North Carolina and John's grant was reaffirmed by that State.

(2) James married Nancy Marshall and had Reverend William Shelton, D. D., who married Virginia Campbell and had William Shelton, D. D., who married Hattie Bass and had Dr. William Albert Shelton, M. D., who married Charlotte Prior and had Dr. Prior Shelton, M. D., of Kansas City, Missouri. There were, other children of James and Nancy, but this is the only complete data I have.

(3) David Valentine was born February 14, 1789, and died in 1864; he married in Halifax County, Virginia, November 16, 1820, Anne Baker who was born November 16, 1800. They moved to Clarksville (then Phillipsville) and bought Buffalo Lithia Springs in 1832. Their children were:

(1) Dr. James, M. D., born January 14, 1822, who lived, practiced medicine and died at Buffalo Lithia Springs. (2) John Bullock (called Jack) M. D., born March 2, 1824. (3) Jesse Harper, born May 10, 1826. (4) David Jayne, born July 7, 1828. (5) Leonard Baker, born June 2, 1830, died April 2, 1832; and (6) William Dozier, born November 12, 1836, a Major in the War between the States.

Dr. James Shelton's first wife was Adeline Overby by whom he had nine children who lived to maturity; they were:

(1) Harper Wilkins who married Rosa Penick; (2) Robert Camillas who married Caroline Pollard; (3) Alice Cornelia who married, first, Beverly Fleming and second, Jacob Reebals: (4) Rosa Pace who married Samuel Briggs; (5) Ada Overby who married William Briggs (brother to Samuel); (6) Nannie, who married W. W. Gresham; (7)

James David who married, first, a Kessler and, second, Minnie Roberts Woltz; (8) Stephen who married Caroline Meherson (descendants living in Washington, D. C., in 1934); and (9) Charles Edwin who married Lelia Kessler.

Doctor James's (1) second wife was Frances Watkins, by whom he had Beverly Watkins Shelton who married Mary Burnette; and Mary Booker Shelton who married Albert Kirkland and had one son, Albert.

Dr. John Bullock Shelton (2) married February 6, 1859, in Rose Creek, Tennessee, Jennie Duke. They moved to Arkansas and lived and died there. Their children who lived to maturity were:

(1) Ida Fintress who married a Mr. Abbott and lives at Roe, Arkansas; (2) Duke; (3) Houston; (4) Anne; (5) William David; and (6) Finley; all married.

Jesse Harper, third son of David and Anne Baker, was a Judge in Sussex County, Virginia. He married Louise Land. Their children were:

(1) Margaret who married a Mr. Stephenson; (2) Louise (single); (3) Nannie; (4) Ruth; (5) David; and (6) John; all married.

David (5) was living in Waynesboro, Virginia in 1932, and had two sons: Walter Heber Shelton and David Jordan Shelton.

David Jayne (the fourth son of David Valentine Shelton, b. 1789, and Anne Baker) died April 19, 1913; his wife was Martha A. Hagerman, and their children were:

(1) John Alexander, born 1862, married Lou Burch; (2) Lillian Mayo, born 1865, married John T. Reaves; (3) Rosa Lee, born 1868, single; (4) Samuel David, born 1870, mar-

ried Nancy York; and (5) William Henry, born 1875, who married Zelma Crement.

John Alexander (1) and his wife, Lou Burch, had:

(1) D. Claud Fuller Shelton (who, by his first wife, Edith Williams, had two children: John Bricket and Martha A. Shelton); (2) Rosa Lee who married Charles Osborne (no issue); (3) Maude Mayo who married Caleb Jones and had four children; (4) Stephen D. who married and had three children; and (5) Noel Burch who married and had two children.

Samuel David Shelton, fourth child of David Jayne Shelton and Nancy York had (1) David Banks Shelton who married Ruth Pegram; (2) Kathleen, single in 1933; (3) Lillian Baker who married Jack Dunn (no issue); and (4) Catherine who married Thomas de Grafenried and had one son, William de Grafenried; David Banks Shelton and Ruth Pegram had two children: David Banks Shelton and Geraldine Pegram Shelton.

The youngest son of David and Anne Baker Shelton, Major William Dozier Shelton, married Sue Crowder and had:

(1) Martha who married a Mr. Clark and had children and grandchildren; (2) William David who married Ivor and lives in Richmond; he has two children; Eleanor and William David; (3) John B., who married Eva Hamilton, and has three sons; (4) Annie, who married Charles Crowder (no issue); and (5) Lucy, single in 1933; a son, Alexander d. s. p.

Harper Wilkins Shelton, son of Dr. James Shelton and Adeline Overby, who married Rose Penick, had:

(1) Harper Wilkins, Jr., who married Susie Creath and

lives in Richmond, Virginia; (2) William Penick who married Edith Keesee and has two children: Edith and Anne; (3) Mary, single, lives in Richmond; (4) Edna Lee who married Arthur Lee Pleasant; (5) Rosalie French who married William Henry Syme; and (6) Sarah Wilson who married Benjamin Brookes Willingham of Macon, Georgia, and has several children.

Robert Camillas Shelton and Caroline Pollard had one child: Carrie Adeline, who married Oscar Curven (no issue).

Alice Cornelia Fleming, Rosa Pace Briggs, Ada Overby Briggs, Nannie Gresham, James David and Stephen, the other children of Dr. James Shelton and Adeline Overby, all left children, but I do not have the records.

MORE NORTH CAROLINA SHELTONS AND NOTES FROM NORTH CAROLINA STATE RECORDS

HE eldest son of David Shelton of Caswell County, North Carolina, was John Shelton of Stokes County who was living in the Salisbury District with his family, in the census of 1785. In 1790, he is listed as John, Sr., head of family, no sons under sixteen and two daughters. John, Jr., is listed as having two sons and three daughters under sixteen. William, with four sons and two daughters under 16; and Daniel with two sons and two daughters under sixteen. Evidently all of John's sons were married before 1790.

William Shelton, son of John of Stokes County, North Carolina, is said by descendants to have married Polly (Mary) Bates, daughter of William Bates of Greenville. They had:

(1) Ellis Shelton who married Mildred Bolling of Greenville, South Carolina; and (2) William Shelton who married Rachel Bolling, a sister of Ellis's wife. The children of Ellis Shelton and Mildred Bolling were:

(1) Martha, (2) William, (3) John Richard who married Caroline Brown and had one child, J. F. Shelton (who married Sarah Love Dahl and had Theodore D. Shelton who was born in North Carolina in 1888 and lived at Asheville until 1917 and is now living (1932) in Eatonton, Georgia; (4) Mary Arena; (5) Elizabeth; (6) Martin; (7) Elliott (called "Bud"); (8) Merritt; (9) Rachael; and (10) Thomas.

Martin (6) lives in Newport, Tennessee, and has a son, Charles; Elliott (7) lives near Blueridge, Georgia, and is in the mercantile business; and Thomas (10) lives in Montgomery, Alabama.

The children of William Shelton and Rachel Bolling were:

(1) John; (2) Ephriam; (3) Mary; (4) Stephen; (5) Thomas; (6) James; (7) Perry; (8) Clorinda; (9) Jane; and (10) Lavadia.

Ephriam (2) Shelton married Mary Davis and had:

(1) William, born 1854, died 1884; (2) Robert Bascom; (3) John Fletcher; (4) Stephen Asbury; (5) Elizabeth, born in 1863 and died in 1884; and (6) Lillian, born in 1865 and living in 1930.

Robert Bascom Shelton, born March 27, 1856, married Rachel Owen in 1883; she is still living (in 1932) but Robert died July 10, 1902. Their children were:

(1) Claudia May, d. s. p.; (2) Coral Elizabeth, born February 22, 1886; (3) William Roy, born December 16, 1888; (4) Ephriam Lowery, born March 12, 1890; (5) Rufus Henegar, born December 16, 1893; (6) Beulah, born September 11, 1896; and (7) John Kenneth, born November 30, 1898, and died July, 1924.

Coral Elizabeth Shelton (2) married Dr. Calvin Michaux Beam, D. S., and lives in Asheville, North Carolina; they have four children: (1) Margaret Elizabeth married Frederick Clare Van Dusen; (2) Coral Alberta, married John Herbert Stone; (3) Claudia Michaux married Gregg Barry; and (4) Robert Shelton Beam, a student in the medical school of Washington U., St. Louis, Mo.

William Roy (3) Shelton married Virginia Hart and has two children: William Roy, Jr., and Coral Jean. Ephriam

Lowery (4) married Lillian Ferne and has two sons: Ephriam L., Jr., and Robert Thomas.

Rufus Henegar (5) Shelton married Hattie Moore Berry of Durham, North Carolina and has Rufus Henegar Shelton, Jr.; they live in Asheville, North Carolina. Beulah (6) Shelton married William F. Lutgen and lives in Los Angeles, California; no issue.

William Shelton, born in 1854, son of Ephriam Shelton and Mary Davis, married Sarah Jane Moody and had four children:

(1) Oliver who married Alda Boyd and has one son, Oliver Hugh; (2) Leonard Shelton, living in the state of Washington; (3) Frances who married David Janes of Waynesville, North Carolina; and (4) Maud who married Gerald Davis.

John Fletcher (3), son of Ephriam and Mary Davis, married Margaret Shoe in 1890; both are living, but there is no issue. Stephen Asbury married Frances Barton and has one daughter, Mary, born in 1900, who married Walter Kettner and lives in Dellwood, North Carolina. Elizabeth married William Owen in 1882, and their daughter, Maud, married a Mr. Moody. Lillian (6) Shelton never married.

Stephen Shelton, son of William Shelton and Rachel Bolling, married and was the father of William Shelton of Waynesville, North Carolina. Perry Shelton, born in 1840, died in 1920; he married Ingals Conley and had two daughters: Bessie and Byrd. Perry was born in Swain County, North Carolina.

I have not been able to trace the other descendants of William and Polly Bates Shelton.

(The above information was furnished by members of

this branch of the Shelton family, from family Bibles.)

The following notes on some North Carolina Sheltons were found in the State Records of North Carolina:

"Patent on land on middle fork of Indian River, formerly Virginia, now North Carolina, issued August 16, 1756 to John Shelton of Hanover County Virginia, for 940 acres, called 'Woods Run' or 'Shelton's Creek', is hereby confirmed." Vol. 24, p. 447.

"Thomas Shelton (son of above John) on muster roll of forces October 25, 1754, in Captain Thomas Hicks' own Company, and commanded by Hon. Col. John Starkey, Esq., Onslow County, North Carolina."

"David Shelton, brother of Thomas, appointed Sheriff of Caswell County, North Carolina, July 20, 1777."

"David Shelton and Robert Dickens—Representatives from Caswell County." House Journal April to May 1782, 1783, 1784.

"David Shelton as head of class of recruits in May, 1782."

"Resignation of David Shelton and of his son, John Shelton, as Justices of the Peace for Caswell County accepted, November 20 and 21, 1789."

"James Shelton, private in Dixon's Company, enlisted May 12, 1781."

"Report from New England on the Battle of Lexington: 'Stamford, April 24th, 10 p. m.'; signed Samuel Shelton."

"Commission to Edward Chilton as Attorney General of Virginia and North Carolina, July 31, 1696."

"List of Admiralty Officers of North and South Carolina: Edward Chilton, Advocate and Attorney General of North and South Carolina, Maryland, Pennsylvania and West Jersey, February 16, 1697/98."

"R. Shelton signs letter of instruction to the Receiver General of North Carolina, June 5, 1712."

"Letter signed 'R. Shelton, Sept. 3, 1713', to Board of Trade of North Carolina."

"Mr. R. Shelton, Secretary to the Lords Proprietors of Carolina, May 7, 1728."

"Mr. R. Shelton, late Secretary, was granted a Barony of 12,000 acres in South Carolina, November 19, 1734."

The above men were Edward Shelton, son of James (2) and grandson of James (1) of Virginia and Bermuda; and Richard Shelton, son of John and grandson of James (1) who was given the grant now known as Sheldon, on which old Sheldon Church now stands at Beaufort, South Carolina.

JAMES SHELTON OF LUNENBERG CO., VA.

Some of Whose Descendants Moved to Missouri

AMES SHELTON of Lunenburg County, Virginia, whose will was proved December 13, 1798, was a son of Henry Shelton whose will is filed in Lancaster County, Virginia, in 1730. Henry was a son of the Benjamin whose brother, William, died in 1748; these wills are filed in Lancaster County, Virginia. James names "wife, Jane" and the following children:

(1) David who married Rhoda Quisenberry; (2) Benjamin who married Annie Austin (Benjamin used the 'Chilton' spelling and lived in Troy, Missouri; he was a grandson of Stephen Shelton, Jr., of Lancaster County, Virginia); (3) Stephen; (4) Thomas; (5) Catherine who married first, a Shelton and had a son, John Shelton; before 1798 she had married a Mr. Mason; and (6) Mary who married a Mr. Harrison. The grandchildren mentioned in James's will were: Winifred and Stephen *Shelton,* James, Thomas, Aaron and David *Quisenberry* and a Patsy *Bell,* and Daniel, Mary, Polly and Jane *Askew* Shelton; Askew was probably the name of James's wife, Jane.

Aaron Quisenberry married Rachel Shelton March 28, 1781.

David Shelton and Rhoda Quisenberry had a son, James David Shelton, who was born in Virginia about 1812 and came to Missouri in 1840, and in 1842 (aged 30) married Mary Irwin; their children were: (1) Winifred who was born in 1856; (2) Sarah Ellen who married Seymour Davis; (3) Elizabeth who married Thomas Wright; (4) Lucy who married John Thurman (John's son, Joseph Thurman, married Lucy's sister, Winifred); (5) Charles David who married and lived in St. Louis, Missouri; (6) Peter (no record); and (7) Creed who married three times.

Creed's children by his first wife were (1) Joseph, (2) Charles and (3) Benjamin.

Judge Nat Shelton of Macon, Missouri, and his sister, Susannah, were children of Meacon Ashley Shelton (son of Crispen Shelton and Susannah Irby), and his second wife, Anna Berger. Susannah married Peachy Gilmer Shelton October 18, 1853, and had a daughter, Willie Claiborne, who married Charles Martin of Troy, Missouri; and a son, Robert Shelton, who married in Troy, Missouri, August 19, 1890, Bird Grandfield; they had three daughters, all married and living in Los Angeles in 1929.

Judge Nat Shelton left a son, Charles, and a daughter, in Macon, Missouri.

(Information furnished from Bible records of Mrs. Charles Martin of Troy, Missouri, and the wife of Charles David Shelton of St. Louis, Missouri.)

WILLIAM SHELTON
of Albemarle Co., Va.

ILLIAM SHELTON, brother of the John who married Eleanor Parks, married first a widow, Mrs. Patience Thomas, who had a son, George Thomas, mentioned in the will of his step-father, William Shelton, filed in Albemarle County, Virginia, in 1789. Wm. was of St. David's Par. King and Queen Co., Va., when he purchased land in Fluvanna Co., Va.

I have no data of death of Patience; a D. A. R. record gives 1736; William had married his second wife, Elizabeth Rogers, before 1740, as she is mentioned in the will of her father in that year as Elizabeth Shelton. By his *second* wife, William had (1) John who married Elizabeth Lawson in 1760; (2) Gideon, no record; and (3) Thomas who married Mary Jameson November 2, 1789 and in 1794 sold the home plantation which he had inherited from his father, and with his wife and mother, Elizabeth Shelton, moved from Albemarle County to Madison County (Kentucky, probably; the record does not state).

By his first wife, Patience Thomas, William had (1) William born in 1731, who married Lucy Harris,[1] daughter of

(1) Their son Wm. Harris Shelton emigrated to Kentucky and died in 1815; their dau. Mourning Shelton mar. Capt. Archibald Woods and her sister Elizabeth married Richard Mobbery; both couples moved to Madison Co., Ky., a sister Ann Shelton mar. Jacob Powers and moved to Harrison Co., Ky. Other children were: Lucy who mar. Elliott Brown, Dabney, Agnes, Weatherston and Thomas. The last two named were living in Augusta Co. Va., in 1817. Sarah and Agnes d. s. p. Henry, son of Wm. (1) married Mary Long, sister of wife of Thos. Garth, Sr., their children were, Susan, who mar. Thos. Smith, Jane, who mar. Jeremiah White, Martha, who married

Chas. Robert Harris and Mourning Glenn, and died in Albemarle County, Virginia, in 1803; and (2) Sarah who married Augustine Shepherd, December 21, 1760, and had twins: Francis and Mary. I have no record of Francis, but Mary married John Haggard; their son, Pleasant Haggard, married Elizabeth Watts, and their daughter, Matilda Haggard, married David Rodes Twyman. Their daughter, Mary Shepherd Twyman, married Ottia Beall and had Matilda Frances Beall who married James Carlisle Lewis and lives in Mount Sterling, Kentucky.

The will of Augustine Shepherd was proved February 15, 1796; it names wife, Sarah, daughters Nancy Foster, Annis Woodson, Mary Haggard, Susannah, Sarah and Henrietta Shepherd, and a son, Augustine Shepherd. (3) Henry, son of Patience Thomas and William Shelton, married Mary Long.

The eldest son of John (1) Shelton and Elizabeth Lawson was David,[2] born June 11, 1761, in Goochland County, Virginia; he married, first, Elizabeth (?) and had a son, Richard, who married Temperance Street.

Sam'l. Mansfield, Mourning, who married John White, Ann, who mar. Achilles Barksdale, Thomas L. who married Susan Ballard (he d. 1859), Mildred—a son Wm. and *Austin* who d. s. p.

Miss Helen Keep of Detroit is a descendant of this Wm. Shelton of Albermarle, as is Mrs. J. E. Lewis of Mt. Sterling, Ky. Dabney, son of Wm. and Lucy Shelton, was married to Catherine Shempe on Dec. 26, 1810 by Rev. Jno. McCue. Wm. son of Henry Shelton and Mary Long, married in 1783—Frances Maupin. The children of Thomas L. Shelton and Susan Ballard, were, Mary, who married David Jeffries, James H., Lucy, who married George C. Omohundro, and Mildred. Thomas L. Shelton died in Augusta Co. Va., about 1900. In Augusta Co. are the marriages of Henry Shelton to Sally Ruple on Sept. 5, 1822, and Thomas W. Shelton to Mary Wilson on April 13, 1842, by B. M. Smith.

(2) Record from Bible of Richard Shelton, son of David Shelton and his first wife, Elizabeth, of Hanover County, Virginia.

Richard Shelton, son of David Shelton and his first wife, Elizabeth, of Hanover County, Virginia, was married to Temperance Street in the year 1797.

David Street Shelton—Born April 23, 1798; died December 25, 1838 (never married).

John Shelton—Born Dec. 9, 1799; married and lived in California; died in ?.

Ralph Shelton—Born Nov. 1, 1801; died Aug. 20, 1866; married Elizabeth Tatum.

Gilliam Shelton—Born Oct. 18, 1803; died March 29, 1865, Marion, Tennessee; married Emma Morgan.

Asa Shelton—Born Dec. 27, 1805; died in ?; married Mattie Ross of Memphis, Tennessee.

William Shelton—Born Sept. 27, 1807; died in ?; (Marion, Tennessee); married Elizabeth Stewart.

Jane Shelton—Born Nov. 28, 1809; died June, 1884; (Georgia); married Howell Tatum.

George Shelton—Born June 2, 1812; died Dec. 23, 1870; (Marion, Tennessee); married Sarah Hornbeck.

Prudence Shelton—Born April 16, 1814; died ?; (Marion, Tennessee); married George Mitchell.

Elizabeth Shelton—Born June 1, 1817; died ?; (Marion, Tennessee); married James Prigmore.

(By his first wife, Elizabeth, David also had a daughter, Nancy Shelton, who married William Henry Street, son of Anthony Street and his wife, Elizabeth, of Hanover County, Virginia.)

David's second wife was Henrietta Thomason, whom he married in 1786 (Marriage Bond in Louisa County, Virginia). This David was the son of John Shelton, (son of William of Albermarle) and Elizabeth Lawson

RECORD FROM BIBLE OF GEORGE SHELTON, SON OF RICHARD AND TEMPERANCE

Mary Adline Shelton—Born April 8, 1838; died ?; married L. D. Westcott of New York State, after Civil War.

Richard Elijah Shelton—Born Dec. 31, 1836; died Jan. 29, 1885; married Elizabeth Thatcher. He was a doctor in the Civil War.

Martha Jane Shelton—Born Dec. 11, 1840; died Aug. 10, 1887; married Washington Lewis.

Temperance Street Shelton—Born Dec. 15, 1842; died Aug. 6, 1902; married Spears Brown.

Prudence Mitchell Shelton—Born Jan. 1, 1844; died June 10, 1850.

Tompson Ashburn Shelton—Born June 14, 1847; died ?; married Jane Bryson.

Nancy Elizabeth Shelton—Born Dec. 4, 1849; died October 10, 1876; married James Kelly.

Esther Carolyn Shelton—Born May 14, 1853; married A. L. Anderson.

Asa Kelly Shelton—Born Jan. 15, 1857; married Minnie Richards.

Ruth Bryson Shelton—Born May 5, 1860; died Sept. 1, 1887; unmarried.

This was sent to the author by Mrs. Esther Anderson of Pikeville, Tennessee, the 8th child of George Shelton and Sarah Hornbeck. In 1934, Dr. Asa Kelly Shelton had the Shelton Clinic at Oliver Springs, Tennessee.

Mrs. Anderson speaks of her father as George W. Shelton. The Bible record does not give an initial. Mrs. Anderson states that her father, George, was only twelve years old when his father, Richard, died. This would fix the death of Richard at about 1824.

Other known children of John Shelton and Elizabeth Lawson were (2) Elizabeth, born February 28, 1763; (3) William, born March 9, 1765; and Nancy (4) (Nannie or Ann, all three names used in records), born October 29, 1767.

Joseph Shelton, another brother of John of "Rural Plains", died d. s. p. His will was probated October 11, 1784; he willed his estate to his brothers, nieces and nephews, and to a sister, Mary Trueheart of whom I have no further record.

SAMUEL SHELTON

of Albemarle Co., Va.
(Brother of "John" of Rural Plains)

AMUEL SHELTON, brother of the John who married Eleanor Parks, married Judith Clough; they had (1) Joseph, (2) Elizabeth, (3) Clough, Captain in the Revolutionary War, (4) Samuel and (5) David.

Clough Shelton married a Miss Fleming and had (1) Nelson Fleming, (2) Maria, (3) Cicely and (4) William A. I have not found the name of David's (5) wife, but his children, Elizabeth and Samuel, are mentioned in the will of their grandfather in 1793.

Cicely Shelton married, first a Mr. Anderson and, second, Reverend Absalom Waller; their son was Dr. Nelson Waller. Samuel's daughter, Elizabeth (dead before 1792) married first on May 30, 1785, John Tindall of Fluvanna County, Virginia; by him she had Elizabeth Shelton Tindall (under age in 1793). Her second husband was John Lewis, Jr., by whom she had Owen, Clough and Sarah Lewis.

Samuel's (1) son, Joseph, was a Colonel in the Revolutionary War; he was a member of the Legislature of Nelson County, Virginia, 1813-1824, incl. He married Mary Harris and had (1) John Marshall, (2) William Harris, (3) Joseph, (4) Robert P., (5) Samuel Henry, (6) Nelson, (7) Elizabeth, (8) Judith and (9) Henry Shelton.

John Marshall (1) Shelton married Nancy Mosby; he was dead by 1828, leaving Dr. John Mosby (1) Shelton who married Mary H. Digges and (2) Joseph Harris Shelton, both small children in 1835.

Joseph (3) married Judith Harris, daughter of William B. Harris and Elizabeth Woods. Joseph, son of Samuel (1), may have been the Colonel Joseph Shelton of the Revolution, whose pension record states "to take effect from 1831 when he was 73 years old". But, the record states "of Goochland Co., Va." Joseph's son James Leslie Shelton, married Elizabeth Watkins Brent of Virginia. Their daughter is Mrs. Robert M. Peck, principal of the Naval Base School, Hampton Roads, Virginia.

Nancy Mosby, wife of John Marshall Shelton (son of Col. Joseph Shelton), was the daughter of Daniel Mosby, grandfather of Col. John S. Mosby of Confederate fame.

Other children of Joseph and Judith Shelton were: John Clifford who married a Miss Garnett of Virginia. Dr. Samuel E., who married Frances Moore, daughter of Judge Moore of the Supreme Court of Texas; Dr. Thomas M. who married Miss Mayo of Texas; Julia Josephine who married William Willis of Orange County, Virginia; Elizabeth (Bettie) who married Judge Henry K. Mann of Galveston, Texas; and Annie, who married Douglas Plummer Denny of New York City.

(2) William H., second son of Col. Joseph Shelton and Mary Harris, was dead by 1828, leaving Maria Louisa and Elizabeth Ann (called Betsy) and a son, Samuel Waddy, all living in 1839.

(4) Robert P. was dead before 1833; (5) Samuel Henry married Pauline Montgomery; (6) Nelson married a Miss Carr; (7) Elizabeth married Lee W. Harris, and (8) Judith married Joseph Shelton of Louisa County, Virginia, a son

of Col. Joseph and his wife Elizabeth Winston. I have no record of (9) Henry, son of Col. Joseph of Nelson County, Virginia.

This record was given me by a member of the Nelson County family. From the wills and court records, I had a note that this Nelson (6) Shelton had married a cousin, Mary (Polly) Shelton, daughter of John Shelton and his wife, Mary Payne, of Louisa County, Virginia, instead of Miss Carr. He may have been married twice, however, or Polly may have married another Nelson Shelton, possibly the son of Clough.

Dr. John Mosby Shelton and Mary H. Digges had a daughter, Rose Evelyn, who married in 1868, John Horsley, and had (1) Dr. John Shelton Horsley, a prominent surgeon of Richmond, Virginia, (2) Frederick Melville Shelton and (3) Guy Winston Shelton, both of Nelson County, Virginia.

James Leslie Shelton (son of Colonel Joseph Shelton) and Elizabeth Watkins Brent had (1) Frances, (2) James L., Jr., (3) Mildred, (4) Samuel W., (5) Joseph H., Jr., (6) Helen Elizabeth, (7) John Woods, and (8) Edwin Houston.

Frances's husband was Robert McNutt Peck, son of Col. James B. Peck, and their children, all single in 1934 and living with their mother in Norfolk, Virginia, are (1) Robert McNutt Peck, Jr., (2) James Leslie Shelton Peck, (3) Mary Grigsby McNutt Peck, and (4) Frances Shelton Peck.

A Joseph Shelton who comes in somewhere on this line was dead by 1828, leaving an infant daughter, Mary Catherine Shelton.

Samuel Shelton, fourth child of Samuel Shelton (1) and Judith Clough, died in 1826, but his will was made in 1801, when he mentions only a son, Joseph, and two daughters. One may have died in childhood as no record is given of her in lists of Samuel's children. His wife was Sarah Waddy, and they had a son, Samuel Waddy Shelton, who moved to Mercer County, Kentucky, and died there May 28, 1833; his wife was Jane Henderson, whom he married in Hanover County, Virginia, in 1781. Issue: (1) William Henderson, (2) Peter, (3) David R. (who married "Patsy" and had son Samuel T.) (4) John H., (5) Thomas, (6) Mary H. (Polly), (7) Elizabeth (Betsy), and (8) Nancy H. Shelton.

Thomas (5) married Pauline Noel at Danville, Boyle County, Kentucky, and had: (1) Peter, (2) William H., (3) Samuel, (4) James Thomas, (5) Lucy, (6) Mildred, (7) Mary and (8) John. William H. (2) married Maria Louise Nevill, February 25, 1862; he died in 1873, his wife died in 1876. They had a son, William Nevill, and daughters: Lillian, Bettie and Lalla Belle who married O. B. Radebough and is living in Nashville, Tennessee (in 1940 the author was told they had moved to Orlando, Florida).

James Thomas (4) was born in 1834 and died in 1917; he married Lucinda Frances Yeager in 1856; she was born in 1840 and died in 1911; both died in Danville, Kentucky. A daughter, Susannah Elizabeth Shelton, married Henry J. Ott and is living (in 1933) in Independence, Missouri. Captain Clough Shelton and Miss Fleming had a son, William A., whose will was proved February 18, 1824; no wife is mentioned, so she evidently predeceased him. Their children were: (1) Dr. Thomas Daniel Shelton (a physician in Albemarle County, Virginia, who d. s. p.), (2) Nelson Fleming Shelton who had land in Nelson County, Virginia, and supposedly d. s. p., and (3) Mildred Clough who married Francis J. Smith and whose grandchildren, Mrs. W. L. Goodwyn and Miss Mildred Harris, were living in 1934, in Richmond, Virginia.

The above Nelson Fleming Shelton may have been the one who married his cousin, Polly, daughter of John Payne Shelton and Massie Shelton of Louisa County, Virginia.

THE SHELTONS OF CAROLINE, STAFFORD
AND SPOTTSYLVANIA COUNTIES, VIRGINIA

OHN SHELTON of Spottsylvania County, Virginia, was a son of John and Ann Shelton (called both Chilton and Shelton) of Caroline and Stafford Counties, Virginia, and a grandson of the John Shelton (called Chilton) who died in 1726, whose grave has been restored at "Currioman". John's will is written August 28, 1805, and proved December 3, 1805. His wife (called Sukie in the records) was Susan Hord who was born April 23, 1742. In the records of his children, given by the late Mr. Brock of the Virginia Historical Society, an Elizabeth who married Mr. Herndon, and a Jane who married a Mr. H. Cook of Alabama, are given and James, son of John, is omitted. The children mentioned in John's will are (1) Richard, heir, of Stafford County, Virginia, (2) Nancy who married M. J. Smith, (3) Thomas H., (4) John Shelton who married Lettie (Lethe) Conyers, daughter of John Conyers (in one record she is mentioned as Sarah), (5) Agnes who married John Brock, (6) William who lived in Spottsylvania County, Virginia, (7) Mary (called Polly) who married Beverly Stubblefield, a Captain in the Continental Army, (8) Lucy, single in 1805 but who, according to Mr. Brock, married a Mr. Wolf of Madison, Virginia, and (9) James Shelton.

The John Shelton, Sr., who died in 1805 had a brother, James, in Stafford County, Virginia. In 1847, there is a record of William S. Shelton's interest in the estate of his father, John (d. 1805) being transferred to O. M. Ford, as trustee; and the interest of his brother, James, transferred from John Moncure. In 1848, the estate of Thomas H., brother of James and William Q., was consolidated under the name of Robert Cropp; this consisted of 350-4 acres on Deep River. I was told that it was one of these John Sheltons who married Ann Cox in Orange County, Virginia.

The *sons* of the John Shelton, who died in 1805, John, Thomas Hord and James, owned the Shelton farm on which the "Battle of the Wilderness" was fought, in the War between the States. One of these brothers had a son, Robert Pierce Shelton, who married Mary Gray; their son, William C. Shelton, is circulation manager of The Washington Times and Herald and has two children, all living in Washington, D. C., in 1934.

The Robert and Barnard Shelton who own the "Shelton Shop" on H Street at Fourteenth in Washington, D. C., are also descendants of one of the Sheltons of Spottsylvania County, Virginia, and are cousins of the above William C. Shelton. The records of James Shelton (brother of John of Spottsylvania County) and his children are given on the register of Overwharton Church as Yellton; just one more alias to add to those that have prevented the history of the Shelton family from being known to posterity many years ago.

A member of the above family has written me that it was this Thomas Hord Shelton, son of John (d. 1805) who married his cousin, Sally Hord. There are so many branches of the family bearing the same Christian names and all cousins that it seems a hopeless task to even try to place each in his or her proper place—the family bible records are the only solution.

A FEW LANCASTER CO., VA., SHELTONS
and Some of Their Descendants

TEPHEN SHELTON (records Shelton, Chilton, Chelton and Charlton) was a member of the House of Burgesses from Lancaster County, Virginia, in 1676. He died in August, 1718. His wife's name was Mary and, from the records, he was evidently a son of the Thomas Shelton who died in Cecil County, Maryland, in 1684. Stephen's children were: (1) Stephen, Jr., (2) John, (3) George, (4) William, (5) Benoni, (6) Andrew, (7) Charles, (8) Thomas and (9) Margaret.

Stephen, Jr., (1) married Elizabeth and had a son, Thomas, mentioned in the will of Stephen, Sr., in 1718. This Thomas bought land in Northumberland County, Virginia, in 1691; his wife was Margaret, and his daughter, Margaret, born in 1683, married the Charles Calvert, Lord Baltimore, who died in 1714. In the later records, this Thomas is called Thomas "Charlton" of Hixham, Northumberland County, Virginia.

John (2), second son of Stephen and Mary Shelton, married Mary and had a son, Robert, and a son, John Shelton (who married Phoebe and died in 1784, leaving a son, John Shelton), and other children; also a granddaughter, Nancy Forrester.

George (3) married a widow, Elizabeth, who had a daughter, Elizabeth, who married Thomas Purcell. This George also had land in Northumberland and Culpepper Counties, Virginia; he died in 1709 and left his estate to his nephew, George, and after him to John (both sons of Benoni (5) and Ann), and to his brother, William (4), who died in 1739. Benoni (5) was dead by 1730; his wife lived until 1777. Andrew (6) died in 1760; he married a widow, Mary Betts Hopkins, who died in 1772. Charles (7) (wife's name not mentioned) left Hanna, Leanna, and Edwin (heir) all under age when Charles died in 1739. Thomas (8) and Margaret (9) were both under age when Stephen, Sr., died in 1718. Thomas married the widow of Thomas Gressert and had Ezekial who died in 1758, and Millicent who was the heir of her brother. I have no record of Margaret (9).

The wills and court records of Lancaster County apparently prove that from the William Shelton (brother of George Shelton, called *Chilton,* who married his cousin, Judith Davis, descends Richard who was the founder of the *Chilton* family of "Catalpa Grove", Lynchburg, Virginia.

The William who was heir to his brother, George, who died in 1709, married Rebecca and died in 1739. Some of their children were (1) William who married Mary Ann Hobson and died in 1748 without issue, naming "a brother, Benjamin (2) and a brother Stephen (3) who had a son, William". There was also a daughter, Rebecca (4) who married a Nicholas Shelton, a daughter, Winifred (5), who married a Mr. Moore, Judith (6) who was left negroes in the will of her cousin, Moses, in 1778, and a Sarah (7) whom I have not been able to trace.

Benjamin (2) had a son, Henry (will 1723, proved 1730) who married Mary; they had (1) William, eldest son and heir, (2) John, heir if William d. s. p., (3) James, (4) Winifred, and (5) Benjamin who married a Craven (her sister, Rhoda, married Thomas Everit and died s. p. in 1748. Benjamin (5) named a God-daughter, Mary Shelton, his heir. James (3) died in Lunenburg County, Virginia; his will was proved in 1798.

The Thomas Shelton (called Charlton and Chilton) who bought land in Northumberland County in 1691, and his wife, Margaret, had, besides the daughter Margaret, who married Charles Calvert, Lord Baltimore, a daughter Mary who married Edmund Scarborough, a son Stephen who married Jemima (?) and probably other issue. Stephen (d. 1761) and Jemima had sons: William (1) (d. 1787), and Stephen, mentioned as youngest child, under sixteen in 1761. Thomas had a brother, George, who went to Maryland; this George had a son, Stephen, who married Judith Fleet in 1748 in St. Stephen's Parish, Northumberland County, Virginia. The records in Annapolis, Maryland,[1]

(1) In Princess Anne Co., Maryland, are a number of *Chelton* wills. The will of Fleet Chelton, is dated July 10, 1839 and probated June 21, 1853. He names Executors, Wm. W. Johnston and John W. Crisfield, and names four sons, Fleet James Chelton, John Wesley Chelton, Geo. Washington Chelton and Wm. H. Chelton; no names of daughters are given, but the family state there were four.

Fleet James, married Leah Anne Adams, dau. of Sampson Adams, John Wesley, b. 1827, d. 7/7/1856, aged 29. Geo. Washington, married a Boughten, Nov. 3, 1830, in St. Mary's Co., Md. Brumbough, v. 1, p. 390.

Wm. H. married and had twin sons, Winfield Scott and Zachary Taylor.

Ellen Francis married a Nevitt and settled in Ohio.

Nancy S. married a Crosswell.

Fleet C. Chelton was born in Somerset Co., Md., Oct. 12, 1782, and died May 22, 1853.

The bible of George *Shelton* is in possession of Mrs. James T. Dorsey, Marion Station, Somerset Co., Md., she was Addie R. *Shelton*, youngest child of Fleet James, called *Chelton* in the Maryland records. In the bible the names are spelled in various ways, for different members of the family, and the same thing occurs on the tombstones.

George W. Shelton evidently a *son* of *George Washington Chelton*, married Sally Cullin in Somerset Co., Md., 8/2/1876 and moved to Baltimore. Geo. was born April 9, 1851, in Somerset Co., Md., and died in Baltimore April 7, 1915, his wife was born March 7, 1862, in Somerset Co., Md., and died in

as well as in the old Shelton bibles, are spelled Chelton, Shelton, Chilton, Charlton, Carlton, Sheldon and Skelton. A will filed John *Charlton* gives name of *wife,* executor, as Martha *Shelton.* The reason for letting these discrepancies in spelling stand on the records for over 200 years is beyond my comprehension. The various spellings for the same family appear even on the tombs in Maryland. However, as Shakespeare signed his own name in a dozen different ways, it was probably "the style" in that period, so "that's that."

General John Ross Key married Ann Roche Shelton (called Charlton) and their son was Francis Scott Key, author of our "Star Spangled Banner". A sister of Francis Key married Roger Brooke Taney, Chief Justice of the United States.

Thomas Chilton (Shelton, youngest son of John (1) of "Carotoman", "Currioman" and "Rural Plains" who died in 1706) and Winifred King had a son, Thomas, born

Baltimore, Feb. 22, 1924, Sally Cullin was the daughter of Sarah Anne Lankford and Severn Cullin.

These *Sheltons* called *Chelton* are descendants of Stephen Shelton, who married Judith Fleet and the marriage and births of their children are on the Parish register in St. Stephens Parish, Northumberland Co., Va. Mrs. Maud Osman Harris, of Chicago, is a descendant of this branch of the family, she has one daughter, Sally.

William S. Chelton, Widow Emma Chelton, administratrix. Ola Chelton, Beatrice Adams, Beulah Johnson, Ruth Chelton and Helen B. Chelton, daughters and W. Guy Chelton, son. S. W. No. 28, folios 11-12. Sept. 1, 1911.

Zachary T. Chelton.

Annie C. Chelton, widow, administratrix. Administration account. Dec. 2, 1914. S. W. No. 28, folio 214.

Emma Chelton.

William G. Chelton, administrator. S. W. No. 28 folio 468. Nov. 26, 1918.

in Lancaster or Middlesex County, Virginia, before 1738 when his mother, widow of Thomas, appeared in Court as executor of her husband's estate.

Descendants of this Thomas moved to Tennessee, then to Kentucky and from there to Missouri where Thomas Chilton, grandson of the above Thomas, died enroute and was buried at St. Charles, Missouri. He is said to have been a son of William Shelton and Ann Lomax; he left a widow and four sons: (1) William, born December 5, 1811; (2) James, (3) John, and (4) Jackson. The widow of Thomas Shelton (spelled Chilton) married one of the Burbridges who, with the Underwoods, had come to Missouri with the "Chiltons". The families have intermarried several times and their descendants are scattered—some of them live in Louisiana, Missouri, and some in Hannibal, Missouri; a grandson of James, Mr. J. C. Estes,[1] lives in St. Louis, Missouri. I have an affidavit from Mr. Estes, written in 1930, stating that his grandfather was never called anything but *Shelton* and that the family never could understand why he spelled his name *Chilton*. Mr. Estes said his ancestors were brought up on the plantation adjoining "Stratford", the Lee Home in Westmoreland County, Virginia. This plantation is "Currioman" called the "Chilton" place. I am glad to state that I have been told that this place was recently purchased by

---

(1) Mr. Estes died in St. Louis, Missouri, January, 1937.

City of St. Louis, May 1st, 1929.
State of Missouri

    John Chilton Estes being duly sworn says, that he is a son of George W. Estes and Mary Augusta Chilton. Mary Augusta Chilton was a daughter of James Chilton of Louisiana, Missouri, whose parents resided on a plantation in Westmoreland County, Virginia, adjoining or very near that of General

a lineal descendant of the family; the location is superb and I am hopeful the place will be restored to some of its old beauty.

The author has made a desperate effort to get photos of some of these old ancestral homes. There do not seem to be any in existence; if there are they must be in the hands of private individuals whom she has been unable to contact.

The drawing on the Court record in Westmoreland Co., Va., of "Currioman", bearing date of 1782, has been photographed and produced here, it covers two very large pages on the Court books, and was evidently a huge estate at that time. As stated in another part of this book, the date seems to be an error, made probably many years ago in copying.

All Westmoreland and Lancaster records, which are *accessible* to the public, seem to bear out the fact that the Col. Thomas referred to on the plat died about 1792 instead of 1782.

This may *someday* be straightened out, if the records stuck away in the Court House at Montross are *ever* investigated.

Robert E. Lee's.

James Chilton and his parents moved from Virginia to Missouri stopping a short while in Kentucky about 1819.

While my grandfather Chilton and all the family spelled their name Chilton, my father, George W. Estes, always pronounced his name as though it was spelled Shelton. I never knew why or the reason for this. It may have been that as my father and his parents came from both Virginia and Kentucky that it was common for both spellings to be pronounced the same way.

Further the deponent saith not.

JOHN CHILTON ESTES

Subscribed and sworn to before me this day May 2nd, 1929.

Wm. Galt Brown, Notary Public

My commission expires Oct. 18th, 1931.

LEE — BALL — RANDOLPH — SHELTON

OL. RICHARD LEE (1) according to his own records, came from "Morton Regis", Shropshire, England; so probably the Lees, as well as the Balls were friends and kinsmen of the Sheltons in England, as well as here in America.

Col. Richard Lee had a grant in York Co., Va., of 1000 acres, Aug. 10, 1642; his wife was Ann. He was Justice, Burgess, Member of the Council of Virginia, Secretary of State and served on numberless Commissions. His will was made in England and is dated 1663; it states "Lately of Stratford, Langton, County of Essex" To his son Richard, he left his plantation in Gloucester Co., Va., called "Paradise".

Col. Richard Lee (1) died prior to April 20, 1664; his eldest son *John* was his heir, but John died very young, and the second son:

Col. Richard Lee (2) became heir and from him descend the "Lees of Stratford". Col. Richard (2) was born in 1647 and died in March 1714 at "Mt. Pleasant", his 2600 acre estate in Westmoreland Co., Va. He was educated at Oxford and at one of the London "Inns" and was a fine Greek, Hebrew and Latin scholar, and was a member of the Council of Virginia from 1676 to 1698, and a Burgess in 1677 or earlier. In 1674, Col. Richard Lee (2) married Letitia, eldest daughter of Henry Corbin and his wife Alice Eltonhead; Letitia was born in 1657 and died in Oct. 1706. The will of this Col. Richard Lee was dated 3/3/1714 and proved April 27, 1715; his eldest son was:

ARMS OF LEE OF VIRGINIA
Two mottoes are used in the Lee Arms—one is *"Ne incautus futuri"*

Col. Richard Lee (3) and *his* fifth son was:

Col. Henry Lee of "Lee Hall" Westmoreland Co., Va., who was born in 1691, and died between 6/13 and 8/25/1747; his will was written on the former and proved on the latter date; he married in 1723/24 Mary, dau. of Col. Richard Bland and Elizabeth Randolph, 9th, child of Col. Wm. Randolph of Turkey Island (born 1695) and his wife Mary, dau. of Henry Isham. The home of Col. Richard Bland was "Jordan's" Prince George Co., Va.

Mary Bland, wife of Col. Henry Lee, was born 8/21/1704 and died between Oct. 1762, when her will was written, and May 29, 1764, when it was proved.

Lettice (prob. Letitia) Lee, dau. of Col. Henry Lee (1) and Mary Bland, was born 1730/31 and married 1746/47, Col. Wm. Ball (5) of "Millenbeck", Lancaster Co., Va. This Col. Wm. Ball was a cousin of the James Ball, who married another *Lettice Lee,* dau. of *Richard* and *Judith* Lee.

"Lee Hall" adjoined "Mt. Pleasant" in Cople Parish, Westmoreland Co., Va. A commission was issued to "Col. Henry Lee of Lee Hall" in June 1737, as Lt. Col. of the Westmoreland Co. Militia. The widow of this Col. Henry Lee, Mary Bland Lee, died in 1764; her will was proved May 29 of that year. In it she leaves "to my beloved daughter, Lettice Ball, all wearing apparel, books, contents of my house, money owed me by my son Richard and the use of all of my slaves for life". She also names a gr. daughter *Mary Ball* and two sons, Wm. (6) Ball of "Millenbeck" and Henry Lee Ball and a daughter Mary Ball, who had married a Graham; she makes no other mention of the son Richard; only that in reference to the money owed her by

him, but names "gr-son Wm. Ball, gr-d's Mary Bland
Ball (prob. the one named above) and Letty Bland Ball,"
and "gr-daughters *Cordelia* and *Florinda Ball,* daughters
of my deceased son Dr. Wm. Ball (6) and d-in-law, Catherine
Ball;" the will is dated Oct. 16, 1788 and proved Dec.
15, 1788.

The will of her son, Col. Wm. Ball (6) is dated 6/17/1785
and proved 7/22/1785, and was witnessed by Wm. *Shelton.*
In it Col. Ball names "wife Catherine" and daughters
Cordelia and *Florinda.* These wills are in the Archives
Division of the Virginia State Library in Richmond; "Lancaster Wills"—Box 207—Fo—88; they are not *indexed* or
classified in any way, so a search there is an herculean task.

One of the most beautiful tributes, of the many paid to
Robert E. Lee, was given over the radio on the birthday of
Lee—January 19, 1941, by Mr. Cameron of the Ford
Motor Co.

I was so impressed by the unusualness of it, that I wrote
to Mr. Cameron for a copy and am printing it here, that it
may be preserved.

"January is the birth month of many great figures in
American history. John Winthrop, Benjamin Franklin,
Israel Putnam, Robert Morris, Paul Revere, John Hancock,
Ethan Allen, Alexander Hamilton, Stephen Decatur, Daniel
Webster were born in the first month of the calendar year
and though each of them is distinguished for service or
character, none of them is honored by the observance of
his anniversary. There is one January anniversary, however, that is observed with pride and reverence—an anniversary that falls today. On January 19, 1807—134 years
ago—was born a man who is beloved of the South and

honored everywhere, whose anniversary, 70 years after his death, was kept today with public exercises in eleven Southern States. That man is General Robert E. Lee.

It is not the fact itself that calls for special remark, but the reason for it. Why was Robert E. Lee chosen for so singular an honor? True, he led the armies of the Confederacy, and that assures him his place in history, but of itself it scarcely explains the place he holds in his people's heart; the leader of the Union armies also is a historic figure but his birthday is not kept. Other great southern names are on the scroll of fame, but to none of them as such has the same depth and extent of public honor been accorded. Military experts agree that General Lee was one of the great captains of the ages; the verdict of History is that he did exploits against giant odds—but neither are these sufficient to account for the devotion he has commanded for at least 80 years.

General Robert E. Lee was of patrician birth, son of "Light-Horse Harry" Lee whose panegyric on George Washington—"first in peace, first in war, first in the hearts of his countrymen"—is known to every American schoolboy. But it is not for his noble descent that Lee is preeminent, and as for wealth, that never was his portion. Must we then ascribe this great affection to the sympathy of generous minds for the devoted leader of a lost cause? No; the emotion that General Lee has evoked is not mere sympathy; it is a positive and masculine admiration rising into a hero-worship and deepening into a veneration that is quite independent of adventitious circumstance.

When all the common sources of public esteem are exhausted and fail to yield the secret of the long-enduring love for Lee, we are confronted with a phenomenon of American life—we are confronted with a fame supported *by the power of character alone.* Men are remembered for political service, for great inventions, for successful military prowess, for literary achievements, for scientific discoveries,—here is one American of many distinctions whose greatest, ennobling all the rest, is *his character as a man.*

It is chiefly to his *character* we owe our interest in the lesser stages of his career. Lee's uneventful youth is notable now chiefly as a background for the charm of an unfolding character. We follow his routine army life before the war because it reflects the devotion to duty that was an essential part of his character. The solemn act of refusing the command of the armies of the United States for the sake of his native State, illumines the deep place that sacrifice had in his character. And what is it that shines through all the years of war, and at Appomattox, and ever brighter after Appomattox as the span of life grew briefer? what is it that still breathes round that chapel tomb at Lexington, Virginia? It is the fairness of judgment, the unfailing self-control, the unforced courtesy toward impatient friend and headstrong foe, the self-forgetfulness in college service, of Robert E. Lee. Not in events and their dates is his real history, but in his qualities as a man.

General Lee was not a dashing soldier, a reckless leader; he was not a personality of earth and fire. The terms his biographers use to designate his qualities are most revealing. Just to look at the names of those characteristics on which all the biographies agree—abstemiousness, amiability and accuracy; boldness, calmness, courage and charm; diligence, devotion and dignity; energy, fairness, faith and frankness; generosity, grace and gentleness; heroism, humor and humility; integrity, justice, kindness, loyalty, magnamity, poise, reasonableness, serenity, tact and wisdom—just to read the list of his attributes as historians have assembled and named them, is to read the whole alphabet of character and to have a portrait of the man.

In a noise-distraught, ambition-strained and fame-hunting generation this is something to think of, that in our national Hall of Fame, and three generations after his death, the nation honors one public man principally for his achievements in Christian character—for it is *that* that first comes to mind on hearing the name of Robert E. Lee.''

BALL — SHELTON

S will be seen in "The Sheltons in Ireland" on page 74 of this book, there were many Ball-Shelton marriages in Ireland.

Six generations of the Virginia Balls lived at "Millenbeck" Lancaster Co., Va.

The first Ball home in Virginia was "Bewdley" built in 1680. This was also the name of the estate of Richard Shelton (called Sheldon) in Worcestershire, England.

The first Col. Wm. Ball of Northampton, England, settled in Lancaster Co., Va., *about* 1650, his wife was Hannah Atherall; they had issue Wm. (2) Joseph, Richard and Hannah Ball.

Capt. Wm. Ball (2) married first a Miss Harris of "Bayview" Northumberland Co., Va. There were no children born of this union. His second wife was Margaret Downman, of "Morattico" Lancaster Co., Va., by whom he had 9 children: an only dau. Margaret, and Richard, James, Joseph, George, Samuel, David, Stretchley and

Wm. Ball (3) who married Hannah Beale in 1744, and by whom he had 5 children: George, Sarah, Judith, Hannah and

Wm. Ball (4) who married his cousin Margaret, dau. of Capt. Richard Ball and his wife Sarah Young and had 6 children: Richard, Williamson, Benjamin, Elizabeth, Sarah and

Wm. Ball (5) whose 2nd wife was Lettice Lee, dau. of Col. Henry Lee of "Lee Hall" Westmoreland Co., Va.

ARMS OF THE BALLS OF VIRGINIA

BEWDLEY-BALL HOME IN VIRGINIA
BUILT IN 1680

BEWDLEY HOME OF THE BALLS IN VIRGINIA, BUILT IN 1680
NAME OF HOME OF RICHARD SHELTON IN ENGLAND

Col. Wm. Ball (6) also called Dr. Ball in the county records, was the only surviving son of this union. This Col. Ball was the 6th. Ball in direct succession at "Millenbeck", his wife was Catherine; I have not been able to find her surname; they had two daughters, *Cordelia*, the elder, who married John Gilmour of "Belmont" Lancaster Co., Va., and *Florinda*, who married Lt. Jesse Shelton, son of Lt. Col. Thos. Shelton of the Westmoreland Militia in the War of 1812, and gr-son of Col. Thomas Shelton, Col. of the *same* Regiment in the Revolution, and who died at his estate "Currioman" Westmoreland Co., Va. (then adjoining the Stratford estate) about 1791 or 92; his will has not been found, but an inventory and division of the estate "Currioman" was made in 1792; a plat of this estate may be seen facing pages 104-105.

This Col. Thomas Shelton, called *Chilton* in many records, was the 2nd son of John Shelton of "Rural Plains" Hanover Co., Va., and his wife Eleanor, dau. of Wm. Parks, the first editor in Maryland and Virginia.

On the Parish Register of Ludlow, a town in Shropshire, Eng., is recorded the birth of a son, Wm. on March 20, 1719/20 to "Wm. Parks and wife Elianor", so he must have been married in England; I have not been able to find the surname of his wife. His estate of 1550 acres in Prince George Co., Maryland, surveyed for him on April 19, 1731, was named "Park Hall".

At Owestry and at Bitterley in Shropshire, are celebrated estates of this name, and in the inventory of his estate he names a negro slave "Ludlow", the name of the town Wm. Parks came from.

A biographer of his states "I believe that Franklin alone

excepted, there was no printer of his period whose service was greater or more distinctive in character that than rendered to the Colonists of Maryland and Virginia, by this pioneer printer.''

In 1749 Wm. Parks undertook a large commission from the Government to print the collected laws of the Colony as revised by the Assembly in 1746-1748. In the Spring of 1750 he decided on a trip to Europe, was taken ill on his ship the ''Nelson'' and died at sea. His will was made on March 30; he died April 1, 1750, and was buried at ''Gosport'', England, a few days later.

In his will Wm. Parks provided that his wife ''Eleanor'' and his son-in-law, *John Shelton,* should complete the task of printing the Laws of Virginia, which he had commenced before his voyage to England. This book appeared about 1752, bearing the name of William Hunter, assistant and successor of Wm. Parks.

The will and inventory of Park's estate are in the Court House at Yorktown, Va. The only child mentioned is Eleanor, who was the wife of John Shelton, the 3rd owner of ''Rural Plains'', Hanover Co., Va.

The youngest child of John and Eleanor Parks Shelton was Sarah, born in 1738, who married Patrick Henry in 1754. They had 6 children; Sarah died very young, and Patrick Henry married Dorothea Dandridge.

Florinda Ball Shelton, wife of Jesse Shelton must have died at the birth of (or soon after) their only child, John Gilmour Shelton, who was born in Lancaster Co., March 1st, 1802, according to his bible.

His aunt Cordelia Ball Gilmour, was his legal guardian, and as he was a very wealthy orphan, the estates *must* have

JOHN GILMORE SHELTON, BORN IN LANCASTER
COUNTY, VIRGINIA, MARCH 1, 1802; DIED IN ST.
LOUIS, MO., FEB. 5, 1869. BURIED IN BELLEFON-
TAINE CEMETERY, ST. LOUIS, MO.

passed through the *Courts,* but no record of any kind has been found. They are evidently among the loose papers, books, etc., in the loft of the old Clerk's office at Lancaster; the vermin and filth have made them inaccessible to the public; it is doubtful whether any thing of value will be left to preserve when Virginia gets around to cleaning out that loft. The author has urged it *for years,* and stressed the value of the old records, but to date, 1941, nothing has been done.

John Gilmour Shelton lived with his aunt, Mrs. Gilmour, until her death in 1815, a year after her marriage to Rawleigh Downman of "Belle Isle", Lancaster Co., Va. After Cordelia's death, John was sent to his gr-aunt, Mary Ball Grayson, wife of Reginald Grayson, at Fredericksburg, Va., where he remained until 1726 when his inheritance came to him, and he went to Lynchburg, Va.; there he married Ann Maria Byrd, daughter of Wm. Byrd (5) and Mary Fitz-Gerald of the "Leinster" family. In 1732 Wm. Byrd (5) and all of his family moved to St. Louis, Mo., where a year later Ann, wife of John Shelton died; she is buried beside him in Bellefontaine Cemetery, St. Louis, Mo.

In 1735 John Gilmour Shelton married the sister of his first wife, Mary Walker Byrd, who lived until May 8th, 1899, and is buried on the other side of her husband, who died at his residence in St. Louis on Feb. 5, 1869.[1]

(1) John Gilmore Shelton of St. Louis, Mo., was too old to serve in the War between the States, but all of his sons served except Frank Grayson who was only 6 years old. The elder sons were graduates of the Uuniversity of Virginia, and fought in the Confederate Army, under Gen. Sterling Price. One son Dr. Charles Oscar Shelton, was wounded at "Pea Ridge" and was taken to New Orleans, where he died at the home of a cousin, the wife of Major Tarleton, of the Confederate Army.

After the war the body of Dr. Shelton was brought home to St. Louis and buried in the family lot in Bellefontaine Cemetery.

The only daughter of John Shelton and Mary Walker Byrd was Maria Genevieve Shelton, who was born in St. Louis, Mo., Sept. 26, 1844, was educated at private schools in the East and on Oct. 29, 1869 was married to Rev. C. D. N. Campbell, D. D., at that time pastor of Centenary Church, St. Louis, Mo. Dr. Campbell was a descendant of John and Priscilla Alden, through the Alden, Edson and Noble lines; his mother was Eunice Noble; the entire line can be found in the "Genealogy" published by the author of this book, in 1927.

Dr. Campbell's father was Benjamin Tillinghast Campbell, descended from Robert Campbell, who came to Voluntown, Conn., in 1719 and his wife Janet Stuart.

This Robert Campbell was a younger son of John Campbell, 1st Earl of Breadalbane, and his second wife; John's first wife was Mary, dau. of Henry Rich, Earl of Holland; she died in 1666 and John married again, and had several children by his second wife, but the author has not been able to find her surname. In his will John passed over his eldest son Duncan, Lord Ormelie and named his 2nd son John as heir. They were sons of the first marriage.

John Campbell, 1st Earl of Breadalbane, was a son of

Even on the Memorial Tablet of the Library of the University of Virginia, the initials of Dr. Shelton's name are wrong. I have his records and his Autograph Album, made during his four years there, and the name is correct on all of them.

Grayson Shelton, the son of Frank Grayson Shelton, volunteered in the World War, at the age of 19; he served as a machine gunner in the 6th Marines of the very famous 2nd Division. After 19 months active service he was killed at the battle of Mt. Blanc, just before the Armistice, and is buried in the American Cemetery at Romagne, France. Facing page 198 is a photo of the home of John Gilmore Shelton of St. Louis, from 1861 to 1866. This house is now (1941) being torn down, as it is in the district for one of the new housing projects.

HOME OF JOHN GILMORE SHELTON OF ST. LOUIS, MO., DURING THE
1860's. IT WAS AT 1117 ST. ANGE AVENUE AND IS NOW, IN 1941, BEING
TORN DOWN FOR A NEW HOUSING PROJECT.

Sir Robert Campbell, Earl of Argyle, who succeeded his brother Sir Colin Campbell who died without issue.

Sir John Campbell, Earl of Breadalbane, was M. P. for Argyleshire, 1669-74.

Robert Campbell, first of his line in America, was born in Campbelltown, Argyleshire in 1673 and married about 1695, as his eldest child *Charles* was born in 1696. His children were all born in Tyrone, Ulster (where he had been given land on his marriage to Janet Stuart) and his eldest son *Charles* was married when the family followed Dr. Dorrance's Colony to America. From this Charles, descended:

Dr. C. D. N. Campbell, D. D., born in Lebanon, Hamilton Co., N. Y., in 1827, died in St. Louis, Jan. 1, 1897; his widow, Genevieve Shelton Campbell, died July 2, 1913, also in St. Louis.

Five children were born of this marriage, Mary Shelton, who married Delmar McCleery and had one child, Genevieve Blackstone McCleery who married Benjamin Franklin Atwood and has two children; they are living in 1941, in Lakewood, Florida. Thomas Campbell, named for his father's kinsman, the poet, has never married; he has been in the U. S. Army for 25 years; he volunteered, at 18 years of age, to serve in the Spanish-American War; he again volunteered to serve in the World War and was in the transport service in the Medical Corps until the Armistice; he made the first trip on the converted troop ship, the *Leviathan,* and 14 trips thereafter, to and from France, transporting troops and bringing back the casualties. After the Armistice, he was in the Army of Occupation, in Belgium and Germany for 18 months, and is still in the U. S. Army. The youngest children of Dr. and Mrs. Campbell were Ada

Lee Campbell (who married Taylor D. Kelley, of St. Louis; he died in 1925, his widow is living in 1941, at "Diamond Hill" Cos Cob, Conn.) and Ethel Claire Campbell, who married Henry Bernard Voges in St. Louis, in 1913, and has three children, Shelton Campbell, Henry Byrd and Ethel Campbell Voges, all of 7056 Tulane Ave., St. Louis, Mo. Mr. Voges died in St. Louis in 1929. The second daughter of Dr. Campbell and Genevieve Shelton, was Mildred Genevieve, who married, in Washington, D. C., March 10th, 1904, Alexander Edward Whitaker of St. Louis, Mo. Mr. Whitaker died in St. Louis, Feb. 20, 1931. They had one child, a daughter, Dorothy, who married October 10, 1928, Arthur Raymond Holden of Milton, Mass. They have one child, Betty Jean Holden, born Oct. 10th, 1930, in Kansas City, Mo. In 1941 they are living in Manchester, N. Hampshire, at 321 N. River Road.

RANDOLPH — SHELTON

ILLIAM (1) RANDOLPH of Turkey Island was born in Yorkshire, England, in 1651 and came to Virginia in 1674. He was a member of the House of Burgesses and of the King's Council; in 1680, he married Mary, dau. of Henry Isham of Bermuda Hundred and his wife Katherine, maiden name (Banks) of Canterbury, Eng., who was the widow of Joseph Royal.

Wm. Randolph and Mary Isham had 7 sons and 2 daughters; the youngest child, Elizabeth Randolph, born in 1695, married Col. Richard Bland, son of Theodorick Bland (one of the first owners of Westover, and who is buried in the private graveyard there).

Elizabeth, dau. of Elizabeth Randolph and Richard Bland of "Blandfield" Essex Co., Va., married William Beverly who was born about 1698; he was the only son of Robert (2) Beverly and Ursula Byrd, dau. of Col. Wm. Byrd of "Westover". Ursula died at 16, leaving a son, William Beverly, who died about 1766, and "Blandfield" reverted to Robert (3) Beverly, who married Maria, dau. of Col. Landon Carter of "Sabine Hall".

Robert (2) Beverly was born about 1675 and spent most of his life on his beautiful estate in King and Queen Co., Va. He was a Burgess for many years and was one of the "Knights of the Golden Horseshoe". The first Robert Beverly, came from "Beverly", Eng., about 1663, and took up land in Middlesex Co., Va. Nothing seems to be known about his first wife, except her name, *Mary;* his 2nd wife,

Katherine, whom he married March 28, 1679, was either the daughter or widow of Theophilus Hone, of James City Co., Va. On the death of Robert (1) Beverly in 1687, his estate of more than 35,000 pounds and containing more than 5,000 acres, was divided among his children. Robert (2) was the son of the 1st wife, *Mary*. It was Wm. Beverly who named the estate in Essex "Blandfield" in honor of his wife, Elizabeth, dau. of Col. Richard Bland and Elizabeth Randolph, his wife. Wm. was born about 1698. Mary Bland, daughter of Col. Richard Bland and Elizabeth Randolph, married Col. Henry Lee of "Lee Hall", Westmoreland Co., Va.

Wm. (2) Randolph, eldest son of Wm. (1) and Mary Isham, was called "The Councillor." He married, at 25, Elizabeth Beverly, dau. of Peter Beverly and Elizabeth Peyton. Wm. (2) was born in Nov. 1681 and died Oct. 19, 1741. He was married to Elizabeth in 1705.

The third Col. Wm. Randolph was known as "Col. Wm. of Wilton". He married Anne, dau. of Benjamin Harrison and his wife, Anne Carter. They had 5 children; their son, Peyton Randolph, married Lucy Harrison, dau. of Gov. Benjamin Harrison (called "The Signer") and his wife Elizabeth Bassett.

Their son, another *Peyton Randolph*, married Helen Mc-Cauley Southall, and their daughter Anne Burritt Randolph was the first wife of Col. John *Shelton*, (4) of "Rural Plains", Hanover Co., Va. This Col. John was the youngest son of Capt. John Shelton (killed on Sept. 11, 1777 at the Battle of Brandywine) and his wife, Eleanor Parks, daughter of Wm. Parks, the editor. The title *Col.* seems to have been an honorary one; he is listed as Capt. John, in the Revolution, but may have been made Colonel later.

TENNESSEE SHELTONS

HERE are many branches of the Virginia Sheltons that came down through the Tennessee line besides those already mentioned. Many of the descendants of Peter[1] Shelton and his wife Susannah Jackson were early settlers in Eastern Tennessee. A Shelton was one of the most prominent settlers of McNary County.

The first settlement in Claiborne County was at Big Spring near Sycamore Creek in 1794-95. This was near the Clinch River.

Grainger County, on the opposite side of the Clinch River from Claiborne County, was created by the first legislature of Tennessee, April 22, 1796. It was formed from the Hawkins and Knox settlements which date from 1784. Many of the first settlers in this region were Scots who located here after the Revolution. It was not uncommon for these pioneers to marry Indian wives and become incorporated into the Cherokee Nation.

Crispen Eliphas Shelton is mentioned in the Annals of Tennessee as one of the early settlers in Hamilton County,

(1) Peter Shelton of Christ Church, Middlesex Co., Va.; was *apparently* the son of Ralph Shelton, son of the first "James Shelton Gentleman" of the early Virginia Colony and later of Bermuda. This Ralph appears in Bermuda records and in some Va. records, but I cannot find any place he lived in Virginia. As Peter's is the only line in which the name *Ralph* was carried down for 200 years and as the Church records state that "All of these Sheltons are one family," it is the conclusion of the author that Peter was a son of Ralph, and a gr-son of James (1) and his wife Ann of Virginia and Bermuda. Peter was born in 1664; married in 1684; died 1718 or 1719.

taken out of Rhea County, and previously he was a resident of Grainger County.

Another pioneer in East Tennessee was Azariah Shelton, son of Ralph Shelton of Henry County, Virginia. According to the book, "Records of Rhea," by the late T. J. Campbell, Azariah Shelton migrated to Grainger County, Tennessee, "in the early Indian days," and later settled in Rhea County. He had sons Ralph, David, Hezekiah and Azariah, the last three all being physicians. The son Azariah was author of a book on medicine.

Ralph Shelton, son of Azariah the elder, remained in Grainger and Claiborne Counties, and established his home on a large farm in Claiborne County, on the Clinch River near the point known as Shelton's Ford. On the opposite side of the river, in Grainger County, is Shelton Bluff, named for Ralph Shelton. This farm is now flooded by Norris Dam Lake, but the hill on which was the family cemetery is above the water line. Great-grandsons of this Ralph Shelton are Samuel Jones Shelton of the editorial staff of the St. Louis, Mo., Post-Dispatch; Frederick DeWitt Shelton, writer and lawyer of Washington, D. C.; and Burleigh Dwight Shelton of Marshfield, Mo.

Peter Shelton was born in Bermuda or Virginia, in 1664, and on March 2, 1684, married Susannah Jackson. They were living in Middlesex County, Virginia, in 1685. They had two sons, Ralph and Peter, and a daughter, Susannah.

Ralph Shelton, son of Peter and Susannah, was born in Middlesex County in 1685 and died in 1733. He married Mary Crispen about 1706. After the death of Ralph Shelton, Mary married William Clark of Amelia County, Virginia. Her will is dated 1750 and was proved in Pittsylvania County, Virginia, in 1770.

Peter Shelton, the second child of Peter and Susannah, was born November 15, 1687. In May, 1708, he married Elizabeth Downing. Both Peter, Senior, and Peter, Junior, died within a year of each other, but the Christ Church Register of Middlesex County, Virginia, does not indicate which died first. One died December 17, 1717, and the other October 1, 1718.

Susannah Shelton, the third child of Peter and Susannah, was born in 1689. She married Thomas Meriwether, son of Nicholas Meriwether (born in Wales in 1631 — died in Virginia in 1678) and Elizabeth Wodehouse, daughter of Henry Wodehouse of Lower Norfolk, Virginia, and granddaughter of Sir Henry Wodehouse of "Waxham", Norfolk, England, and his wife Ann, daughter of Sir Nicholas Bacon. Thomas Meriwether died in 1708, making Ralph Shelton, brother of Susannah, his heir (Essex County, Virginia, Records). The infant daughter of Thomas and Susannah Meriwether, Susannah, married John Armistead of "Hesse", Gloucester County, Virginia.

Susannah Jackson Shelton, wife of Peter Shelton, Sr., must have died at the time of, or soon after, the birth of her daughter Susannah in 1689. Peter Shelton's second wife was Abigail ———, and her children were: Henry, baptized September 20, 1691; Thomas, baptized September 20, 1693; and Zebulon, baptized August 4, 1700. After the death of Peter Shelton (presumably the Peter who died first, December 17, 1717) his widow married Robert Holderness on February 11, 1719. Zebulon Shelton married Mary Goar, February 20, 1720. The birth of two of their children is recorded in the Christ Church Register—Sarah, baptized October 15, 1721, and Abby (Abigail), baptized February 9, 1723.

The eldest son of Ralph Shelton and Mary Crispen was Thomas, born 1707, and died March 24, 1742. He married Mary Probert, January 4, 1730. They had a son Reuben, baptized June 10, 1733; a son Thomas, baptized May 2, 1740; and a daughter Mary, baptized February 21, 1737-38.

The second son of Ralph Shelton and Mary Crispen was Ralph Shelton, born in 1709, who died in Henry County, Virginia, where his will was proved March 30, 1789. His first wife was Mary Daniel whom he married June 10, 1731. He lived in Amelia County, Virginia, for many years, and sold his land there and moved to Henry County in 1763. I have found no record of the death of his first wife, Mary Daniel, but "wife Susannah" is mentioned in a deed shortly before his death, and in his will he names "my four last children, Easop, Abigail, Mary and Liberty Shelton," to share equally in his estate with his elder children. Other children named in his will are his sons Ralph, Palitiah, Eliphas, James, Hezekiah, Jeremiah, Azariah (moved to Tennessee), Roger, and a son John whom he cut off with a bequest of 25 pounds so that he could not claim kinship; the daughters named are Katherine Rutherford, Sarah Robertson, Elizabeth Arnold, Rina McGhee and Susannah Jones.

Azariah Shelton, son of Ralph Shelton of Henry County, Virginia, married Sarah Holt. It probably was in the 1890's that he migrated to East Tennessee. His son Ralph, probably his eldest, is recorded in the Census of 1850 as having been born in Virginia, and since he was listed as "age, 63" he would have been born about 1786 or 1787.

Ralph Shelton, son of Azariah and Sarah, who lived on the Shelton farm at Shelton's Ford on the Clinch River in Claiborne County, Tennessee, was married twice. His first wife was a Bunch and is thought to have been a daughter of Martin Bunch who was one of the signers of a petition in Henry County, Virginia, April 22, 1794. By her he had Jincie, Susan, Annie and Sallie.

Ralph Shelton's second wife was Ann Taylor (born in 1809 in Tennessee), a sister of Joel Taylor. Their children were: Ralph, Louisa (married a Hurst), Letie (married a Watson), Mary A. (married a Greer), Elizabeth (married Joel Dotson), Mark (married Ollie Quail), Anderson (married Mary Hurst), Penelope who married Robert Beeler and moved to Neosho, Missouri, and Malinda. In the Census of 1850 there are also listed in the household of Ralph Shelton young children who probably are his grand-children —Jasper Shelton, Houston Shelton, Edmond Shelton, Chrisly Shelton (evidently Crispen), all boys, and Thury (spelling indistinct) and Louisa, girls. Annie, a daughter of Ralph by his first wife, married a Carroll and moved to Indian Territory. Their daughter, Martha, married James Randolph; and their daughter, Laura Ann, is said to have married Jackson Barnett, the millionaire Indian who figured in much litigation.

Ralph Shelton, son of Ralph and Ann Taylor Shelton, was born in Claiborne County, Tennessee, August 23, 1829. On May 22, 1851, he married Frances Cheatham (or Chitham) Owen, born March 25, 1827, daughter of Job F. Owen and Franky Cheatham (Chitham) who "came from North Carolina." Ralph and his wife Frances made their home in Lauderdale County, Alabama, on a farm on the banks of the Tennessee River, near the town of Waterloo, Alabama. Ralph was a boatman on the Tennessee River steamboats. He died August 29, 1862, and his wife Frances died August 9, 1889.

Children of Ralph Shelton and Frances Cheatham (Chitham) Owen, all born in Lauderdale County, Alabama, were Frances Jane, William Hezekiah, Samuel Azariah, David Jefferson, and Lucinda Ann. Ralph's widow Frances and her five children moved to Webster County, Missouri, in 1869. These children were:

Frances Jane Shelton, born April 8, 1852, who married Abner Hargus.

William Hezekiah Shelton, born August 27, 1854, who married Sarah King, and had Roxie, Lillian, Pearl, and William, who died as a young man, unmarried.

David Jefferson Shelton, born September 23, 1860, died as a young man, unmarried.

Lucinda Ann Shelton, born March 6, 1863, married Oscar Craig, and their only child was Frances.

Samuel Azariah Shelton, born September 3, 1858, now (1941) lives in Marshfield, Missouri, where at the age of 82 he still maintains his law office and takes an active interest in local and public affairs. On October 30, 1881, in Webster County, Missouri, he married Jincie Napier who was born March 2, 1862 in Ozark County, Missouri, and died January 12, 1938. She was the daughter of Cyrus Napier and Nancy K. Bennett Napier, and was the great-great-great-great granddaughter of Dr. Patrick Napier who came to Gloucester County, Virginia, in 1655, and married Elizabeth Booth. Samuel A. Shelton grew up on a farm, became a school teacher, and later a lawyer. At various times he served as Clerk of the Circuit Court, Prosecuting Attorney, and Postmaster at Marshfield. He served as member of the U. S. House of Representatives, 1921-1923, but refused to stand for re-election.

Children of Samuel Azariah Shelton and Jincie Napier Shelton, all born in Webster County, Missouri, are Ashford Mark, Michael David, Ada Belle, Samuel Jones, Frances Maude, Frederick DeWitt, Ethel and Burleigh Dwight. Both Ashford Mark and Michael David died during childhood.

Ada Belle Shelton was born February 24, 1887. She married John C. Ketcham of Hastings, Michigan, in 1924, and was his second wife. Mr. Ketcham was a member of the U. S. House of Representatives for 12 years. They have one daughter, Mary Shelton Ketcham, born August 3, 1925.

Samuel Jones Shelton was born October 2, 1889. On September 20, 1916, he married Edith Clay Case, of Springfield, Mo. Their two children are Cloy Catherine Shelton, born October 9, 1918, and Samuel James Shelton, born March 8, 1925. Samuel Jones Shelton graduated from Colorado College, Colorado Springs, Colorado, in 1912, and soon afterwards joined the staff of the St. Louis, Mo., Post-Dispatch. In the World War, although exempt from service as a married man he volunteered and served ten months in France as a member of the Tank Corps. His daughter Cloy was born while he was in France. From 1922 to 1927 he was editor of Motor Age, weekly national magazine of the automobile industry, in Chicago. Since then he has been on the editorial staff of the St. Louis Post-Dispatch. His home is at 232 Hawthorne Ave., Webster Groves, Missouri.

Frances Maude Shelton was born June 24, 1891, and married Elijah S. Warden in 1911. They live in Raytown, Missouri, and have two children, William Samuel Warden, born in 1914, a lawyer, and Kathleen Warden Muir, born in 1916.

Frederick DeWitt Shelton was born September 11, 1894. He married Charline McCanse, daughter of Charles A. McCanse and Virginia Ann Hopper McCanse of Mount Vernon, Missouri, the wedding taking place in Philadelphia, Pa., June 14, 1930. They have one son, Napier Shelton, born December 2, 1931. Their home is at 4411 Hadfield Lane, N. W., Washington, D. C. Frederick DeWitt Shelton is a writer and lawyer. He graduated from Drury College, Springfield, Missouri, in 1916, and later studied at Columbia University, Georgetown University, Brookings Graduate School, and George Washington University Law School. Rejected for combat service in the World War because of a lame foot he volunteered for non-combat service and served until January 15, 1919 at Camp Joseph E. Johnston. After about two years working as field secretary for the American City Bureau of New York, he joined the staff of the Chamber of Commerce of the United States, Washington, D. C., where he was employed for eleven years. He then became associated with W. M. Kiplinger in the publication of the Kiplinger Washington Letter, a business in which he is still interested. In 1935 he and Mr. Kiplinger wrote a book, "Inflation Ahead," more than 75,000 copies of which were sold within a few weeks after publication.

Ethel Shelton 7th child of Samuel Azariah Shelton, and Jincie Napier, was born June 28, 1898, and married George A. Childress who is now County Collector of Webster County, Missouri. Their home is in Marshfield, Mo. They have a son, Robert Lucas Childress, born in 1923, and a daughter, Nancy Kay Childress, born in 1930.

Burleigh Dwight Shelton, youngest of Samuel's children, was born August 11, 1900. He graduated from Drury College in 1922, and while there served in the Student Army Training Corps. He was in the hotel business at Joplin, Missouri, for several years, and is now in business at Marshfield, Missouri. He and his wife Lois Frank, whom he married December 5, 1935, have twin adopted daughters, Lucinda Lou and Linda Lois.

DESCENDANTS OF JAMES SHELTON
Born in Christ Church Parish, Middlesex Co., Va., in 1726

NOTHER Tennessee branch of the Shelton family whose descendants came to Missouri was that of James Shelton, the brother of Ralph who married Mary Daniel. The children of Ralph and Mary Crispen (later Mrs. Wm. Clark of Amelia and Pittsylvania Counties, Va.) were: Thomas (1) born in 1707, married Mary Probert 1-14-1730, d. 3-24-1742; Ralph (2) born 1709, married 1731, d. 1786/87; Elizabeth (3), born 1711, married Wm. Davis Oct. 9, 1728; Crispen (4) born 1713, married Letitia Shelton. Crispen d. 10-29-1787. They had a son, Wm. Shelton, born in 1735.

Reuben (5) born 1715, d. Oct. 8, 1715; Catherine (6) born 1719, married a Blakey; her daughter Patience Catesby Blakey is mentioned in her gr-mother's will. Reuben, son of Thomas (1) is also mentioned in this will; John (7) born 1722; Benjamin (8) born 1724 (wife's name Mary), and *James*, b. 1726.

Thomas (1) Shelton and Mary Probert had Reuben, b. 1733; Mary, b. 1737, d. 1742); Thomas, b. 1740, and Micajah, b. 1742.

The wife of *James* Shelton, b. 1726, was *Jincie* according to Mrs. Catherine Moser, a descendant of this James; whether James was married more than once she did not know, but the wife *she* knew of was *Jincie*. Mrs. Moser said James had 13 sons and gave me the names of 12 of these: Thomas (1), James (2), Joseph (3), John (4), Mark (5), Anderson (6), Frederick (7), Jarrett (or Garrett) (8),

Porter (9), George (10), William (11), and David (12). She did not know the order of their births; I give the names as she gave them to me, she thought there was a Rawleigh.

David (12) was the founder of the "Shelton Laurel" branch of the family in the North Carolina mountains. Thomas Shelton (1) was born in Virginia about 1745 and died in Jefferson County, Tennessee. His will is dated 1/4/1807. His wife's name was Sapphira. Thomas had a son James, who married Nancy Clark, August 1, 1796 and a son Thomas Boggs Shelton, b. in 1775 in Virginia. He married (1) February 13, 1802, Susannah Inman and his second wife was Betsy McCain.

James, brother of Thomas (1) married and had a son, Thomas Coot Shelton, who married 7-13-1813, Rebecca Daniel. Both of these men are said to have been named after English Generals under whom their father had served in the Colonial Armies, "Boggs" and "Coot".

Thomas and Sapphira had a daughter who married John Inman and a daughter who married George Larve; all of these are mentioned in the will of Thomas, 1807.

Joseph (3) married Minerva Scruggs, and had Catherine, who married Wm. Moser and John Love Shelton who married Mary Eliza Eckel.

Mrs. Moser stated that Joseph died when his son John was only 12 years old. John Love Shelton and Mary Eliza Eckel had Joseph who married a Miss Sutton, Sam Porter who married Isabel Starnes, and is in business in Knoxville, Tenn. Love Ernest, who married Frank H. Taylor, Jane Evelyn who married Alfred H. Taylor, brother of Frank, and Deeta Katherine, who married R. H. Miller.

The will of James Shelton (called Chilton) son of Thos.

(1) and husband of Nancy Clark is filed in Madison Co., Mo., 12/26/1829, Will Bk. A, p. 25. He names "widow Nancy, execrs. Francis, Raleigh and Jesse Chilton, sons"; other children named are John, William, Thomas and Jarrett, daughters Mary, wife of Elijah O'Bannon, Lucinda, wife of Richard Britten, Susan, wife of Eleazor Green Clay and Nancy, wife of Joseph B. Stone. In the partition Sale Bk. G., pp. 358, March 10, 1855, all of the above are named as *proven* heirs.

Susan Shelton, born in Madison Co., Mo., in 1824, married Eleazor Green Clay Nov. 9, 1841 and died in Wayne Co., Ill., in 1870. Her husband Eleazor was born in Grainger Co., Tenn., in 1818, and died in Dallas, Texas, in 1869 (rec. from the bible of his father, Eleazor Clay).

Lucinda Clay, d. of Susan and Eleazor, was born Jan. 2, 1844, and died May 10, 1921; she married Peter Hanger Lewis in Iron Co., Mo., in 1861; he was born in Iron Co., Mo., in 1838 and died Dec. 11, 1896; both he and his wife died in Columbia Co., Ark.

Kate Lewis, daughter of Lucinda Clay and Peter Hanger Lewis, was born Dec. 9, 1881, and married Wm. H. Arnold, Feb. 3, 1903; they live at 503 Hickory St., Texarkana, *Ark.*, and have one son Richard Lewis Arnold who was born Dec. 30, 1906 and married, in Washington, D. C., Jane Sheppard, d. of Senator Sheppard, on June 9, 1934. They have a son, born March 26, 1936, Richard Sheppard Arnold, and live at 2001 Laurel St., Texarkana, Texas.

Raleigh Chilton, son of James and Nancy Clark Chilton, died Dec. 28, 1864, adm. Jan. 20, 1865; he names his heirs as:

Heirs of John Chilton of Mo. and Ark.

Heirs of Mary O'Bannon, part in Mo.

Heirs of Francis Chilton, part in Mo.

Heirs of William Chilton in Kansas.

Heirs of Thomas Chilton in Ill., Mo., and Calif.

Heirs of Nancy Stone in Mo.

Heirs of Jarrett Chilton in Mo.

Heirs of Susan Clay in Ill.

Heirs of Lucinda Britten in Mo.

Marriage Records in Madison Co., Mo., Bk. A, p. 37.

Aug. 2, 1838, Lindsay *Shelton* and Richard Britten (dau. of James *Chilton*), all of this county. Book A, p. 73.

Nov. 9, 1841, Jesse N. Pollard, Methodist Minister, married Susan *Shelton* of Madison Co., Mo., to Eleazor Green Clay of St. Francois Co., Mo. Recorded Dec. 23, 1841.

A sister of Mrs. Arnold is Mrs. Ella Lewis King, who was born in 1865 on Sept. 23 in Wayne Co., Ill.

James Shelton, his brother Thomas Boggs Shelton and their 1st cousin Thomas Coot Shelton all came to Mo. from Rhea and Jefferson Counties, Tenn., in the early 1800's. The mother of James and Thos. Boggs, Sapphira, was said to have been one-fourth of Indian blood.

Thos. Boggs Shelton and his 1st wife Susannah Inman had 10 children:

Clementine, b. 1803	= Zimri Elly Carter — had 15 children
Mark, b. 1804	= Betsy Carter, sister of Zimri —had 2 children
John, b. 1805	= 1st Letitia Carter — had 4 children
	= 2nd Sophia Chilton (a cousin) —had 10 children
Chas. Truman, b. 1807	= Nancy Kelley—4 children

Shadrack, b. 1809   = Patsy Harrison—6 children

William, b. 1811   = Eliza Allen—6 children

James, b. 1813   = Miss Alley and moved to Waco, Texas

Thomas Jefferson, b. 1815 = 1st Martha Watkins in Tenn.
          = 2nd Mary Josephine Chilton (cousin)—12 children

Joshua, b. 1817   = Elizabeth Chilton, 2nd cousin —8 children

Frank, b. 1819   = Abt. 1845 Mrs. Margaret Fancher Stearsman and had 5 children

Thomas Boggs Shelton married his 2nd wife about 1835; by her, Betsy McCain, he had 3 children: Andrew Jackson Shelton who married Emeline Nesbit and had 4 children. Susan who married William Hawkins of Shannon Co., Mo., and Mathias or Mathew of whom I have no data. Mrs. Hawkins lived on what is known as "The Barnes Farm" near Freemont, Mo.; her father Thos. Boggs Shelton died there, in 1862.

Thomas Coot Chilton, born in Tenn. in 1790, son of James *Shelton* who served in the Colonial Army under Gen. Coot and named his son for him, was married in Dandridge, Jeff. Co., Tenn., Sept. 3, 1813, to Rebecca Daniel. In the marriage bond the name is spelled *Shelton,* they had 11 children:

Iby, b. 1815   = Saml. Davis in Shannon Co., Mo.—2 children

Mary Josephine, b. 1817 = Thos. J. Chilton, son of Thos. Boggs Chilton—12 children

Sophia, b. Aug. 20, 1820 = in 1841 John Chilton, son of Thos. Boggs Chilton — 10 children

Betsy, b. 1828 = Joshua Chilton, son of Thos. Boggs Chilton—8 children

Ann, b. 1822 = John B. Wood, no issue

Malvina, b. 1838 = d. s. p.

Louise, b. abt. 1840 = Benjamin Sinclair, abt. 1860— 2 children

John = a Miss Sinclair in Shannon Co., Mo., and moved to Phelps, Co., Mo.

James Coot = Charlse Hudleston, abt. 1856— 4 children

Thos. Coot = a Miss Sugg, abt. 1850 — 5 children

Joshua = d. s. p.

The family state that Thos. Coot Shelton moved to Shannon Co., Mo., from Knox Co., Tenn., about 1836; Dr. Thos. Reed came with him. Both settled on the Current River; Chilton's farm is 2 miles below the junction of Jack's Fork, and the Reed farm is 6 miles below the Chilton's in Shannon Co., Mo.

Dr. Reed's wife was a daughter of a Truman Chilton. Truman's wife was Betsy Inman, a sister of Susannah, wife of Thos. Boggs Chilton. Betsy did not come to Mo. with her husband and he was thrown from his horse and killed shortly after he arrived. This Truman was thought to be a brother of Thos. Coot Chilton. A sister Patsy = Truman Douglas in Rhea Co., Tenn., about 1800 and moved to Carter Co., Mo.; they had Samuel, Joseph, Thomas Truman and 1 dau. Minerva. Another sister Sophia = George

Larne or Larve in Rhea Co., or Knox Co., Tenn., abt.
1805-06. She moved to Shannon Co., Mo., after the death of
her husband, but a few years later moved back to Tenn.;
she had a son George.

I think the family have this Sophia mixed up. I feel sure
that she was a daughter of the Thomas whose will is filed
in Jefferson Co., Tenn., 1/4/1807, and in which is mentioned
his son-in-law, Geo. Larve. It is hard to read the name on
any of these old records; it could be *Lowe,* Larue, Larve or
even Love; there are many of the last name in these Tenn.
Counties.

The marriage bonds of Margaret Love and Hezekiah
Shelton, Apr. 17, 1828, and of David *Shelton* and Elizabeth
Witt, Sept. 5, 1822, are at Dayton, Rhea Co., Tenn. These
were both doctors and sons of Azariah—son of Ralph Shelton, who died in Henry Co., Va., 1786/87.

Samuel Shelton of Franklin Co., Mo., attorney, and David
Shelton of Gasconade Co., Mo., were sons of William Shel-
ton of Grainger Co., Tenn. The land of William was on the
Clinch River. Granger Co. Rec. Oct. 15, 1828.

St. Louis, Missouri,
August 31, 1940

To Whom It May Concern:

This is to state that I (Mrs.) Mildred C. Whitaker, for
the past twenty-five years historian of the Shelton-Chilton
family, interviewed on Saturday, April 20, 1940, in Jefferson County, Tennessee, Mrs. Catherine Moser, aged 86. Mrs.
Moser gave me the following data on her line of this family:

That she is the daughter of Joseph Shelton, given later in
their records as "Chilton" and Minerva Scruggs; that
Joseph was the son of James and Jincie Shelton from Vir-

ginia. She could not state whether Jincie was the first or a later wife of James Shelton. She also stated that James had thirteen sons, one of whom was Thomas, whose wife was Sapphira and whose will is filed in Jefferson County, Tennessee, in 1806; *that* James Shelton was the son of Ralph Shelton and Mary Crispen. Mrs. Moser could not give dates of births, marriages or deaths but she was very clear in her statement of facts.

The birth of said James Shelton is registered in Christ Church Parish, Middlesex County, Virginia, in 1726; his father Ralph in 1685, was married in the same parish to Mary Crispen and Ralph died in 1733. His widow, Mary Crispen Shelton, married William Clark of Amelia County, Virginia, and her will is dated June 30, 1750; she died in 1765 and her will was proved August 20, 1770. Her son James is named with her other children.

The Christ Church records state that Ralph Shelton and the Sheltons of "Carotoman" Lancaster County, Virginia, "Currioman" Westmoreland County, Virginia, and "Rural Plains" Hanover County, Virginia, were "all of one family." There were no other Shelton, Chilton, Skelton, Sheldon or Charlton families in America in the early 1600's or the 1700's.

The various spellings of the name has caused endless confusion and so many of the records in Virginia have been lost or burned or otherwise destroyed that it is utterly impossible to get all dates of births, marriages or deaths.

The record, however, is a continuous one, so I am making this statement after working on the family history for over twenty-five years, to assist those who wish to join Colonial Societies on this line and are unable to get the necessary data.

The Ralph Shelton born in Middlesex County, Virginia, in 1685 was the son of Peter Shelton, born 1664 and his wife, Susannah Jackson. Peter was a grandson of the "James Shelton gentleman" who came to Virginia in the Second London Company in 1609 with his cousin, Lord Delaware. This James Shelton was a member of the First and Second Court of Virginia and moved to Bermuda about 1630; he was the son of Sir Ralph Shelton and his first wife, Jane West, daughter of the First Lord Delaware. This Sir Ralph Shelton was killed at the Isle de Rhe in 1628. The Thomas Shelton who died in Tennessee in 1806 had a son James, who married Nancy Clark and came to Missouri in the early 1800's. His will is filed in Madison County, Missouri, in 1829.

(MRS.) MILDRED C. WHITAKER

State of Missouri
City of St. Louis
Subscribed and sworn to before me this 31st day of August, 1940.

Perry Topping, Jr., Notary Public.
My commission expires March 21, 1941.

IN GRAINGER CO., TENN., ARE THE FOLLOWING MARRIAGE BONDS

Ralph Shelton ⎫ Jan. 9, 1828,
Ann Taylor ⎭ Benj. Lewis, Minister
Rebecca Shelton ⎫ March 27, 1838
Wm. Vittito ⎭
James Helton ⎫ June 2, 1838 (I think this is meant for
Sally Boatman ⎭ *Shelton*)
David Helton ⎫ Aug. 19, 1938 (I think this is meant for
Jane Jones ⎭ *Shelton*)

Eliz. Shelton
Peter Sampsel } Jan. 15, 1839

Jacob Shelton
Martha Box or Bok or Bon } May 11, 1839

Frederick Shelton
Arena C. Jones } Feb. 23, 1845

Mary A. Shelton
Henry Greer } Aug. 2, 1850

Fred Shelton
Kath. Easley } Dec. 27, 1850

Jacob Shelton
C. Shelton } March 13, 1852

David Shelton
Marg. I. Dennis } March 25, 1852

Eli. Shelton
Sarah Lovell } Nov. 27, 1854

Peter Messer
Sarah Shelton } June 7, 1855

Emily Virginia Shelton
John Wesley Bulling } May 24, 1857

Mark Shelton
Jestin Adkins } Aug. 27, 1857

George A. Shelton
Sarah Easterly } Sept. 16, 1857

SLAYDEN, DICKSON CO., TENN., SHELTONS

From Family Bible Records and County Court Records, Clerk's Office, Pittsylvania Co., Va.

ILL of Thomas Shelton (father of William, who died in 1827) b. 1723, married about 1741. Will signed June 1, 1808, recorded July 18, 1808.

Legatees

Wife—Jane (called Jennie, *probably Bennett*).

Niece—Betsy, dau. of nephew, Charles, dec'd.

Son—William, who married Ann Lomax.

Son—Thomas, b. 1742, d. 1846, married 1st in 1762 Jane *Clopton* (b. 1744), 2nd Cousins, 3rd a *Crump;* Thomas is said to have lived to be 103.

Son—Bennett, married and had a daughter who married a Henderson and had a son Bennett Henderson.

Son—James, married Susannah Wall, abt. 1800.

Dau.—Nancy Slayden, b. 1761, living in Pitts Co. in 1839, aged 78.

Dau.—Lucy Slayden.

Dau.—Sally Johnson, wife of William Johnson, executors sons, Thomas and William.

Will Book 1-134—Nov. 19, 1827—Will of William (son of Thomas) Shelton; d. Aug. 4, 1827.

Legatees

Wife—Ann (Lomax, married Feb. 12, 1779. Ann was born in 1757 in Charles Co., Maryland, and died in Pitts Co., Va., in 1842).

Son—Thomas, b. 1780 (moved to Missouri).

Son—Robert.

Son—John.

Son—Bennett (b. Jan. 3, 1784, married first a Miss Cloud and moved to North Carolina; children: Andrew Jackson, Nancy and Martha. 2nd wife Sarah Hill, married Feb. 1, 1819; one child Lydia. Andrew Jackson Shelton was born May 6, 1816, d. Feb. 13, 1899 in Erie, Tenn.; married 1/17/1841 Rachel Cassady, who was born 1/5/1820. Their son Joseph Robert Shelton was born Nov. 15, 1851 in Erie, Tenn., d 4/22/1893 in Rockwood, Texas. Jos. Robt. was married in Lorena, Texas, on Dec. 27, 1880 to Betty Jane Brusenhen, who was born on Dec. 8, 1860 in Rienze, Miss. A daughter of this union, Miss Annie Shelton, is living in Brownwood, Texas, in 1941).

Son—Noah.

Dau.—Sarah Shelton.

Dau.—Elizabeth Shelton.

Dau.—Nancy Williams

Dau.—Martha Yeaman.

REPORT OF VETERANS ADMINISTRATION, WASHINGTON, D. C.

William Shelton (or Chelton), resident of Pittsylvania County, Virginia, enlisted April 1776 and served three months as a private in Captain John Donelson's Virginia Company and went out against the Indians on New and Holston Rivers. He enlisted May 1, 1781 and served as a private in Captain Henry Burnett's Virginia Company and was discharged August 4, 1781.

He died August 4, 1827, in Pittsylvania County, Virginia.

The soldier married February 12, 1779, at the house of Thomas Shelton, Ann Lomax.

The soldier's widow, Ann, was allowed a pension on her application executed October 2, 1838, while a resident of Pittsylvania County, Virginia, aged 81 years.

In 1839 the soldier's sister, Nancy Slayden, was aged 78 years and resided in Pittsylvania County, Virginia.

The names of the following children of William and Ann Shelton are shown:

John Shelton.
Thomas Shelton.
Bennett Shelton, born January 3, 1784.
Noah Shelton, born August 3, 1787.
Sarah Shelton, born November 30, 1789.
Robert Shelton, born October 4, 1792.
Ann Shelton, born October 18, 1794. (Probably Nancy who married a Williams.)
Elizabeth Shelton, born February 1, 1797.
Martha Shelton, born April 7, 1799. (Married a Yeaman.)

GENERAL ACCOUNTING OFFICE, WASHINGTON, D. C.

The last payment made to Ann Shelton, pensioner of the Revolutionary War, Virginia Agency, and widow of William Shelton, was made to her attorney December 7, 1841. On November 2, 1841, the pensioner certified that she had resided in the County of Pittsylvania, State of Virginia, for a period of seventy years and prior thereto she resided in Charles County, Maryland.

PITTSYLVANIA COUNTY, VIRGINIA, CLERK'S OFFICE

Bennett Shelton made a deed of trust of his personal

property, August 8, 1821, to Alexander Carter for Bruce and Hagood, of Halifax County.

MARRIAGE REGISTER

February 1, 1819, Bennett Shelton-Sarah Hill

Sec.—William Shelton

Father—Joseph Hill

OATH OF ALLEGIANCE

Males sixteen years of age and over.

Subscribed and sworn to before George Carter,

4th day of October, 1777

Thomas Chelton, William Chelton, Charles Chelton.

SLAYDEN GRAVEYARD, 2 MILES ON BARTON'S CREEK (TENN.)

Three graves, enclosed with heavy stones and three tombstones.

Arrena Slayden, born Dec. 19, 1822; died May 29, 1841; age 19-5-10.

Rhoda Shelton, wife of Wm. E. Slayden, born Aug. 22, 1788; died Sept. 27, 1853, age 61-1-5.

William E. Slayden, born May 16, 1789; died Jan. 29, 1861; age 71.

SHELTON GRAVEYARD, NEAR SLAYDEN, DICKSON COUNTY (TENN.)

John H. Shelton, Mar. 14, 1817; Dec. 21, 1853 (mar. Sophia Patterson).

Richard, son of F. and W. F. Shelton, Sept. 28, 1854; Sept. 14, 1855.

John J. Shelton, son of J. W. and M. J. Shelton, Sept. 11, 1855; Feb. 3, 1856.

James M. Shelton, Nov. 13, 1851; Feb. 27, 1856, son of J. W. and M. J. Shelton.

Emma J. Shelton, dau. of J. W. and M. J. Shelton, May 18, 1853; Feb. 23, 1856.

William Shelton, Aug. 10, 1767; Dec. 4, 1857.

Priscilla, wife of Wm. Shelton, June 6, 1779; June 24, 1850.

Mary A. Shelton, dau. of W. & P. Shelton, Jan. 18, 1801; June 25, 1848.

Colmon J. P. Shelton, Dec. 23, 1845; May 3, 1888. Masonic emblem on stone. Two graves with field stones at head and foot. Frank Shelton said these were the graves of Coleman Shelton and wife Dorcas Stone.

Mollie McCollom, wife of Colmon Shelton and dau. of Robt. J. McCollum.

Robert J. McCollum, Feb. 10, 1821; Jan. 10, 1904.

Mrs. Nancy Harvy, Sept. 27, 1827; July 17, 1895.

Mary L., consort of R. Murphey, died Aug. 6, 1842, in 22nd year of her age.

Susan Carroll, Dec. 22, 1835; Mar. 9, 1918.

Data found near Slayden

Martha Shelton mar. Joe Turner.

Julia Ann Shelton mar. Joseph Shelby Slayden, Mar. 8, 1839.

Liza Shelton mar. Talbot Slayden.

Nancy Shelton mar. Owen Edwards.

These are daus. of "Little" Billie Blue Shelton who mar. Patsey Paine. He is buried on Williamson Branch below Trinity Church. The Wm. Shelton called "Big" Billie Blue Shelton, was born in Virginia and came to Tennessee in the latter part of 1700 and married a

Miss Hamblen. They settled in the southern part of Dickson Co. (Slayden is in that Co.) Issue: Coleman, b. 1803; George W., b. 1809; Wm. M., b. 1807; John, b. 1817; James W., b. 1820; Albert G., Presbyterian minister, b. 1822; Marshall Ferriss, b. 1825, d. 1893, mar. 1853 Winnifred Fowler Pope who d. 1892. Issue: Richard, Robert, Elisha, Wm. Coleman, James W., Albert E., John Price, Geo. Marshall.

The William Shelton, b. Aug. 10, 1767, d. Dec. 4, 1857 (and Priscilla, his wife, b. June 6, 1779, d. June 24, 1840), was a son of Abraham Shelton and his wife Chloe Robertson. Abraham was a son of Crispen Shelton of Pittsylvania Co. who was a son of Ralph Shelton and Mary Crispen. Crispen was born in 1713 in Christ Church Parish, Middlesex Co., Va. The children of Abraham Shelton and Chloe Robertson who were married Jan. 16, 1760, were Lettice who married a White, Ann, dead by 1803 when her mother's will was proved; Jane who married John Stone, Abram, Crispen, who married Susannah Irby, William who married Priscilla Slayden, Dr. Tavenor C., Frederick, Meacon, dead by 1803, Robertson, a daughter who married a Field Payne and a daughter who married a Grasty.

Crispen Shelton, b. 2-28-1761, and Susannah Irby, b. Aug. 6, 1762, had issue: Chas. Irby who married an Ashley and moved to Georgia. He was in the war of 1812. Abram Cowper, b. 12-21-89, d. Sept. 1840, who married Mary Leigh Claiborne, daughter of Bathurst Claiborne; Chloe Robertson, b. Sept. 2, 1792, d. 1873, married in 1812, Thompson Robert. son; Ann, b. 1797, d. 8-11-1873; Meacon Ashley, b. 7-7-97, d. 8-11-1873, married 1st Ann Evans (1824), 2nd Anna Berger 6-3-1828, daughter of Jacob Berger of Pittsylvania Co., Va., and Martha Irby.

Abram Cowper Shelton and Mary Leigh Claiborne had:
Charles who married and d. s. p. Nathaniel d. s. p.
Wm. Claiborne, died aged 73, Peachy Gilmer who married
Susannah Catherine Shelton, (a cousin, daughter of Meacon
Ashley Shelton), and had 4 children, 2 of whom died in
infancy. Peachy Gilmer Shelton and Susannah Catherine
Shelton (b. Nov. 2, 1839, d. Oct. 8, 1912) had a daughter,
Willie Claiborne Shelton, b. Aug. 30, 1854 in Lincoln Co.,
Mo., who married May 9, 1875 Charles Martin of Troy, Mo.,
son of Judge Chas. Martin and his wife Mahala. Mrs.
Martin was living in Troy, Mo., in 1930.

Meacon Ashley Shelton and his family moved to Lincoln
Co., Mo., from Va. in 1844.

Jacob Berger's wife was Catherine Nowlin, daughter of
Bryan Ward Nowlin and Lucy Wade. Jacob and Catherine
were the parents of the 2nd wife of Meacon Ashley Shelton,
Anna Berger.

In the will of Crispen Shelton (b. 1713) brother of Ralph
(b. 1709) written Oct. 29, 1787, proved Feb. 17, 1794, in
Pittsylvania Co., Va., he names "wife" Lettice, sons Abraham, Gabriel, Lewis, Beverly, Spencer, Armistead, Vincent,
gr-son Crispen (son of Abraham), daughters Elizabeth
Hurt, Jane Todd (wife of Col. Todd—g-gr-f of Abraham
Lincoln), and Susannah Dickerson.

When proved in 1794 Beverly and Vincent Shelton were
the only surviving executors. Mrs. Levi Tyler of Louisville,
Ky., is a descendant of the above *Spencer* Shelton and his
wife Clara.

Corp. Thomas Shelton, b. 1742, d. 1846, son of Thomas,
b. 1723, d. 1808, married 1st Miss Clopton, 2nd Miss Cousins
and 3rd Miss Crump.

James Shelton,
his son,
Married
Susanna Wall
abt. 1800
and had

{
Nancy Bates Shelton, born June 26, 1801
  (Married Mr. Haymes)
Ursula Shelton, born Feb. 22, 1803
Jane Bennett Shelton, born Aug. 4, 1806
  (Married Byrd Shelton—2nd cousins)
Thomas Jefferson Shelton, born Jan. 11, 1809
  (Married Motley and lived in Pittsylvania Co.)
Elizabeth Shelton, born Sept. 5, 1811
Polly Shelton, born Dec. 10, 1815
Susannah Shelton, born April 13, 1816
  (Married Haymes)
James Byrd Shelton, born July 25, 1818
  (Married a Cardwell and lived in Pittsylvania Co.)
}

Thomas Jefferson
Shelton
Died May 15, 1896
Married
Sarah Elizabeth
Motley

{
James Samuel (Dead)

Susannah Wilmoth
  (Married John Bannister Anderson)

Thomas Wall (Norfolk, Va.)

Charles Fleming
}

Charles Shelton
Married
Miss Flippen
(Died in Tenn.)

{
Byrd
Gabriel
Charles
John
Irwin
2 Daughters
}

Byrd Shelton
Married
Jane Shelton
(See below)
(Second cousins)

{
Gerard Shelton
  (He had 12 living children)
}

Aurelius Blankenship
Married
Jane Shelton
(Died April 15, 1924,
aged 83)

{
Aurelia P. Blankenship
Charles A.
Ellen I. (Atkinson)
Lillie Bryce—Trevillian's mother
Young Henry
Mary Lillie (Lisk)
Howard (dead)
}

From History of Halifax County, by Carrington, Richmond, 1924:

P. 205 Daniel Shelton witnessed Thomas Howerton's Will, January 26, 1829.

P. 376 Patsy Shelton married James Crenshaw, March 4, 1797.

P. 391   Dorcas Shelton married David Hunter, March 15, 1767.

P. 392   Alice Shelton married Hezekiah Jackson, October 22, 1787.

P. 398   Ruth Shelton married Jessie Murphy, June 14, 1792.

P. 406   Mark Shelton married Nancy Dobson, 1794.

P. 409   Josiah Shelton married Fathey Ford, May 25, 1798.

P. 453   G. Gunter married Betsy Shelton, February 10, 1802.

P. 453   Jackson Guthrie married Mary Susanna Shelton (known as Polly) February 8, 1843.

P. 457   Edward Haymes married Nancy D. Shelton, January 5, 1825.

P. 477   William Norman married Eliza Shelton, October 18, 1832.

P. 493   Byrd Shelton married Jane B. Shelton, his second cousin, December 18, 1834.

P. 493   William Shelton married Mary Arnett, December 22, 1851.

MISCELLANEOUS OFFICIAL RECORDS OF SHELTONS
in Virginia, North Carolina and Tennessee

HE following are records which I have found and examined in various Court Houses and libraries in the states mentioned:

RECORDS OF ORIGINAL LAND PATENTS IN VIRGINIA GRANTED BY THE CROWN

Book 7—years 1679 to 1689:
William Shelton. 150 acres. Page 82.

Book 10—years 1710 to 1719:
William Skelton (Shelton). 150 acres, Page 39.

Book 11—years 1719 to 1724:
John Shelton. 1198 acres. Page 232.

Book 11—years 1719 to 1724:
James Shelton. Four grants of 1200, 400, 400, 400 acres respectively. Pages 338 and 339.

Book 12—years 1724 and 1725:
John Shelton. 400 acres. Page 245.
John Shelton. 600 acres. Page 378.

Book 13—years 1725 to 1730:
James Skelton. 1600 acres, 1600 acres, 750 acres, and 393 acres in four separate grants. Pages 14, 15, 434. (The handwriting of that time often made an "h" look like a "k" and thus copied records are apt to make a Skelton out of a Shelton. And sometimes it is hard to tell whether it is an "h" or a "k".)

Book 15—years from 1732 to 1735:
James Shelton. 393 acres. Page 290.

Book No. 22—years from 1743 to 1745:
Ralph Shelton. 400 acres. Page 561. Date of grant was September 20, 1745. This is the tract in Amelia County lying on the great Nottaway River.

Book No. 24—years from 1745 to 1746:
Joseph Shelton (or Skelton). 400 acres. Page 358.
Edward Shelton (or Skelton). 125 acres. Page 383.

Book No. 28—years from 1746 to 1749:
John Skelton (or Shelton). 335 acres. Page 1.
John Skelton (or Shelton). 150 acres. Page 2
Ralph Shelton. 400 acres. Page 592. June 20, 1749. This tract was in Lunenburgh County, on Ledbetters Creek.

Book No. 29—years from 1749 to 1751:
James Skelton (or Shelton). 10 acres. Page 178.

Book No. 33—years from 1756 to 1761:
John Shelton. Separate grants of 650, 1400, 940, 995, 150 and 1000 acres, respectively. Pages 196, 202, 210, 268, 269, 319.
William Shelton. 82 acres. Page 471.
Joseph Shelton. 98 acres. Page 502.
Benjamin Shelton. 119 acres. Page 550.

Book 34—years from 1756 to 1762:
Henry Shelton. 29 acres and 250 acres. Pages 201, 488.

Book 35—years from 1762 to 1764:
William Shelton. 80 acres and 50 acres. Pages 175, 436.

Book No. 36—years from 1764 to 1767:
Palatiah Shelton & c. 400 acres. Page 1006.

Crispen Shelton. 1515 acres. Page 589.

Book No. 38—years from 1768 to 1770:

William Shelton. 99 acres. Page 829.

Book No. 40—from 1771 to 1772:

James Shelton. 400 acres. Page 819.

Book No. 41—years from 1772 to 1773:

Mark Shelton. 399 acres. Page 126.

James Shelton. 500 acres. Page 131.

Abraham Shelton. 249 acres. Page 133.

Gabriel Shelton & c. 400, 404, 794 acres respectively. Pages 416, 417, 442.

Halifax County, Halifax Virginia:

Deed to Palletin Shelton of Halifax County. 140 acres, lying on Sycamore Creek. Consideration, 100 pounds. (This is a misspelling of Palatiah Shelton, who bought 165 acres on Irvin River, Aug. 29, 1771— once in Halifax County.)

Pittsylvania County, Chatham, Virginia—This County and Henry County were once parts of Halifax County:

Deed to Palatiah Shelton of Pittsylvania County. 165 acres, lying on Irvin River, date, August 29, 1771.

Deed from Palatiah Shelton and Mary his wife. Nov. 29, 1770. 130 acres on Smith River at a place known by the name of Rock Castle. (Smith River flows by city of Martinsville.)

Deed from Mark Shelton, "Planter, of Pittsylvania County." December 16th, 1779.

Henry County, Martinsville, Virginia. Henry County was once part of Pittsylvania County after the latter was cut off from Halifax County. The following deeds are recorded here:

1779—Palatiah Shelton.
1780—William Shelton.
1780—Samuel Shelton.
1791—Hezekiah Shetlon.

Royal land grant to Ralph Shelton: I personally inspected the official records in the State Land Office in Richmond of lands granted by patent from the King of England, and found a grant from George II dated June 20, 1749 for 400 acres to Ralph Shelton. There are no words to indicate the residence of Ralph. This tract of land is described as being in Lunenburgh County, located on the lower side of Ledbetters Creek. Description of the land shows that this tract touched the land of John Ingram, Samuel Ingram, Jonathan Davis, and "Johnson's line." Part of what was then Lunenburgh County later was cut off to form Amelia County.

I found record of a land patent granted to Ralph Shelton on September 20, 1745, for 400 acres, and it bears the same description as stated in deed from Ralph Shelton to Richard Burks, in 1763, the land lying on north side of the great Nottaway River. This definitely identifies Ralph, the patentee of 1745, as the man who sold out in Amelia County and moved to Henry County. This patent shown in Book No. 22, page 561.

Sale of Amelia land by Ralph Shelton: In the present Amelia County records, Deed Book 8, page 374, I saw on July 7, 1939, a record of a deed from Ralph Shelton of Nottaway Parish, Amelia County, to Richard Burks. Date of the deed was February 22, 1763. Tract was of 686 acres, and the consideration was 400 pounds. Description of land showed it to be on the lower side of Snales Creek, and on the north side of the great Nottaway River, 400 acres of the tract "being land which was granted to Ralph Shelton by Patent, September 20, 1745. The other 286 acres was land bought by Ralph Shelton from Samuel Jordan on October 23, 1751.

The deed to Richard Burks was witnessed by *John Shelton.*

Record of this tract bought by *Ralph Shelton* from Samuel Jordan is in Amelia County records, Deed Book 4, page 179. Date is October 23, 1751. Ralph is described as of Parish of Nottaway, Amelia County. Consideration was 30 pounds. 286 acres. It is stated in deed to have been patented to Samuel Jordan by King George II, September 20, 1748. It is described as being on lower side of Snales Creek, beginning at Bagley's corner white oak, etc.

Then Ralph Shelton moved to Henry County, Virginia. This is shown by Amelia County Records which show sale of land by *Ralph Shelton of Henry County, Va.,* the land being the same as that previously owned by Ralph Shelton of Amelia County.

Deed from Ralph Shelton of Henry County to Thomas Dudley. Deed Book 15, page 34. Consideration, 250 pounds. Tract described as 400 acres granted to Ralph Shelton by patent, September 20, 1745, and lying on lower side of Snales Creek, on north side of great Nottaway River. James Shelton signed as a witness to this deed.

It is the same land previously deeded to Richard Burks. That may have been a deed of trust to secure a loan, or the deal may have fallen through for some reason. Date of this deed to Thomas Dudley is November 28, 1778.

Then a few days later there was another deed for sale

of land from *Ralph Shelton of Henry County* and Richard Burks to John Knight. Date is December 2, 1778. Recorded in Amelia County Deed Book 15, page 205. Consideration was 300 pounds. Detailed description of land is not given in deed. *Stephen Shelton* was a witness.

Other records of Ralph Shelton while he was a resident of Amelia County:

February 19, 1747: Ralph Shelton petitioned the County Court for permission to build a water mill on his land on the great Nottaway River. Court ordered a committee of 12 freeholders of the vicinage to view the site and report damage that might be done to other property. This supports the record that Ralph had patented land in 1745 in this county and was living on the great Nottaway prior to record of a patent to Ralph Shelton of land in Lunenburgh County in 1749.

In 1763, Samuel Jordan sued Ralph Shelton on a debt, and a jury heard the suit and gave judgment against Ralph for 52 pounds and seven shillings with interest at the rate of 5 per cent from November 1, 1756.

Ralph Shelton in Henry County, Virginia: Ralph Shelton bought land in what is now Henry County in July, 1763, after having sold his land in Amelia County in February of the same year. Land bought by Ralph in Henry County was then located in Halifax County, later in Pittsylvania County, before Henry County was formed.

Record in Halifax County Deed Book 4, page 357. Date July 21, 1763. Deed from Darby Callahan of Orange County, North Carolina, to *Ralph Shelton of Amelia County.* 400 acres, lying on both sides of the South Fork of Mayo River. Consideration, 70 pounds of the current money of Virginia.

Record in Pittsylvania County Deed Book 2, page 309. Date, May 6, 1771. Deed to *Ralph Shelton of Pittsylvania County* to 400 acres on South Fork of Mayo River. Consideration, 25 pounds. (This land is now in Henry County.)

Pittsylvania County Court, July Term, 1770: *Ralph Shelton* got an injunction to stay proceedings against him by Ross and Leak under a previous judgment of this Court. *Daniel Shelton* was security for Ralph.

In 1776, in Henry County, there is record of a deed to *Ralph Shelton, Senior,* for 119½ acres of land, for consideration of 100 pounds. (He sold this about a year later for 140 pounds.) Note the use of the suffix "Senior". Apparently the *son Ralph* was coming to an age to have business transactions of his own.

Sale of land in Henry County by Ralph Shelton:

In 1784, *Shelton, Senior,* of Henry County, sold 400 acres to his son, *James Shelton* of Henry County. (In this, or one other sale in Henry County, it provided in the deed that Ralph was paid the consideration "in hard money". The customary payment was "in current money of Virginia".)

In 1788, a deed to land in Henry County was executed by *"Ralph Shelton and Elizabeth his wife of Henry County".* It was for 250 acres, and the consideration was 100 pounds. It is interesting to note that the suffix "Senior" was not used. Also there was no mention of a wife in the deed from Ralph, Senior, in 1784. It seems to be a deed from Ralph, the son.

Last records of Ralph Shelton in Henry County: The above two deeds from *Ralph Shelton* are the last records of any kind found in the County records of Henry County, for Ralph Shelton.

James Shelton: February 24, 1780. Deed TO his son-in-law Gregory Durham, as a gift. 150 acres, on both sides of Ironmonger Creek, touching the lands of *William Shelton.* Witnessed by William Shelton. Deed Book 2, page 4.

Jeremiah Shelton: July 1, 1784. Deed TO Charles Pigg. £35. 154 acres on the North Fork of Mayo River, "being land granted to said Shelton, September 1, 1780. Deed Book 2, page 499.

Ralph Shelton, Senior: March 13, 1784. Deed TO James Shelton "his son." £5. 400 acres on both sides of South Fork of Mayo River. Witnessed by *Eliphaz Shelton.* Deed Book 3, page 29.

Samuel Shelton: September 8, 1788. Deed FROM George Hairston. £25. 87 acres on South Side of North Mayo River. Deed Book 3, page 460.

Palatiah Shelton: October 27, 1785. David TO James MacBride. £20. 251 acres on Neidgon Creek. Deed Book 3, page 167.

Palatiah Shelton: September 15, 1786. Deed TO Blizard Magruder. £400. 309 acres on Middle Fork of little Dan River. Deed Book 3, page 250.

Palatiah Shelton: September 24, 1786. Deed TO Stephen Lyon. £60. 50 acres, the place on which Palatiah Shelton now lives on Russell Creek. Deed Book 3, page 256.

William Shelton et al: October 21, 1786. Deed TO Alexander Hunter. £200. 400 acres on Horse Pasture Creek. Deed Book 3, page 257.

William Shelton, "heir at law of James Shelton late of Henry County, deceased," et al: Deed TO John Marr. "£500 species." 810 acres on North Fork of Mayo River. Deed Book 3, page 375.

Palatiah Shelton: September 10, 1788. Deed TO Stephen Lyon. £300. On Russell Creek . . . 204 acres in one tract, another tract of 250 acres, and another tract of 109 acres. Agreed to by Annie, wife of Palatiah Shelton. Deed Book 3, page 466.

Ralph Shelton and Elizabeth his wife of Henry County: April 10, 1788. Deed TO Jacob Adams. £100. 250 acres on Mathews Creek. Witnessed by Eliphaz Shelton. Deed Book 3, page 468. (This Ralph must have been the son of the Ralph Shelton, Senior, whose will was filed in 1789.)

SHELTON MARRIAGE RECORDS IN HENRY CO., VA.

Nathan Shelton to Polly Hatcher, April 13, 1802. Hubbard Hatcher, Surety.

Aaron Mills to *Sally Shelton,* September 9, 1803. James Shelton, Surety.

Archibald Hatcher to *Nancy Shelton,* October 22, 1807. Nathan Shelton, Surety.

Austin Jones to *Ruth Shelton,* January 2, 1817. John Shelton, Surety.

William F. Abington to *Fanny Shelton,* May 9, 1818. Pinias Allen, Surety.

James Shelton to Unity Gilley, November 8, 1818. John Shelton, Surety.

Thomas S. Shelton to Elizabeth Norman, February 2, 1819. Will Norman, Jr., Surety.

James Penn to *Mary Shelton,* November 10, 1818. John Shelton, Surety.

RECORDS OF SHELTON WILLS IN HENRY CO., VA.

Zebulon Shelton: Inventory of his estate is recorded in

Will Book One, page one, February, 1777. Total amount of estate was £75 12' 6".[1]

James Shelton: Will Book One, page 100. Will dated May, 1784, and ordered recorded by the Court March 26, 1785. To his wife Philapinea Shelton he left five slaves and his plantation where he lived. He named his children as Nathan, James, Molly, Nancy and Sally (Nathan and James, minors), and provided that his estate should go to them after his widow's death. Separately he mentioned another son, William, and named him as one of the executors of his will.

Inventory of James Shelton's estate, totalling £397, is recorded in Will Book One, page 102.

Will of Ralph Shelton, Senior, of Henry County, is recorded in Will Book No. One, page 170, Martinsville, Virginia. It was dated April 23, 1787, and was presented in Court of Henry County on March 30, 1789. Executors named were "my sons Ralph Shelton and Eliphaz Shelton". It was Eliphaz who presented it in Court in 1789. No record of the actual death of Ralph, Senior. And there is no mention of a wife.

His son John Shelton he cut off in the will with a bequest of 25 pounds sterling, so that he could not "claim kinship".

Then he named his children as follows, ordering that the estate be divided among them: Ralph Shelton, Palatiah Shelton, Eliphaz Shelton, James Shelton, Ezekiah Shelton

---

(1) This Zebulon was the son of Peter Shelton of Middlesex Co., Va. Zebulon and Mary Goar, his wife, had a son Henry Shelton who went to Goochland Co., Va. He served in the Rev. as a private in Capt. Wm. Sanford's Co. 2nd Va. Reg., commanded successively by Col. Alex. Spottswood and Col. Christian Febriger. He was transferred Aug. 1778 to Capt. Alex. Parker's Co., same Reg., and discharged Sept. 11, 1779.

(other records spell it, Hezekiah), Jeremiah Shelton, Azariah Shelton (who moved to Tennessee) these are children by his 1st wife: and Roger Shelton, Easop Shelton, Abbegal Shelton, Mary Shelton, Liberty Shelton, were children of the 2nd wife, and Kathern Rutherford, Sarah Robertson, Elizabeth Arnold, Rina McGhee, Susanah Jones, were his grandchildren.

He mentions ''my four last children namely Easop Shelton, Abbegal Shelton, Mary Shelton, Liberty Shelton'' by way of including them with his other children as sharing equally in his estate.

Inventory of Ralph Shelton's estate was filed in Court, June 29, 1789. Total was 51 pounds (mostly live stock, tools, no slaves).

Further accounting for the estate of Ralph Shelton was made to Court, July 23, 1789, by Eliphaz Shelton. It showed total of 67 pounds net, and included board for widow and five children, although no widow was mentioned in the will.

Eliphaz was one of many sons of Ralph Shelton, and was named as co-executor with another son Ralph Shelton.

One son mentioned in the will was *Azariah Shelton,* who migrated to *Grainger County, Tennessee,* and later to *Rhea County, Tennessee;* he was the father of *Ralph Shelton,* of *Claiborne County, Tennessee.*

Eliphaz Shelton, of Henry County, Virginia, son of Ralph Shelton, was a Captain in the Revolutionary War; in 1779.

James Shelton, of Henry County, Virginia, was a Captain in the Revolutionary War, 1777.

(This information is taken from a plaque placed in the Henry County Court House by the Daughters of the American Revolution.)

James Terry: In his will he devised to his wife (not named by name) all "my land that I have bought of *Ralph Shelton*." He mentions a daughter Peggy, and gives a slave girl Fillis "to my daughter Sarah that is married to *Cuthbert Shelton*." This Cuthbert Shelton was later active in the early days of Grainger County, Tennessee. The will named also sons (probably gr-sons) John Shelton and Richard Shelton. James Terry in his will appointed his wife and Cuthbert Shelton as executors. Will was attested by Ralph Shelton and three others. Will was proved in Court, July 14, 1788 "by oaths of the witnesses thereto," indicating that said Ralph Shelton was there in person. Will is recorded in Will Book One, page 161, and was dated March 18, 1788.

Nathan Shelton: Inventory of his estate was filed in Court, May 4, 1814, totaling $169. Will Book 2, page 245.

James Shelton: Inventory of his estate was filed in Court, June 2, 1814. Will Book 2, page 277.

William Shelton: Will Book 2, pages 277, 309. Inventory of estate totaling $3091.81, filed Sept. 26, 1807. Accounting by Administrator of estate of William Shelton was filed in Court in 1819, in which is mentioned the payment to John Shelton on December 25, 1809, of £3.6 to "buy leather," and also a payment to James Shelton on December 15, 1807.

RECORDS OF SHELTON DEEDS IN HENRY CO., VA.

Ralph Shelton: February 10, 1776. Deed from John Sims. £100. On Green Creek, a branch of Mayo River, 119½ acres. Deed Book One, page 25.

James Shelton: April 21, 1777. Deed from J. F. Miller. £300. 350 acres on North Fork of Mayo River. Deed Book One, page 33.

Palatiah Shelton: February 15, 1779. Deed from William Robert Hinton. £1800. 246 acres on waters of Russell Creek and Mayo River. Witnessed by Eliphaz Shelton. Deed Book One, page 206.

Ralph Shelton, Sr. and Susanna his wife: September 10, 1777. Deed TO Robert Baker. £140. 119½ acres on Green Creek (tract bought in 1776). Deed Book One, page 70.

This is the Ralph Shelton whose will was filed in 1789. *Susanna* must have been his second wife, mother of the four younger children mentioned in his will.

Palatiah Shelton and Mary his wife: March 25, 1779. Deed TO Joseph Reynolds, son of Richard Reynolds. £250. 165 acres on both sides of Irvin River. Book One, page 209.

James Shelton and Philipiah his wife: April 30, 1778. Deed to Josiah Smith. £216. 216 acres on Horse Pasture Creek, "being part of the tract said Shelton purchased from Thomas Mann Randolph." Witnessed by William Shelton. Deed Book One, page 132.

James Shelton: February 24, 1780. Deed TO William Shelton "his son," as a gift. 200 acres which "corner on the land of *Samuel Shelton.* Deed Book 2, page 1.

James Shelton: February 24, 1780. Deed TO *Samuel Shelton.* Consideration, one bay stallion. 130 acres on both sides of Horse Pasture Creek, "part of the tract said James Shelton purchased from Thomas Mann Randolph," touching corner of lands of Wm. Shelton and James Shelton. Witnessed by Wm. Shelton. Deed Book 2, page 2.

Ralph Shelton and Elizabeth his wife, of Henry County: April 10, 1788. £100. 145 acres on Mathews Creek, beginning at Ralph and Thomas Shelton's corner . . . to John Shelton's line. Witnessed by Eliphaz Shelton. Deed Book 3, page 470.

Samuel Shelton: April 27, 1789. Deed TO Samuel Staples. £150. 130 acres, beginning at corner of lands of James Shelton deceased and William Shelton, on the north side of Horse Pasture Creek. Deed Book 3, page 527.

Elizabeth Shelton: April 27, 1790. Discharge of William Jones as her Attorney in Fact. Deed Book 4, page 115.

Elizabeth Shelton: October 15, 1790. Appointed her "friend Ezekiah (evidently Hezekiah) Shelton of Henry County" as her attorney to recover for her from Eliphaz Shelton, John Nite, and Thomas Dudley the sum of £500, to take legal courses, etc. Deed Book 4, page 153.

James Shelton: April 25, 1791. Deed TO Hezekiah Shelton. £13. 209 acres on both sides of Mayo River. Deed Book 4, page 251.

William Shelton: March 12, 1796. Deed FROM Peter Leak. £60. 50 acres, on Horse Pasture Creek. Deed Book 5, page 259.

Ralph Shelton: September, 1788. Deed TO Elizabeth Terry. £200. 78 acres, on each side of Big Dan River. Signed, "Ralph Shelton." Deed Book 4, page 149.

Shelton records in Tazewell County, Virginia:

The only record I found was of the appraisement of the estate of *John Shelton* in 1867 (Will Book No. 4, p. 109).

Pendleton in his book, "History of Tazewell County," however, says that the first survey made in that county was made for a John Shelton in 1748. (This was John of Hanover Co., Va.)

Shelton records in Russell County, Virginia, at Lebanon: Deed from *Jeremiah Shelton* and *Nancy Shelton* to

Benjamin South, May, 1797. 230 acres on the Clinch River. (Deed Book 2, page 322.)

Shelton records in Washington County, Virginia, at Abingdon:

Deed to *Joseph Shelton* "of Washington County" from John Coles. February 12, 1827. 150 acres on a branch of South Fork of Holston River, called Gropes Creek. (Deed Book 9, page 360.)

Shelton records in Scott County, Virginia, at Gate City:

Deed to *John Shelton* "of Scott County" from Solomon Potter. April 17, 1818. 25 acres on Opossum Creek. (Deed Book 2, page 68.)

Deed from *John Shelton* "of Scott County" to David Winegar. December 7, 1833. 25 acres on Opossum Creek. (Deed Book 4, page 325.)

SHELTON RECORDS IN GRAINGER AND CLAIBORNE COUNTIES, TENN.

Grainger County, Tennessee, Census of 1830, lists as heads of families: Eli. Shelton, with family of 10. Gabriel Shelton, with family of 2 (apparently children if any grown and gone away). James Shelton, with family of 11, 3 of them males under 15 years old.

The first record I found of Ralph Shelton of Grainger County was a deed to him in 1796. There are other deed records of him in 1798, 1800, 1804. His main farm and home seems to have been on 400 acres ''on the south side of Holston River in Grainger County opposite the mouth of German Creek (I think this site is now in Jefferson County).

By the year 1811 this Ralph Shelton was living in Knox

County, Tennessee, as shown by a power of attorney he executed to Richard Shelton to sell his (Ralph's) land on Holston River. This power of attorney was witnessed by David Shelton and George Shelton, both of whom had died before 1834.

Captain David Shelton was very active in Grainger County affairs in the period 1796 to early 1800's. So was Cuthbert Shelton.

William Shelton deeded land to Samuel Rail, 1803, Grainger County.

Sarah Shelton shown, 1809, as widow and admr. of William Shelton.

Crispian E. Shelton, 1814, bought land from John Cocke in Grainger County.

John Shelton, 1817, of Knox County, deeded to Richard Shelton of Grainger County one negro woman and her 3 children for $1200.00.

Crispian E. Shelton, 1818, deeded land to Ralph Shelton.

Crispian E. Shelton, 1821, "of Rhea County, Tennessee," deeded land to Ralph Shelton "of Claiborne County."

Samuel Shelton "of Franklin County, Missouri" as attorney in fact for his brother David Shelton "of Gasconade County, Missouri" conveyed the interest of David Shelton in Grainger County land of William Shelton, deceased, who was father of said Samuel and David Shelton. Lands were on Clinch River in Grainger County. (Grainger County record, Oct. 15, 1828.)

David Shelton, 1796, granted license to keep a public house.

In 1796, County Court appointed Palatiah Shelton, Cuthbert Shelton, Ralph Shelton and David Shelton, et al, to view the nearest and best way from the Waggon Road between Riggs and Martins to Shelton's Ford on Holston River and make report to the next court. (Grainger records)

The following notes are all from Grainger County records unless otherwise indicated:

Deed Records Book A, page 10—James McNare conveyed to *Ralph Shelton* 200 acres, on south side of Holston River. Aug. 5, 1796.

Deeds Records Book A, page 35—June 12, 1797—James Nicholas conveyed to *David Shelton* 25 acres, on north side of Holston River.

Deed Records Book A, page 77, March 24, 1798—*Ralph Shelton* conveyed to *Cuthbert Shelton* 150 acres, on south side of Holston River, opposite the mouth of German Creek, "it being the same place whereon the said Cuthbert Shelton now lives." Boundary runs along the line of "Ralph Shelton's back line" and follows that line "to where it strikes the river."

Deed Records Book A, page 116, June 10, 1798—Isam Chisum conveyed to *David Shelton* 100 acres, on the north side of Holston River, about two miles below the mouth of German River. Consideration, $130.00.

Deed Records Book A, page 116, February 20, 1799 — *David Shelton* sold to Joseph Noe the same 100 acres described in last above record.

Deed Records Book A, page 126, October 6, 1798—John Davis conveyed to *Captain David Shelton* 100 acres, adjoins property of John Davis and Ephram Guffee.

Deed Records Book A, page 177, January 22, 1800—*David*

Shelton conveyed to Joseph Cobb, 100 acres, same tract conveyed to him Oct. 6, 1798.

Deed Records Book A, page 210, November 24, 1800—John Little conveyed to *Ralph Shelton* 150 acres for $600, on south side of Holston River, beginning on Holston River opposite the mouth of German Creek and adjoining land already owned by Ralph Shelton.

Deed Records Book A, page 333, May 23, 1804—*Ralph Shelton* sold 80 acres of the farm on which he lived, opposite the mouth of German Creek, on the south side of Holston River, to William Street. Deed shows that *Richard Shelton* owned a farm adjoining or near.

Deed Records Book A, page 334, November 19, 1803—Sheriff Robert Yancey executed a sheriff's deed to Jesse Riggs, conveying land of *David Shelton* to satisfy a judgment against David Shelton, in the amount of $18.46, 100 acres "lying on Panther Creek Road."

Deed Records Book A, page 334, May 23, 1804— *Ralph Shelton* conveyed to *Richard Shelton* 123 acres for consideration of $100, on the south side of Holston River, being part of the tract where Ralph Shelton now lives.

Deed Records Book A, page 68, October 6, 1798—*David Shelton* conveyed to William Kirkham 200 acres on the north side of Holston River.

Deed Records Book A, page 190, March 10, 1800—*David Shelton* conveyed to John Little, for $500, a tract of 150 acres on the south side of Holston River, opposite the mouth of German Creek, being the same tract where *Cuthbert Shelton* formerly lived and which he conveyed to David Shelton by deed of April 15, 1799.

Book A, Deed Records, page 303, August 15, 1803—

William Shelton conveyed to Samuel Rail 100 acres on the north side of Holston River, the tract once granted by the State of North Carolina to John Duncan.

Deed Records Book B, page 292, May 12, 1809—100 acres on south side of Holston River to *Sarah Shelton,* widow and administratrix of estate of *William Shelton.*

Deed Records Book B, page 429, August 24, 1801—William Evans conveyed to *David Shelton* 100 acres on the great road leading from Dotson's Ford to Knox.

Deed Records Book B, page 305, May 12, 1809—*Sarah Shelton,* widow and administratrix of William Shelton deceased, conveyed to Jesse Cheeck, 100 acres in Grainger County, on the south side of Clinch River, about one mile above Kentucky Ford.

Deed Records, April 11, 1814—John Cocke conveyed to *Crispian E. Shelton* 100 acres in Grainger County on the Clinch River.

Deed Records, October 28, 1817—*John Shelton* of Knox County conveyed to *Richard Shelton* of Grainger County, one negro woman slave and her three children for $1200.

Deed Records, May 8, 1818—*Crispian E. Shelton* conveyed to *Ralph Shelton "of Claiborne County,"* 29 acres in Grainger County, at the fork of Puncheon Camp Creek and Clinch River. Deed was witnessed by *David Shelton* and Sarah Harris.

Deed Records, Book E, page 129, January 1, 1820 — Thomas Johnson conveyed to *Ralph Shelton "of Claiborne County,"* 87½ acres in Grainger County on Puncheon Camp Creek.

Deed Records Book E, page 241. November 21, 1821—*Crispian E. Shelton* "of Rhea County, Tennessee," to

Ralph Shelton of "Claiborne County," 29 acres on Puncheon Camp Creek, "adjoining Ralph Shelton's land."

Deed Records Book F, page 614—*Ralph Shelton* "of Knox County" in 1811 had appointed *Richard Shelton* of Grainger County as his attorney to sell his, Ralph's, land on Holston River in Grainger County. The instrument of appointment was witnessed by *David Shelton* and *George Shelton*, both of whom had died before January 14, 1834, necessitating other proof of signatures.

Deed Records Book F, page 24, February 15, 1828— *Ralph Shelton* of Claiborne County sold 24 acres he had bought from *Crispian E. Shelton.*

Deed Records, August 15, year (?)—*Ralph Shelton* of Claiborne County sold 87½ acres in Grainger County on Puncheon Camp Creek.

September 12, 1796—County Court of Grainger County granted *David Shelton* a license to "keep a Public House where he now lives."

September 13, 1796—County Court of Grainger County appointed *Palatiah Shelton, Cuthbert Shelton, Ralph Shelton, David Shelton,* and others "to view the nearest and best way from the Waggon Road between Riggs and Martins to *Shelton's Ford* on Holston River and make a report to the next Court."

Grainger County Court Records are well preserved, showing proceedings of the Court from the time the County was created in *1796*. These additional notes are from the County Court records:

March 15, 1797—County Court ordered a road built "from *Shelton's Ford* on the Holston River to the Kentucky Road."

December 13, 1797—Last Will and Testament of *Nancy Shelton* was proven in open court, and ordered to be recorded. (The original Will is in the file boxes.) In it Nancy Shelton, daughter of *William Shelton,* left all, which was not very much, to her sister, *Dotia Austen.*

February, 1798 — *Cuthbert Shelton* was appointed a Justice of the County Court. And Cuthbert Shelton was appointed to take the tax lists in *"Captain David Shelton's District."*

November 19, 1798—*Captain David Shelton* was appointed Overseer of the road "from Shelton's Ford on the Holston River to the Grainger line."

In the years 1796 to 1800 the name of *David Shelton* appears many times as a member of the Grand Jury. From the records it appears that David Shelton and Cuthbert Shelton were especially active in County affairs in the first few years after the County was formed in 1796.

William Shelton died in Grainger County intestate. His widow, *Sarah Shelton,* was appointed administratrix of his estate. Her report filed with the Court in 1809 showed $340 realized from public sale of his live stock and tools. Sarah Shelton married a Lucas after William Shelton's death.

James Shelton and M. Shelton to Charles McAnally, 1818, Deed Book D, page 443.

Richard Shelton to Charles Read, 1820. Deed Book E, page 236.

Samuel Shelton to Charles McAnally, 1822, Deed Book E, page 308.

Ralph Shelton to Joel Dotson (Ralph's son-in-law), 1823, Deed Book E, page 364.

R. Shelton to J. Bullen, 1829, Deed Book F, page 24.

David Shelton to Charles McAnally, 1831. Deed Book F, page 270.

Ralph Shelton to John Boils, 1831, Deed Book F, page 272.

James Shelton from George and Thomas Bristow, 1840. Deed Book H, pages 157, 159, 160.

Ralph Shelton to Richard Shelton, 1834, Book F, page 614.

Nancy Shelton to Harbin L———, 1843, Book J, page 157.

Ralph Shelton to Abednego Farmer, 1843, Book J, page 262.

David Shelton to R. T. Cabbage, 1851, Book L, page 495.

William Shelton of Grainger County had sons *David Shelton* and *Samuel Shelton*. County Court records clearly show this. David Shelton moved to Gasconade County, Missouri, sometime prior to October 15, 1828. And Samuel Shelton moved to Franklin County, Missouri, sometime before the same date.

Nancy Shelton of Grainger County and *Dotia Austen,* sisters, were daughters of a William Shelton of Grainger County, who probably was the same William Shelton as the father of Samuel and David . . . records indicate this, but not conclusively so.

This is the county in which *Ralph Shelton* lived, on the Clinch River at "Shelton's Ford." His son, *Ralph Shelton,* was born here.

Jeremiah Skelton (Shelton), in 1835, conveyed to James Dickinson, a tract of land. Consideration, $100. Deed Book L, page 143.

Ralph Shelton, in 1817, had conveyed to him, from

Thomas Johnson, 100 acres on the north side of the Clinch River. Consideration, $60. Deed Book E, page 251.

Marriage Records of Claiborne County, Tennessee:

Anderson Shelton and Mary Hurst, 1859. Book 3, page 111. Anderson Shelton was a younger brother of the Ralph Shelton who married Ann Taylor.

Minutes of the County Court of Claiborne County, Tennessee:

Ralph Shelton was sworn to attend grand jury, February term, 1815.

Ralph Shelton, Constable, attended on the Grand Jury for 3 days, February Term, 1815, and was allowed to receive out of county monies $3.00.

SHELTON RECORDS IN GREENE CO., TENN.

Greenville, Tennessee, county seat of Green County, is one of the oldest cities in the state, closely tied up with the history of the settlement of the state.

Armstead G. Shelton, in 1826, recorded a deed from John McAmish, for 70 acres. Deed Book 14, page 119.

SHELTON RECORDS IN KNOX CO., TENN.

Cuthbert Shelton, January 31, 1806, conveyed to Robert Marley, 100 acres on Beaver Creek Valley. Deed Book M, pages 299, 300. He apparently is the Cuthbert Shelton who moved to Grainger County, Tennessee, from Henry County, Virginia.

Gabriel Shelton, May 11, 1810, conveyed to Thomas Reed, 25 acres on Beaver Dam Creek. Deed Book N-1, page 297.

Ann Shelton, November 9, 1810, conveyed to Thomas Reed, Sheriff, 33 1/3 acres. Deed Book O-1, page 154.

Cuthbert Shelton, October 19, 1811, conveyed to John Calloway, 160 acres in Beaver Creek Valley. Deed Book O-1, page 219.

Cuthbert Shelton, by attorney, conveyed to Robert Marley, 50 acres in Beaver Creek Valley, April 6, 1813. Deed Book O-1, page 319.

Ralph Shelton, January 9, 1815, conveyed to John Shelton, some slaves. Deed Book P-1, page 120. This apparently was the Ralph Shelton who figures in early Grainger County history, who lived on the Holston River, and who in his old age moved to Knox County. He apparently was the Ralph Shelton who came to Grainger County from Henry County, Virginia, son of the Ralph Shelton who died in Henry County about 1789.

Ralph Shelton, August 2, 1815, conveyed to John Shelton, 300 acres on Hickory Creek, Hynds Valley. Deed Book P-1, page 341.

Cuthbert Shelton, July 19, 1816, conveyed to Luke Lea, 52½ acres on Beaver Creek, Deed Book Q-1, page 97.

Agesiah (Azariah) Shelton, June 5, 1832, conveyed to William C. Frazier, a tract of land on Turkey Creek. Deed Book Y-1, page 119.

Palatiah Shelton, May 4, 1853, conveyed to Azro F. Smith, 242 acres on north side of Beaver Creek. Deed Book T-2, page 72.

Palatiah Shelton, February 26, 1856, conveyed to John Beeler, 102 acres on Beaver Creek. Deed Book U-2, page 426.

Mark Shelton and Ollie Shelton his wife, August 3, 1908, conveyed to William Clapp et ux, 1½ acres, in 5th District, Emory Road. Deed Book 225, page 410. Mark Shelton was the brother of Ralph Shelton. He married Ollie Quayle.

Mark Shelton, April 9, 1912, conveyed to Ida Cooper, 8 acres in 5th District, on Tazewell Road. Deed Book 239, page 343.

Cuthbert Shelton "of Knox County," had conveyed to him, March 14, 1800, from Luke Lea, 200 acres on Beaver Creek which flows into Clinch River. Consideration, $1000. Deed Book F-1, page 350.

Ralph Shelton had conveyed to him, April 28, 1806, from Edward Cateham, 65 acres on Black Oak Ridge and 300 acres in Hines Valley, Hickory Creek. Deed Book L-1, pages 314, 316. Ralph Shelton is described as "of Knox County." Land is on the creek that empties into Clinch River, second creek below Beaver Creek (in vicinity of land of Cuthbert Shelton and other Sheltons).

Azariah Shelton had conveyed to him, October 23, 1830, from Thomas Hindman, 2 acres. Azariah Shelton is described as "of Knox County." Deed Book W-1, page 194. This probably is a son of the Azariah Shelton named as one of the sons of the Ralph Shelton whose will was probated in Henry County, Virginia, in 1789.

Palatiah Shelton "of Knox County" had conveyed to him, from Ann Duren et al, October 21, 1823, 250 acres on the north side of Beaver Creek. Deed Book V-1, page 133.

Palatiah Shelton had conveyed to him, July 30, 1853, from Edward Prince, 100 acres on Beaver Creek. Deed Book R-2, page 328.

SHELTON RECORDS IN HAWKINS CO., TENN.

Hawkins County is one of the oldest and most historical counties in Tennessee. It was Hawkins County, North Carolina, before the State of Tennessee was formed.

Polly Shelton: On September 6, 1790, Jesse Riggs conveyed to Polly Shelton "of Hawkins County and State of North Carolina," (now Tennessee) 245 acres, on the north side of the divide that divides French Broad River and Holston River. Consideration, 150 pounds. (In two places in the deed the name is spelled Pally Shelton, and may be meant for RALLY Shelton, or a corruption of Pallatiah Shelton.) Deed Book No. 1, page 59.

William Shelton: In 1813, Robert Hamilton conveyed a tract of land in Hawkins County to William Shelton. Deed Book No. 3, page 249.

Hezekiah Shelton: On December 7, 1814, John Clayton conveyed a tract of land to Hezekiah Shelton, in Hawkins County. The record is transcribed from the original deed book, and the spelling is confusing. In the same deed it is spelled "Shalton," "Shutton," and Strutten." (Hawkins County is near Claiborne County.) Deed Book 3, page 329.

James Skelton (Shelton): In 1833, James Lions conveyed a tract of land in Hawkins County to James Skelton. Deed Book 14, page 150.

Reuben Skelton (Shelton): In 1833, C. Arnold conveyed a tract of land in Hawkins County to Reuben Skelton. Deed Book No. 14, page 170.

Reuben Skelton (Shelton): In 1833, Francis Goddard conveyed a tract of land in Hawkins County to Reuben Skelton. Deed Book No. 14, page 171.

James Skelton (Shelton): In 1834, Crispin Goin conveyed a tract of land in Hawkins County to James Skelton. Deed Book No. 14, page 471.

Alexander Shelton: There are numerous deed records in Hawkins County of conveyances to and from Alexander

Shelton, from the early days of the county up to 1882. And beginning in 1875 there are numerous records of Alexander Shelton, Jr.

SHELTON RECORDS IN JEFFERSON CO., TENN.

Dandridge, county seat of Jefferson, is the third oldest town in Tennessee.

Pallatiah Shelton: On January 24, 1795, Pallatiah Shelton ''of County of Hawkins and Territory of the United States'' conveyed to John Loe 245 acres ''lying in County of Jefferson.'' Consideration, 200 pounds. Deed Book B, page 182. (This deed was proven in Court at February, 1795, Sessions, and recorded in Minute Book No. 1, in which the spelling is John Low.)

Thomas Chilton (Shelton): In 1795 he served on Jury at May Sessions of County Court of Jefferson County.

Thomas Shelton: In 1796 he served on Jury at May Sessions of County Court of Jefferson County. Also, again at February Session of County Court in 1797.

Thomas Shelton: In 1797, Michael Bacon conveyed to Thomas Shelton a tract of land in Jefferson County. Proven in February Sessions of County Court, 1797.

James Shelton: He served on Jury at February Sessions, 1797, of County Court of Jefferson County.

Marriage records of Jefferson County:

Thomas Shelton to Rebecca Daniel, Sept. 3, 1813.

Eli. (evidently Eliphas, son of Ralph, Sr.) Shelton to Peggy Adamson, Sept. 3, 1814.

James Shelton to Jane Langdon, June 8, 1816, by Henry Bradford, Justice of the Peace.

Sarah Shelton: In a deed record of January 10, 1809, she is referred to as the widow of *William Shelton* of Grainger County, Tennessee, and as the daughter of Miller Doggett, who was a brother of Jesse Doggett. Deed Book I, page 278.

(Minute Book No. 7)

Page 416—James Chilton, working on road, June 15, 1824.

Page 53—John Chilton, security for John Welch, March 13, 1819.

Page 161—Bill of sale from Rebecca Shelton and Clever Shelton to Fred. Pulse for a negro slave named Jess. Duly proven in Court (Sept. 13, 1820).

Page 25—Clever Shelton vs. Chas. Hodge, Jr., T. V. A. dismissed Dec. 15, 1818.

Page 435—Clever Shelton and his hands working road Sept. 15, 1824.

Page 90—Thomas Shelton to James Shelton, a deed of relinquishment, Sept. 16, 1819.

Page 296—John M. Shelton on a Jury, June 12, 1822.

Page 82—John Shelton on a Jury to view, 1819.

Page 244—Case—Randolph Sims vs. Martin Shelton, Sept. 14, 1821.

Page 316—Nelson Shelton working on road Dec. 9, 1822.

Page 344—Hands on James Shelton plantation working road March 9, 1829.

Page 398—John M. Shelton, Traverse Jury, Sept. 25, 1827.

Page 279—John M. Shelton, admr. on estate of Noah T. Shelton, June 9, 1828.

Eliphaz, Noah F. and John M. Shelton were on the tax list of Jefferson Co. in 1822.

Page 198—James Chilton's Deed of Conveyance to Jane and Geo. Laverty—140 acres, Mar. 15, 1827.

Page 490—James Chilton on Jury Sept. 15, 1830.

Page 308—Clever Shelton, Deed of Conveyance to John Fain for 50 acres of land, Sept. 10, 1828.

Clever Shelton, Deed of Trust to Jesse Moore, Jr., 50 acres, July 28, 1826—$200—Jos. Hamilton, Clerk.

Clever Shelton, Deed of Trust to John Fain, Jan. 4, 1829 —$25—50 acres.

Clever Shelton, Deed of Trust to John Fain—2 tracts containing 271 acres—Sept. 23, 1829. Cons. $200. Test, Shadrach Inman, I. M. Gillespie.

Clever Shelton, Deed of Trust to Caswell Lea; land and slaves. Test., Saml. F. Clawson, George Tabler, Aug. 5, 1826.

William Love (or Low), Deed to James Shelton. Reg. Feb. 7, 1838. Cons. $300—100 acres. Test., Shadrach Inman, John Love—Wm. Love (seal).

N. K. Shelton, Deed to Saml. M. Hughes, Nov. 12, 1838. $500—75 acres.

John M. Shelton, Deed to Nelson V. Shelton for 133½ acres—$300—April 17, 1852, 9 o'clock a. m. Jas. M. Nicholson, Clerk.

Michael Bacon's deed to Thomas Shelton, April ye 14th, 1797: County and territory south of the river Ohio, consideration £50, where Michael Bacon lived.

Present: Thomas Kinkade Jurat, John Tillery. Michael (X his mark) Bacon.

Palatiah Shelton to John Loe (Love?) registered 9th March 1795. County of Hawkins and ter. of U. S. Cons.

200£ — 245 acres — Delivered in presence of Christopher Hussy. Palatiah Shelton (seal).

Sarah Shelton to Jesse Doggett—no record.

John Green and wife, deed to Clever Shelton for 196 acres of land—Reg. 2 July 1822. Cons. $800—196 acres— in presence of John and Mary Green (X mark).

Jacob Miller, Deed to Clever Shelton for 50 acres, July 28, 1826. $200. In pres. of Robert Craig, Wm. Crook.

Page 65—Chilton, Jas., working road, Apr. 7, 1845.

Page 66—Chilton, Jas., helping lay off a road, Apr. 7, 1845.

Page 293—Chilton, Jas., helping lay off a road, Apr. 7, 1845.

Page 361—Chilton, Jas., witness to will of Henry Randolph, March 6, 1848.

Page 486—Chilton, Wm., overseer of a road.

Page 520—Shelton, John, and hands working road.

Page 502—John M. Shelton, dec'd, list of sales, inventory, Apr. 2nd, 1849.

Page 489—John M. Shelton, last will and testament presented in spec. Court, Feb. 5, 1849.

Page 490—Cassandra Shelton, executrix to John M. Shelton, Feb. 5, 1849.

NORTH CAROLINA RECORDS

UNCOMBE COUNTY COURT HOUSE, Asheville, North Carolina. This County in the early days included most of what is now Madison County and the section known as ''Shelton Laurel'', bordering on the Tennessee line.

Deed from John Strother to *David Shelton* for 30 acres on ''Laurel Branch''. Consideration, $13.00. July 28, 1815. This was part of a large tract of 326,000 acres originally granted to John Gray Blount, later sold by Sheriff for taxes. Deed Book H, page 270.

Deed from State of North Carolina, No. 931, to *David Shelton* and his assignee *Rodrick Shelton.* 100 acres on Bald Mountain Creek. December 10, 1801. Deed Book 4, page 622.

Deed to *David Shelton.* 418 acres on Laurel Creek. April 12, 1823. Deed Book 13, page 418.

Deed to *Rodrick Shelton.* August 27, 1800. Deed Book 11, page 75.

Deed to *Lewis Shelton.* 12 acres on Laurel Creek. July 28th, 1815. Deed Book H, page 219.

Lewis Shelton and *James Shelton* are described as sons of Rodrick Shelton.

Also there was a *Martin Shelton* as grantee of a deed in Laurel Creek County about the time of the first deeds to any Sheltons.

No mention of a *Ralph Shelton* in the early deed records of Buncombe County.

There probably are earlier records in the North Carolina

State Capitol, records of deeds prior to formation of Buncombe Co.

Shelton's Gap in Buncombe Co.: An Order of the Buncombe County, N. C., Court, April Term, 1800, reads as follows:

"Ordered by the Court that the Sheriff summon the following persons to serve as a Jury to View, mark and lay off a road the nearest and most convenient way from the road leading from Asheville to the head of the Catawba to Shelton's Gap," etc. . . . (From "History of Buncombe County, N. C." by F. A. Sondley.)

Census of 1790 shows a *David Shelton* in the list of taxpayers of the Caswell County, North Carolina, of the "Richmond District."

David Shelton of Caswell County, North Carolina, was a member of the State Legislature in the year 1782. This David was the one who was at Valley Forge; he was a son of John Shelton and his wife Eleanor Parks of "Rural Plains", Hanover Co., Va.

The founder of the "Shelton Laurel", North Carolina Sheltons, was David Shelton, son of the James Shelton, born in Virginia in 1726, whose descendants were in Jefferson County, Tenn.

Sons of David Shelton: William, James, Isaac, Eliphas, David, Alex, John.

Daughters: Nancy, Kate, Sally, Judith, Molly. (There were said to have been 14 children but only these names could be recalled by old settlers.)

Facts about these children:

William had sons Andy and William.

James had sons (who grew to manhood) John A. and Calvin.

Isaac had sons, names not known.

Silas died in boyhood.

Alex lived to be over 100 years old, had four wives, 30 children; among sons were Nick, Merriman, Mandy, Richard.

Judith married, but her sons took Shelton name, among them were Frank, Dan, Soloman.

Molly, married and went West, no other information.

Nancy, Kate, Sally—no information.

John was a captain in the Union Army in the War between the States; he lived for years with Calvin, son of his brother James, on a Virginia farm between Lynchburg and Richmond.

One of David Shelton's descendants claims to have a deed for Shelton Laurel as early as 1793. David's wife was Catherine; he was said to have married her in Indiana and brought her here while a bride when he was a very young man.

CHILDREN OF DAVID SHELTON
(As remembered by Reuben Hensley)

Sons in order were: William (had 12 children), Isaac, Alexander (born 1804), Eliphas, David, James, John, Captain in Army.

Daughters: Nancy—oldest of all children, Sally, Katie, Judith.

CHILDREN OF WILLIAM SHELTON
(Son of old David)

Sons: James, Noah—died in Civil War, John, William Riley, Peter, Eliphas, Montgomery.

Daughters: Matilda, Nancy, Minerva Jane, Ibby Damsel, Iona.

CHILDREN OF ALEXANDER SHELTON, Son of David
(As remembered by Reuben Hensley)

1. By wife *Nancy Hall:* Nancy, David, Silas—shot and killed while crossing river in Civil War, Alexander (Little Alex), William Rock, Lida, Katie.

2. By wife *Nancy Riddle:* Linnie, Elizabeth, Cloe, Celie, Mandy (son), Nicholas, Augustus.

3. By wife *Margaret Hensley:* Dolly, Barbara Allen, Melvina, Elzira, twins, George, Valentine, Jane, Reuben.

4. By wife *Rhoda Norton:* Mary and Elie.

THE SHELTON MASSACRE AT SHELTON LAUREL
January 19, 1863

Those massacred were: James Shelton (son of old David) and his two sons, James and David. David Shelton (an old man—related to but not a descendant of David, the original settler). William Shelton, Azariah Shelton, Rod Shelton, James Metcalf, Halen Moore, Wade Moore, Ellison King, Joe Woods, Jasper Chandler.

"SHELDON CHURCH", BEAUFORT, S. CAROLINA
and
BERMUDA RECORDS

HE first grants of South Carolina were to the Earl of Carlisle of Barbadoes in 1624-29, and to Lord Baltimore of Maryland, in 1632. In 1663-65, grants were given to eight "Proprietors", two being Lord John Berkeley and Sir George Cartaret. The next grant to the proprietors was March 24th, the fifteenth year of Charles II.

In October, 1683, John Moore, "Proprietor, Deputy and Secretary of the Provinces", arrived and with him came from Bermuda, John Shelton, son of James (1) of Bermuda, who was given 300 acres of land. This John died in Bermuda, August 15, 1691, and his son, Richard Shelton, became Secretary to the Proprietors, which office he held up to 1731. In 1734, he was granted a Barony of 12,000 acres by Sir George Carteret, Palantine. The entire tract was called "Sheldon Plantation". Why *Sheldon,* is hard to understand as all of the North and South Carolina records are *Shelton.*

The plantation adjoined the parish church of Prince William, now Beaufort County, South Carolina, and the church became known as *"Sheldon"* Church and is still so called.

I understand that a beautiful Easter service is held there every year; it was burned by the British in 1780 on their march from Savannah to Charleston, and again by the Federal troops in 1865, but its massive walls survived both conflagrations. It is said to be the "most elegant and complete" country church in America.

Richard Shelton lived at "Sheldon" until his death. He married Frances Lake in Bermuda, May 27, 1683. "Sheldon" later became the country seat of Lieutenant-Governor William Bull who is buried there; he was born at "Ashley Hall", April, 1683, and died at Sheldon, March 21, 1755. His wife, Mary Bull, died there in September, 1771 and is buried beside her husband in "Sheldon" Church Yard. Richard Shelton died on a visit to Bermuda (History of South Carolina Under the Royal Government, p. 292; South Carolina History and Genealogical Society Publications, Vol. I, p. 18).

This Richard Shelton and Frances Lake had issue: Richard who died in Bermuda, March 23, 1693; Elizabeth, born November 6, 1684, died November 11, 1684; Sarah, born April 18, 1686, died November 17, 1700; and Robert (Captain) born December 7, 1689, baptized May 25, 1693. There may have been other children; these are all I have found in the Bermuda records.

Captain Robert Shelton married Mary Lyte on August 12, 1712. They had two children that died in infancy and Richard (1), baptized September 23, 1716; Mary (2) born December 13, 1717; Robert (3) baptized November 5, 1720; and Sarah (4) born April 6, baptized April 13, 1723.

Frances, wife of Richard, Sr., died December 6, 1692. On October 13, 1739, Richard (1), son of Robert and Mary, married Mrs. Elizabeth Woodward (widow); he died in July, 1744 and his widow died February 10, 1747. A child, Sarah, was baptized January 8, 1745.

Captain Robert Shelton died November 16, 1742. His wife, Mary, died September 23, 1737; their son, Robert (3), baptized November 5, 1720, died May 17, 1723. There may have been other children of all of these marriages, but those listed are the only ones I found recorded.

Other Bermuda records: Robert and Freswith Shelton had a son, Thomas, baptized June 24, 1663.

Robert and Angelica Prince Shelton had Robert, baptized September 1, 1668. William, baptized July 7, 1671 and Elizabeth, baptized April 22, 1672.

Samuel and Margaret Shelton had Samuel baptized December 4, 1673 and Thomas, baptized December 7, 1675; Samuel Shelton, Sr., and Margaret Molyneux were married in Bermuda, February 27, 1673; Margaret died November 26, 1681, and Samuel married Grace, by whom (?) he had Jane Shelton, baptized July 26, 1678. She died December 22, 1679.

Samuel, Jr., son of Samuel and his first wife, Margaret Molyneux, married December 2, 1697, Mary Wilmouth, and had a daughter Sarah, baptized December, 1702. (The record of Jane as a daughter of Samuel and Grace must be wrong; Jane was evidently a child by his first wife, Margaret. The Census gives: "Samuel and Grace, no children" in 1686.)

Thomas Shelton, son of Samuel and Margaret, married Mercy and had: Mary Shelton, baptized October 12, 1712; James, baptized December 10, 1715 (born same day); and Mercy Ann Shelton, baptized March 16, 1719 (born March 14). I find no marriage for Mercy Ann, but the death record is Mercy Ann "Shilom". This was November 21, 1776, and may be another spelling of Shelton, or her marriage name. There is no record of the marriage of Thomas and Mercy, nor of the death of either one of them in

Bermuda, that I have been able to find. Other Shelton marriages in Bermuda:

Mary married John Harden (?)—name not plain—in October, 1653.

William married Susanna Green, March 23, 1669.

Elizabeth married John Smith (whose son, Oliver Smith, married Elizabeth Lake, sister of Frances Lake who married Richard Shelton) December 26, 1675.

Rebecca married John Wingatt, July 9, 1682.

Mary married Henry Sandiford, September 28, 1686.

William married Latitia Cook, August 2, 1687.

Robert Shelton married Mrs. Honnor Biddle, August 31, 1695.

William Shelton married Alice Alexander, April 23, 1702.

Mrs. Jane Shelton married James Matthews, November 4, 1703.

Mrs. Honor Shelton (probably widow of Robert) married September 28, 1704, John Millington.

Charles Shelton married Mary Daw May 23, 1706.

Mrs. Sarah Shelton married John Poor, November 19, 1726.

Temperance Shelton married William Harrison, November 13, 1734.

There is also a record of a Guy Shelton and wife, 1680, and wills of William Shelton, 1667; Joseph Shelton, 1673; Richard Shelton, 1744; Ralph Shelton, 1766; and Richard Cure Shelton, 1782. The death of William Shelton, mariner of Virginia, is recorded January 6, 1695.

The will of Richard Cure Shelton names a number of family connections. It is dated December 12, 1780, and was proved August 23, 1782. He must have had a very large estate, from the number and sizes of the bequests. It gives him "Now of St. Michaels"; the name of his plantation was "The Good Hope in the Colony of Essequebo". Following are some of the provisions of his will:

"To eldest son of brother, Thomas, deceased, by his wife, Ann".

"To his eldest sister, Ann".

"To my sister, Suky, or the male heirs of her body" (children of his sister, Mary, wife of Hill Collicott of Bristol, to inherit share of Sukey in case of decease of her and her sons).

"To nieces, Mary and Elizabeth Collicott".

"To Richard *Shelton* Collicott, eldest son of Hill Collicott".

"To Hill, 2nd son, to Thomas, youngest son, and to the youngest daughter of my sister, each 200 pounds".

"To my brother, Thomas' son, Thomas *Shelton,* or his male heirs, all the residue of my estate".

The above Richard Shelton Collicott, Esq. is given as of "Weston" in the notice of the London Gentleman's Magazine of his "marriage, November 8, 1791, to Miss French at Reading."

An interesting account of Henry Wodehouse, Governor of Bermuda, is given here, showing the Shelton intermarriage. Captain Henry was a member of the expedition to the Isle of Rhe when Sir Ralph Shelton, father of James (1) of Virginia and Bermuda and founder of the American line, was killed.

Edward W. James, the author of the article from which

this sketch is taken, uses the *Woodhouse* spelling; most of the English *Shelton* records use Wodehouse—so this latter spelling is used in this history of the family.

HENRY WOODHOUSE

APTAIN HENRY WOODHOUSE was the Governor of the Bermudas from October, 1623, to January 13th, 1626-7, and was present "At a Counsell Table I March, 1626-7." He was in the expedition to Re and Rochelle, 1627-28. Was recommended by the Lords of the Admiralty to be Captain of Tilbury Fort, and was master of the muster of Suffolk County, England. He said that King Charles, in 1631, promised him the governorship of Virginia, and in 1634 and in 1635, he petitioned the King to fulfill his promise, and at one time it was thought he had done so. A friend of Governor Winthrop of Massachusetts wrote from London, "that there were ships and soldiers provided, and given out as carrying the new Governor, Captain Woodhouse, to Virginia." Among the papers in Her Majesty's Public Record office, London, is the following:

"To the Kings most Excellent Ma'tie,
The humble peticon of
Henry Woodhouse,

Humbly sheweth that whereas your Matie hath been graciously pleased neere four yeares past to promise your Peticoner the Governor's place of Virginia, the settling of wch Plantacon hath bene of suche long continuance that your peticoner starveth with the expectation, and having lost £600 of his arrears, and £60 of yearly intertainment in Suffolk, never having received one penny for his employment on the Isle of Rey and Rochelle. Hee, therefore, humbly prayeth your Matie will graciously declare your pleasure, and make your peticoner enjoy the happiness of your Maties favour by giveing your warrant for the drawing of his Commission whereby your Peticoner shall avoid further troubling of your Matie who is absolutely undone without yor Maties immediate dispatch. And hee shall (as is duty ever bound) daily continue his prayers for your Maties long and most prosperous raigne.''

In 1634, he took a lease for six shares of land in Hambleton Tribe, Bermuda, for 99 years, of his nephew, Sir William Killigrew, the dramatist, dated October 29th, at a rental of one hundred oranges, one hundred lemons and one hundred potatoes, to be paid at the Feast of the annunciation of the Blessed Virgin Mary. In 1637, Sir William Killigrew reclaimed the land as the rent had not been paid, but requested his agent to grant Woodhouse another lease at a higher price—''Three hundred of the largest and best oranges, one hundred of the best potato roots, and one hundred of the best lemons.'' Woodhouse declined the proffer, and his name does not again occur in connection with the Bermudas. His course while Governor has been severely censured by Lefroy, who says he was tyrannical and arbitrary, but he has been defended by William Frith Williams, who says he was compelled to enforce the law. In 1630-1, the ladies of Southampton Tribe caused such a disturbance by quarreling about the right of precedence in being seated in church that the Governor and Council had to be called in to settle the dispute.

Capt. Woodhouse on the 7th of August, 1628, purchased of John Gering of London two shares of land in the Bermudas, and on the 27th of July, 1632, gave them to his son Henry, who, born in 1607, settled in Virginia in 1637, and received a grant of 500 acres of land for the importation of Henry Woodhouse, Mary Woodhouse, Eliz: Woodhouse, Henry Brightman, Lam Wilson, Jacob Bradschaler, Jon Symons, Tho. Symons, Kaemu of Camena, Thomas of Poluxon; he was a member of the House of Burgesses, 1647-1652, County Commissioner from 1642 to 1653, member of the vestry, Lynhaven Parish in 1640, and died in 1655. He left four sons, Henry, Horatio, John and William, and several daughters, Elizabeth who married Giles Collins, Mary, who married Edward Attwood, Rachel, who married John Totne, and one who married Hercules Low, and one by the name of Judith, who may have been Mrs. Low.

"In the name of God, Amen, I Henry Woodhowse doe make ordeyne, Constitute and appoint this to be my last will and testament, ffirst and principally I bequeath my soule unto Allmighty God, my maker and Jesus Christ my Redeemer by whose death and passion I hope to have remission of all my sinnes, and my body to be buried. I will and bequeath unto my wife, Maria Woodhowse one third pte of all my moveable estate that I am Estated in, And I doe likewise will that my wife shall enjoye the use of my plantacon untill my Sonne Henry Woodhowse shall be Twenty yeeres of age or longer if shee sholde continue a widdowe. I doe will and bequeath unto my sonne Henry five hundred acres of land whereon now I doe live. I doe will and bequeath unto my sonne Horatio Woodhowse two hundred acres of land lyeing by a Creeke commonly called by the name of Gregories Creeke. I doe will and bequeath unto my sonne John Woodhowse two hundred and Seaventy foure acres of land lyeing and being at a place called the head of the dammes. There be two shares of land in Bermudes wch I sold unto my brother in lawe, Mr. Charles

Sothren, but if in Case the said Charles died wth out Issue
of his body lawfully begotten then the said land to return
to me and my heires, wch said land I will and bequeath unto
my son Willm[1] being so returned to mee. I doe likewise
will that after my debts are paied out of my whole estate
that then my wife to have hir third pte of the estate, and
the remaynder to be equally divided amongst my children
as they shall come to age, my sonnes at Twenty and my
daughters at Sixteen I doe bequeath unto my daughter,
Elizabeth Collins, and Judith, five shillings a peece, or the
worth of it. I doe desire my loveing wife, my friends, Mr.
Lemuell Mason and Thomas Allen to see this my last will
and Testamt pformed. But in case any of my children
sholde die before they come to age then my will is that
theire part soe dieing be equally devided amongst the
liveing, onely the land, and that to goe by Succession, first
unto the heires males. I doe likewise give unto my wife all
that little plate I have, Except to each of my Children by
this wife, one Silver Spoone. In pformance hereof I have
hereunto sett my hand this Sixteenth of July, One thousand
Sixe hundred fiifty five. Signed in the pr sence of

Tho: Allen,   HEN: WOODHOUSE.

the mke (E) of
Joane Henley

Jurat in Curp Tho: Allen tant 15th Novembris, 1655.

Test Wm Turner Cl: Cur:''

The arms given in Blomefield's History of Norfolk
County, England of the Woodhouse family of Waxham,
Hickling and Kimberley are Quarterly, azure, and ermin,
in the first quarter a leopard's head, or. The arms in Burke,
which agree with those now in the possession of the elder

branch of the family in Princess Anne County are, Quarterly erm. and az. in the 2nd and 3rd quarters a leopard's head or: Crest—a griffin segreant or.

"John Woodhouse married Alice, daughter of William Croft, Esq.; they had (1) Sir Thomas of Waxham, who d. s. p., and (2) Sir William, whose first wife was Ann, daughter of Henry Repps, of Thorp Market, Esq.; there was no issue.

The second wife of Sir William Woodhouse was Elizabeth, daughter of Sir Philip Calthorp, and widow of Sir Henry Parker. Their children were: (1) Sir Thomas who married Ann, daughter and co-heir of John Wootton of Tudenham. (2) Mary, who married *Sir Ralph Shelton* (whose son married Jane West, daughter of the first Lord de la Warr). (3) Sir Henry Woodhouse whose first wife was Ann, daughter of Sir Nicholas Bacon, Lord Keeper. Their children were: (1) Sir William Woodhouse, Knt. of Waxham, Norfolk, who married Frances, daughter of Sir Robert Jermyn of Rushbrook, (2) Henry Woodhouse, Governor of Bermuda, (3) Francis and (4) Thomas of Kimberley, Norfolk.

The son of Henry Woodhouse,[1] Governor of Bermuda, was Henry Woodhouse of Virginia, whose wife was Maria (?). The second wife of Sir Henry Woodhouse, son of Sir William Woodhouse and Elizabeth Calthorp, was Cecilly Gresham."

(1) The land which the Ex-Governor bought in 1628, and gave to his son Henry in 1632, the latter sold his brother-in-law, Charles Sothren, to be returned to him if he died without heirs, in 1640, and in his will left the same to his son, William if it was returned. This land was in the possession of Sothren in 1663.

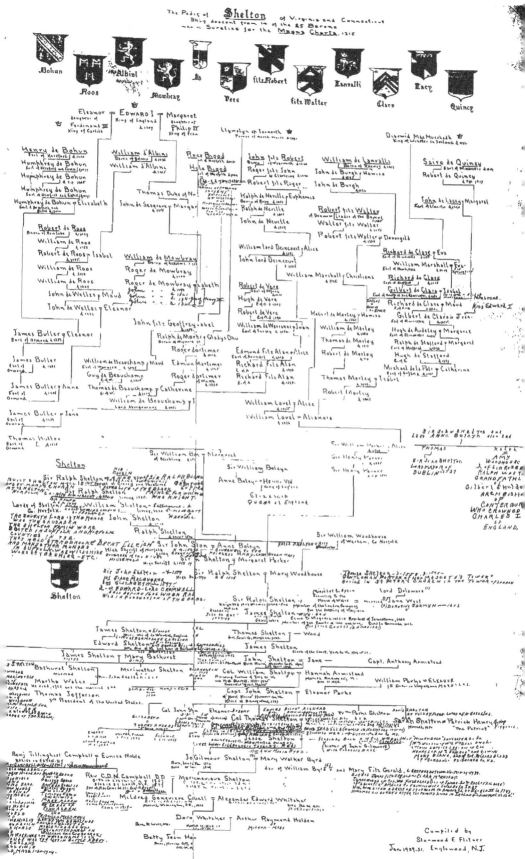

The Pedigree of **Shelton** of Virginia and Connecticut
Shewing descent from 1 of the 25 Barons
who were Sureties for the **Magna Charta** 1215

Compiled by
Stanwood E. Flitner
Jan 1929-31. Englewood, N.J.

and of the commonwealth the twenty...th, between Henry Fields on the one part and Jesse Chilton of the county of... in the commonwealth of the other part, ... that the said Henry Fields and Alice his wife for and in consideration of the sum of... one thousand and eight hundred and thirty dollars current money of Virginia lawful money of Virginia to them in hand paid by the said Jesse Chilton at or before the sealing and delivery of these presents the receipt whereof they do hereby acknowledge and therewith and of every part thereof acquit and discharge the said Jesse Chilton his heirs exors and administrators, have given, granted, bargained, sold, aliened, enfeoffed, transferred, conveyed and confirmed, and by these presents they the said Henry Fields and Alice his wife doth themselves their heirs exors and administrators give grant bargain sell alien enfeoff transfer convey and confirm unto the said Jesse Chilton his heirs and assigns forever... the third part of a certain tract or parcel of land lying and being in the said county of... commonly called and known by the name of Fields tract together with all the members of... Fields tract, heirs and... of the said Henry Fields by the last will of his deceased father, and which said line... Chilton is owed and had effected the said Henry Fields heirs and exors of the other three hundred and ninety acres of land and three... given in a certain bond, to the same more or less... under bounded as followeth;

Beginning at a white oak corner... on the south... at... in S 82½° W 351 poles crossing the... run to the corner of the fence, a corner with the said..., thence N 10.45 W 31 poles to a pine another corner with Gilmore, thence N 58.30 E 78 poles... the... and... and... another corner with Gilmore, thence N 83 E 228½ poles... Gilmore, thence N 26 W 188 poles on the south... west of the said road thence S 37.30 E 267 poles crossing the... of Fergusons creek to the beginning aforesaid to have and to hold the said several tracts and parcels of land and singular the said third part of the said tract of land together with the reversion of the other third part, all the members of the said several tracts, and all and singular the premises with the appurtenances belonging and the said Jesse Chilton his heirs and assigns forever... and defend the right and title of the said several tracts and after... title... unto the said Jesse Chilton his heirs and assigns forever... whatsoever: And the said Henry Fields and Alice his wife do for themselves their heirs exors and administrators hereby covenant promise and... to and with the said Jesse Chilton his heirs and assigns that they the said Henry Fields and Alice his wife and their heirs shall and will warrant and defend the right and title of the above therefore... of the said tract of land together with the reversion of the other third part of... we... mentioned in the... of... whereof... the said Jesse Chilton his heirs against the claim and demand of... and every person whatsoever, to his the account of the said tract unto the said Jesse Chilton his heirs... them deceased Jesse Chilton his heirs... assigns forever. Provided whereof the said Henry Fields hath hereunto set their hands and seals the day and year above written.

Signed sealed and delivered
in presence of
Jefferson Payne   Ephraim Payne
William George   William Robinson

                        B Robinson
                        Nancy Payne ...

This Indenture made and entered into this Eighteenth day of January, one Thousand seven hundred & ninety eight, Between William Lawson agent for Gaven Lawson who ... in fact for Bogle Somervell & Co — John McGilmour as heir at Law of ... at Gilmour Dec'd who was a partner in trade of aforesaid Firm Helen Gilmour ... of aforesaid Robert Gilmour Dec'd & Cordelia ... wife of aforesaid John Gilmour of the one part & Elias Edmonds Junior of the other part Witnesseth that for & in consideration of the sum of Four hundred & fifty Dollars to them ... paid by the aforesaid Elias Edmonds & the receipt whereof they do hereby knowledge & for every part thereof do acquit the aforesaid Elias Edmonds & ... granted bargained sold aliened confirm'd & delivered unto the aforesaid ... Edmonds ... a certain tract parcel or lot of land lying being situate in ... County of Lancaster & State of Virginia Known by the name of Kilmarnock ... containing two & half acres more or less being that lot purchased by aforesaid ... Gilmour dec'd from William Stapton for the proper use of aforesaid ... & at present occupied by aforesaid Elias Edmonds & Together with all ... & c. Thereon & all appurtenances thereunto belonging — The aforesaid ... Lawson agent & c & John McGilmour Helen Gilmour their Heirs, & c do for covenant with the aforesaid Elias Edmonds & & do warrant that he the aforesaid ... Edmonds & his heirs & c shall peaceably & quietly hold occupy & possess the afore... premises free from the molestation of any person or persons whatever — as also to ... & defend the right of aforesaid premises & c unto the aforesaid Elias Edmonds ... heirs & c for ever against the lawfull claim of all persons whatsoever. In ... whereof we have hereunto affix'd our seal/signatures & seals the day & year before ... ...

... Gilmour
... Cullen
...nda Ball
... Mitchell
... Taylor

William Lawson
John M Gilmour

...

Cordelia Gilmour

Rec'd from the within mentioned Elias Edmonds &c the within
mentioned sum of Five hundred & fifty dollars—being full
payment for the within mentioned premises——

Robert Gilmour   William Lannon &c

Henry Pullen   John McGilmour

nich. P. Mitchell   Ellen Gilmour

Wm Taylor   Amelia Gilmour

    At a court held for Lancaster county on the 17th day of September 1798,
indenture of bargain and sale from and receipt hereon endorsed, were proved by
oaths of Henry Pullen, Daniel P. Mitchell and William Taylor three of the witnesses thereto and ordered to be
recorded——

              Teste   Henry Fowler clk

to E Edmonds

Sept. 1798 proved

recorded—

Received of John Clifton this day, a receipt(?) which within
this within mentioned sum of nine hundred and thirty
seven pounds sixteen shillings being lawful money of
Virginia, being the full consideration money within
mentioned to be paid to me at or before the ensealing
and delivery of these within written indenture

(Inry received me)

Matthew Laporte

Signed Sealed
&c

At an event over for hundred commission the Hillsborough
from 13th this the of August same (endorsed)
from Henry Foster and others his son to John Clifton
was proved by the oaths of William Bridges and
Francis Lewis ... of the acknowledged(?)...
court order for the same ... on the 8th day of July 1800
the and order was further and fully proved by the oaths of
William Robinson another witness thereto and ...
receipt thereon endorsed ordered to be recorded, and the
of the said deed by the said Alice appear by a commission ...
... also ordered to be recorded

Teste,
James Fowler clk.

Received this day of
Clifton

1800 James Foster & wife
Deed from by and and Wife
Received and registered
Fowler Clerk

CPSIA information can be obtained at www.ICGtesting.com
Printed in the USA
LVOW01*1040120813

347467LV00004B/10/P